CONTEMPORARY COMMUNITY HEALTH SERIES

THE PSYCHIATRIC HALFWAY HOUSE

THE
PSYCHIATRIC

Richard D. Budson, M.D.

HALFWAY HOUSE

A Handbook of Theory and Practice

University of Pittsburgh Press

Published by the University of Pittsburgh Press, Pittsburgh, Pa. 15260
Copyright © 1978, University of Pittsburgh Press
All rights reserved
Feffer and Simons, Inc., London
Manufactured in the United States of America
First printing 1978
Second printing 1978

Library of Congress Cataloging in Publication Data

Budson, Richard D
  The psychiatric halfway house.

  (Contemporary community health series)
  Bibliography: p.
  Includes index.
  1. Mentally ill—Rehabilitation. 2. Halfway houses.
I. Title. II. Series. [DNLM: 1. Halfway houses—
Handbooks. 2. Mental disorders—Rehabilitation—Hand-
books. 3. Mental health services—United States—Hand-
books. WM27 AA1 B9p]
RC439.5.B8   362.2'2   77-74548
ISBN 0-8229-3350-0

To Sandy, Andrew, and Vickie

About the Author

Richard D. Budson, M.D., is Assistant Professor of Psychiatry at the Harvard Medical School, Associate Psychiatrist at McLean Hospital, Belmont, Mass., and the former Director of Community Residence Programs for the Massachusetts Department of Mental Health.

Contents

Tables

Figures

Preface

This book is intended to be a handbook for a wide spectrum of citizens involved in developing community residence programs for the mentally ill. Likely readers include all those who are planning or operating individual community residences or regional programs. This work is also intended to be an educational resource for all other citizens who find themselves having to make decisions about community residences in one capacity or another. The community residence has become a subject of legislative control and funding; the courts have been ordering and monitoring less restrictive means of caring for the mentally ill; and city officials have had to make zoning decisions regarding the location of halfway houses. This volume is intended to help such officials in their deliberations. Citizens representing the local neighborhoods also need a guide to residence programs. Further, it is hoped that this text will be useful in the social, psychological, and rehabilitative curricula offered by the modern university.

This work builds on, and departs from, previous halfway house literature. Previous works included descriptions of single individual programs, brief descriptions of geographically unrelated programs, and a descriptive analysis of a national survey.[1] This book, however, more nearly approaches the ideal of a general textbook on the subject of halfway houses.

The book comprises three parts. The text addresses the community residence initially as a concept, because all planning and structure must follow from a sound theoretical base. Thus, a serious effort is made in the first part to describe a comprehensive theoretical rationale and ideology. Next, the book relates ideology to a potential network of community residences when viewed from the perspective of state and local government. The issues discussed include quality control as set out in regulatory standards; the adoption of safe and suitable building codes; the establishment of minimum standards for the self-preservation of the inhabitants; and existing zoning laws as they relate to the problem of community entry. Finally, we will look at the community residence as a singular entity, with its own set of developmental and clinical management problems.

The following pages represent my best effort to share experiences gained over a six-year period during which I served as director of both a statewide and an individual community residence program. Wearing the hats of provider and state official significantly contributed to my understanding of the complexity of the problems at both levels. Ultimately, this work embraced the federal level too, resulting in legislation establishing the community residence as an essential component of community mental health centers throughout the nation.

Throughout this experience, the most difficult task was to prevent bureaucracy from wiping out essential programmatic elements. This was accomplished with compromise where appropriate, but with absolute steadfastness of position where critical clinical principles were at stake. My own principles and clinical strategies developed slowly. In psychiatric training and beyond, much of my energy was spent in trying to achieve change in traditional "medical practices" which were, in my view, too often based more on tradition than on sound ideology or proven effectiveness.

It is not irrelevant that my first experience treating the mentally ill started before I was even a medical student. At Harvard College in 1956 I participated as a student volunteer working with patients at the Metropolitan State Hospital. Our student group was enthusiastically supported and supervised by Dr. Milton Greenblatt, whose career has influenced and continually interrelated with my own. Dr. Greenblatt had a special talent for encouraging young, unsure idealists to forge ahead into unknown waters.

My first encounter with the Metropolitan State Hospital was a little scary. The hospital was big, bleak, overcrowded, and under-staffed. Six psychiatrists treated and followed nearly two thousand patients, most of whom were considered beyond help. I asked to work with a patient individually and was assigned a woman who had been in the hospital for twenty-seven years. She spoke a dialect of schizophrenese no one understood. I saw her biweekly, concentrating on understanding her, being reliable, honest, and helping her to separate out socially acceptable speech and behavior from the unacceptable. Eventually we began to go into town regularly for ice cream and shopping, opportunities for her to exercise her new social skills. After a year and a half, she was hired to work at Goodwill Industries in Boston and was able to live in a lodging house near her work.

At the time it was an entirely novel idea that an untrained, non-professional person could have an ameliorative effect on seriously ill patients. Dr. Greenblatt presented the program at the World Congress of Psychiatry in Montreal the next year. Now the use of volunteers on a one-to-one basis is commonplace. How far we have come in twenty years!

Clearly, this experience had a major, and optimistic, impact on me; a great deal could be done for the mentally ill after all. Further, the experience suggested that the hospital itself helped to maintain the pathology of the patient; in my experience, social contact with the community helped to alleviate it. In 1969, after my residency, I set out to develop and subsequently to direct the first American psychiatric halfway house affiliated with a private psychiatric teaching hospital—Berkeley House, affiliated with the McLean Hospital, a Harvard Medical School teaching hospital. At the request of Dr. Greenblatt, who was then Commissioner of Mental Health, I accepted the position of Director of Community Residence Programs for the mentally ill for the Commonwealth of Massachusetts. In addition, as I developed the state program, it became apparent that there were overlapping issues relating to the entire halfway house program in Massachusetts. This program included halfway houses not only for the mentally ill, but also for the retarded, drug abusers, alcoholics, children from broken homes, and youthful and adult offenders. Eventually, I organized and chaired the Interdepartmental Rehabilitation Facilities Board of the Executive Office of Human Services. This board became a vehicle which could initiate and contribute to the drafting of needed legislation, regulations, and codes. It was both gratifying and ultimately necessary that Governor Francis W. Sargent and his wife, Jessie, were particularly interested in our work. They opened doors and smoothed the way where we needed help in being heard and taken seriously.

Finally, I spent considerable hours and days working with Stanley B. Jones, staff director for Senator Edward Kennedy's Senate Health Subcommittee. This led to the drafting and passage of the new Community Mental Health Center Act, which for the first time recognized the psychiatric halfway house as an essential component of the community mental health center.

Much remains to be done, and my hope is that the readers of this book will form an alliance to accomplish it. Elitist professionals are not what we need. Just plain human beings—citizens who are concerned about the afflicted among us—are the solution. I chose to become a physician and psychiatrist in order to be in a position *as a citizen* to help implement changes in the system of mental health care. My hope now is that the audience to which this book is addressed will become the essential partners in the realization of humane and effective care for the mentally ill.

Acknowledgments

First and foremost I owe a great debt to The Mailman Foundation and Mr. and Mrs. Joseph L. Mailman, without whose dedication and generosity there would be no community residence program at McLean Hospital. Francis de Marneffe, M.D., McLean's Director, was steadfast in his enthusiastic support for a pioneering venture.

My assistants at the Massachusetts Department of Mental Health, Justine Meehan, M.D., and Emily Barclay, served with industry, intelligence, and devotion. Cheryl and Robert Jolley, Mary Theresa and Vincent Lynch, Constance and Erik Johannessen, and Rona Klein, M.D., the staff of Berkeley House, contributed to making a dream a reality and provided the substance upon which this book is based.

I appreciate the unstinting encouragement of Evelyn Stone, Shervert Frazier, M.D., and Milton Greenblatt, M.D. I thank Suzanne Gordon for her helpful suggestions and Lloyd Linford for his editorial assistance. I am particularly grateful to Beth Luey, Associate Editor of the University of Pittsburgh Press, for her expertise, which she cheerfully made available, and for her sensitive understanding of the subject matter of this volume.

Finally, special thanks go to my long-time friend and associate, Peter A. Martin, M.D.

PART I

The Development of an Ideology

CHAPTER 1

Crisis, Concept, and Challenge

For over one hundred years the primary locus of care for the mentally ill has been the remote state hospital. Today this system is no longer fixed and unquestioned. Major attempts at reform have resulted in a complex system of contradictory demands and requirements—that patients not be incarcerated without treatment; that patients not be released into the community before there are adequate community care programs; that large, expensive institutions not continue to drain dwindling state coffers; that unscrupulous private entrepreneurs not victimize again the vulnerable population of discharged patients.

In general, destruction and reform of the old have outstripped creation of the new, and inadequate development of proper rehabilitative facilities in the community has had serious consequences for patients. In several parts of the country there has already been a sudden influx of discharged patients into unprepared communities. With no prearranged residential program designed to meet their rehabilitative needs, patients have too often drifted into blighted urban areas, into single-occupancy hotels, living in isolation and without meaningful activity. Ghettos of former mental patients tend to form in the most undesirable areas. In this setting deterioration is the rule, with the outcome for the patient too frequently suicide, destructive behavior, or a return to intense withdrawal. In addition, the ex-patient is victimized by the predators of society who frequent the same parts of the urban jungle. This situation has attained high visibility in the local community through an attentive press.

Community reaction has been based partly on annoyance with an unsightly nuisance. But there has also been a genuine movement toward increased community involvement with the discharged patient. In this context, the psychiatric halfway house has become increasingly important. Pressures for deinstitutionalization make the establishment of sufficient numbers of psychiatric halfway houses a crucial issue for the coming decade. However, if these facilities are to be accepted and truly integrated into the structure of society, they must be established in a manner which assures their clinical integrity, their physical safety, and their fiscal soundness.

The Setting

The beginnings of the halfway house movement preceded and anticipated the current crisis. It evolved not only in response to the abominable conditions of the typical state hospital, but also in response to other medical and social movements. The advent of psychotropic medications in the mid-1950s made rehabilitation and community care a potential reality for the first time. At the outset, attention centered on making the hospital itself more therapeutic,[1] but delays and bureaucratic inertia fostered a move toward an entirely new environment for the mental patient. The search for an alternative to large institutions and the alienation they engender was proceeding on many fronts. Examples come readily to mind. The rush to participate in the Peace Corps in the early 1960s reflected youth's search for an opportunity to work together in small groups on a common, manageable project. The Vietnam war, which caused many young adults to feel acutely disfranchised, undoubtedly contributed to the lowering of the voting age, giving those who were to be ordered to battle a voice in selecting their government. Students pressured universities into reorganizing their curricula and governing boards. The poor and the black rebelled against large city governments which they felt were unresponsive to their needs. Upheaval and riot ensued, leading to constructive efforts at creating neighborhood arms of centralized city government—for instance, Boston's mini-city halls.

In addition to this reaction against bigness and remoteness, the 1960s also saw a reaction against a unique, isolated smallness that was part of the American scene—the isolated nuclear family. The extended family had almost ceased to exist two decades after the end of World War II. National corporations shuttled nuclear families from location to location according to corporate-economic needs. The commune was but one reaction to this isolation, representing an attempt to re-create the ethos of the extended family of the past.

Thus, for many reasons and on many fronts, impersonal bigness and isolated smallness fostered a yearning for new social groupings. And it was in this context that small groups of mental health workers began, largely on their own, to develop spontaneously and simultaneously in different parts of the country a new modality—a living situation for ex-patients which attempted to avoid the "too big" of large institutions and the "too small" of nuclear families. The new modality, the psychiatric halfway house, was typically a familylike group of ten to fifteen residents, living in a big old house with a live-in couple. Ancillary personnel, consultation, and outside daily activities complemented the basic living program.

The Concept

Gradually, an explicit rationale for the halfway house emerged. There was a desire to alleviate four basic deficiencies of the traditional large institution:

Largeness. The traditional state mental hospital housed at least a thousand patients, with groups of fifty to sixty on a ward. Because of inadequate resources, functional staff frequently consisted of a single ward nurse or attendant who could do little but maintain order and attempt to meet the most basic needs of the patients. This situation contributed to what has been described as the "social breakdown syndrome"—a social withdrawal caused by the loss of meaningful interpersonal exchange leading to an increased retreat into a patient's inner world. Administrative decisions which affected the daily life of the ward were typically made at some central administrative office of the mammoth institution. The ward itself was remote from the site of the decision-making. Neither staff nor patients were in a position to affect these decisions, or even understand the reasoning behind them. This also contributed to patient withdrawal, as the immediate environment tended to be not only unresponsive, but also inexplicable.

Universal medical model. The patient was considered sick twenty-four hours a day, reinforcing his image of himself as defective and helplessly dependent on the hospital staff. The patient-nurse relationship was one of a passive recipient to an active purveyor of health. Little distinction was made between acute psychotic episodes and periods of diminished symptomatology. The patient was considered "sick" even when going to bed, eating, or sitting in the day room. Healthy functions tended to be disregarded, as the very identity of the professional staff depended upon a focus on the patient's pathology. Even activities providing a variety of living experiences in the institution were identified as recreational, occupational, music, or art "therapies." In short, the hospital was a place to be "sick."

A closed society. Like other closed social systems (the military, prisons, and religious orders, for example), the state hospital had its own unique social order, with its own rules and codes of punishment for transgressions. The attendant—the lowest caste in the staff hierarchy and the least trained—usually had the most direct contact with the patients and the most power over their daily life. Attendants decided whether the patient went into seclusion, was allowed privileges on the grounds, or was assigned extra chores on the ward. The code of acceptable behavior varied from staff member to staff member. This condition led patients increasingly to disregard outside standards, and to become increasingly compliant to the power system under which they lived. Frightened, compliant patients inevitably became less willing to take initiatives toward health or any other life situation.

Isolation from the community. Traditionally, the state or county hospital was in a rural area, separated from the main road by landscaped hills and reached by winding driveways. This physical isolation made interactions in a normal setting next to impossible for the patients. Even if they obtained privileges to leave the ward and be on the grounds, the outside world remained remote.

The large, impersonal ward, run on a universal medical model, and imposing its own standards of conduct in a remote physical setting generally reinforced pathology and perpetuated the "patient" state. The end result was too often an institutionalized chronic schizophrenic patient, withdrawn and hopeless, maintaining bizarre symptomatology.

The psychiatric halfway house, or the community residence, explicitly alleviates these four problems and has the following attributes:

Smallness. The typical community residence for people with emotional problems is either a large old house or an existing lodging house, with approximately fifteen residents. The house is usually operated by a small, nonprofit, private corporation with two houseparents as employed staff and other relief and ancillary personnel available. The houseparents live in the community residence twenty-four hours a day; in contrast to the eight-hour rotations of three different sets of hospital staff. All administrative decisions affecting the life of the house are routinely discussed by the houseparents and the residents in regular house meetings. Typically, the community is small enough to encourage members of the group to know each other well and to relate supportively to individuals in temporary difficulty.

The family model. The typical community residence is based on an attempt to re-create a sound, familylike living situation. The setting is usually an old, large, family house furnished warmly and comfortably. The occupants are known as residents, not patients. The staff are houseparents or house managers who live in the community residence as parents do. Often one of the house managers works or attends school outside the house during the day, not unlike the usual home situation. The entire group has dinner together nightly, family style. That the resident may have a problem is not ignored, nor is the fact that he may need medical supervision. As in a home situation, he obtains medical supervision at medical facilities outside the domicile, within the community, either at a day hospital or at an outpatient department, such as a local community mental health center. The houseparents are skilled at recognizing and fostering the health of the individual resident, as opposed to his pathology.

An open setting.   The relatively small, familylike group lives in a neighborhood to which it relates in various ways. The group shops for its food there, attends churches, takes advantage of recreational and entertainment facilities, and uses social-service facilities. In its turn, the community residence accepts the mores of the neighborhood. Excessive noise, illicit drugs, and belligerent behavior are precluded by general community codes. Behavior is not determined by the idiosyncrasies of the staff. Compliance with codes is therefore meaningfully related to successful living in the real world.

Integrated within the community.   To achieve the programmatic goal of reintegrating the citizen into the community, his domicile, if at all possible, should be in the community. Services are nearby, but on a separate site to which the resident travels. Bringing services *into* the community residence defeats the programmatic goal. The resident's trips to the market, the drugstore, the laundromat, the bank, the doctor, or a movie challenge him, stimulating him to higher levels of functioning and more adaptive modes of behavior.

These four attributes of the psychiatric halfway house—as a small, familylike domicile naturally open to the mores of the community and located truly within it—provide a rich contrast to the stark environment of the traditional state mental hospital.

Different Models

The halfway house was initially conceived as an aftercare facility to assist in community entry of the discharged mental patient. Over the years, however, it has come increasingly to be viewed as the potential domiciliary base for patients in a variety of clinical conditions at different times in the history of their difficulty. Thus, a more general term—"community residence"—began to be more appropriate than "halfway house," a term which connotes temporariness.

The newly defined community residence was then viewed as a program which had the potential to alter its goals according to the changing needs of the population it served. Among the variables in the design of the community residence are the following five:

Time in the history of the illness. The community residence can provide initial care at the onset of an acute psychologic disturbance or aftercare, following a course of institutionalization. These can be provided exclusively or concurrently.

Length of stay in the residence. The community residence can be a short-stay, transitional facility with a specific maximum length of stay, or an indeterminate, potentially long-term facility with no deadlines or explicit expectation for the resident to move out.

Staffing. The community residence may have live-in staff; an increased staffing pattern consistent with an increased degree of dependence and disability in the residents; no live-in staff (in this instance there usually would be visiting staff from an affiliated psychiatric program); or volunteers used as healthy role models.

Daily program. The community residence may be what has been called a high-expectation facility requiring the residents to be enrolled and attending school or working; or it may have intermediate expectations, with residents actively engaged in a day hospital program, an ex-patient social club, or (if the members are capable of vocational rehabilitation) in a sheltered workshop program, either transitional or terminal.

Meals. Meals are usually provided (evening meals and perhaps breakfast), except in a cooperative apartment facility.

Various combinations of these programmatic aspects are possible. For example, the high-expectation, transitional halfway house would provide initial care or aftercare, with staff living in and providing dinner and with residents who were working or in school expected to leave within a prescribed period. The intermediate-expectation, long-stay community residence would typically provide aftercare for the chronic former mental patient, with a live-in staff initially providing meals; the residents would all be in day care, a sheltered workshop, or a combination of the two. The cooperative apartment would provide neither meals nor live-in staff, and there would be no expectations for the residents to move out in any specified period. These are only three of many possibilities.

Different types of community residences can be viewed on a scale ranging from greater dependence to greater independence. However, a program that segregates patients in this manner should be approached with caution, as it risks repeating the patient caste system of the hospital. The segregation of the more disabled from residents who could be more rapidly rehabilitated would tend to reproduce the demoralized atmosphere so well known at the hospital. It is to the advantage of both groups to mix them in one community residence. This gives the more able residents an opportunity to help the more disabled; while the natural movement and success of the healthier bestows a hopeful mood on the entire facility.

The Challenge

Today's crisis in the delivery of mental health services can be solved if an integrated system of community rehabilitative programs can be developed. The psychiatric community residence is a key element in this system, providing a supportive alternative domicile, and allowing the resident to leave a noxious living situation without being cut off from community, job, and friends. The hospital-induced social breakdown syndrome could become extinct. We are far from attaining the numbers of facilities needed, however. There were only 289 community residences in the entire United States in 1974. Assuming that an average of fifteen hundred people per state need such care, some five thousand community residences are needed nationally.

Our first challenge in attaining this goal is adequate funding. The rule has been a complex system of income from a multitude of sources—federal, state, county, city, mental health, vocational rehabilitation, and social security—funding a variety of legal entities. These sources and agencies must be coordinated, rationalized, and handled in a way that does not rob the resident of monies that are his. National health insurance and all other insurance programs must address themselves to this modality of care. Existing state budgets must be reviewed and funds reallocated from the institutions that currently drain them. Job retraining and education must be provided for employees transferred from the institution to the community.

It is important to reemphasize that the community residence, as a mental health service, had a unique beginning. It did not begin as part of a directed, unified, official policy, coming from above. (Indeed, the five essential services defined in the original Community Mental Health Center Law in 1963 left out the community residence entirely.) Rather, the community residence began with a low profile, as an offspring of antiestablishment experimentation. There were no grand announcements in the press, no laws, no regulations, no building codes, no licenses. The mid-1960s was a time of innovation without such encumbrances. Only recently has this state of affairs begun to change. In 1974, the bill to continue the Community Mental Health Center (S. 3280, Health Revenue Sharing Acts) included the community residence as an essential service for the first time. (It became law in 1975.)

Legitimation, then, is a second major challenge. The community residence, born outside the mental health system, must become part of this system without letting the system destroy the basic clinical concepts outlined earlier. The task of the system, in turn, is to legitimate the community residence in its interfaces with the community. Appropriate systemic concerns include quality control, building codes, and zoning requirements. Carefully and judiciously developed standards will be a distinct asset to the entire range of interested parties—the client, the provider of services, the community, the state legislature, and national bodies. Such standards will ensure that the client is protected from potential abuses by the provider; that the provider is protected from discrimination by the community; that the community is protected from undue saturation by these facilities; and that the state legislature is protected against fiscal mismanagement. Arbitrarily stringent or irresponsibly lax

standards alike are potential threats both to the community residence programs and, indirectly, to the whole effort to deinstitution-
alize the care of large numbers of our troubled citizens.

The third and final challenge confronting the community residence program is perhaps the most profound. How can we preserve
and build on the initial creative spark that launched the community
residence program in the first place? Once established, this system
will increasingly be staffed by workers who did not help start it.
Working in a community residence should never be "just a job."
The retrained mental health workers moving into the community, as
well as newcomers to the field, must educate themselves and join in
the spirit of relating to former patients as people.

CHAPTER 2

In Search of a Conceptual Model: Historical Perspectives

A comprehensive understanding of the community residence requires attention to three essential operational levels: the residence's interfaces with the external community; its internal functions, organization, and structures; and, finally, its impact upon the individual resident. The exploration of all possible parts of these operations could so complicate the picture as to make formation of a unifying concept seem impossible. Yet without a unifying concept, the conflicting requirements of disparate groups can lead to contradictory decisions which threaten basic community residence programmatic goals. This chapter introduces the concept that the *family*, when viewed as a complex social system, can provide a conceptual framework for the community residence. The family, so conceived, can be used as a crucially important reference point in relation to each potential decision in planning, developing, and operating an individual halfway house or a system of several community residences. With this unifying conceptual model acting as a programmatic safeguard, it is more likely that the intended rehabilitative goal of the entire program will be achieved.

The interfaces with the external community are numerous and must be taken into account when establishing a community residence. The local community, itself far from homogeneous, can be subdivided into a variety of groups. Reacting to a planned community residence, different groups may speak with different points of view, according to their special interests. The immediate neighbors might be concerned about their families being somehow contaminated by the project; the surrounding neighborhood may worry about diminishing property values; neighborhood associations may tend to protect *their* enclave from the ostensible intruder. Nonpolitical social leaders, especially the clergy and health professionals, are usually allies. But the politicians on the planning board and town councils, who often play deciding roles in determining town zoning and other ordinances, will be swayed by the opinion of the electorate. Public opinion is molded by many factors, especially local newspapers that willy-nilly fan the flames of local sentiment. Natural allies are the local mental health associations and other human-service advocate groups, the state mental health area office, and the area board in the community. Frequently neutral prior to the opening of the community residence, but potentially powerful allies of residence programs once they are in operation, are local social-service agencies, community centers, churches, libraries, and hospitals.

The outside community also includes the state agencies which play crucial roles in developing community residences. The state licensing agency may set standards for all programs. The legislature and executive decide on financial support. Building or public safety departments determine building codes. In addition to filling technical roles, the state government—especially the executive, but also the legislature—can exert powerful moral leadership. Overall state policy as to the site of rehabilitative care can be extremely important in affecting public opinion. This general sentiment—as reported through the media—has a ripple effect throughout the entire society, forming the waves that rock local officials.

Interfaces at the national level include a variety of requirements related to funding. Programs potentially involved are national health insurance, the community mental health center, social rehabilitative services, and supplemental security income payments to the residents as administered by the Social Security Administration. In addition, standards may be set by private national bodies such as the Joint Commission on Accreditation of Hospitals.

Not only must a developing community residence address itself to the external interfaces, but each party in this outer sector must in its turn relate responsibly to the community residence. Guidelines are needed for external entities to understand the essence of the program upon which they pass judgment; to help them decide what type of dwelling to permit, what programmatic standards to adopt, and what requirements to demand.

Obviously, then, the outside community also needs conceptual guidelines so that *its* decisions can be fair, judicious, and constructive. The very nature of the conceptual framework will establish a natural pattern of *exchange* between the community residence and the public sector—to their mutual benefit, it is hoped. For example, a residence program provides the community with a certain service for which it receives recognition and is valued by the community.

Internal functions requiring decisions of the community residence and its organizing body include choosing location, the type and size of the building, and decor and furnishings. The level of disability to be served affects size and location. Adequate day rehabilitative services must also be available for the participating group residents.

Internal activities of the program that require decision-making include the entire range of internal responsibilities and expectations, chores, and restrictions. Divisions of labor must be agreed upon. Some crucial questions are: Which responsibilities should be given to the staff, the residents, or both? How large a staff should there be? What personal qualities should they have? What standards are expected of residents and staff with regard to noise, alcoholic beverages, hours, sexual behavior, bringing strangers into the house, bringing family into the house, dress, nudity, cleanliness, and attendance at meetings? All these internal decisions must be made within the context of the unique social organization of the house. Should they be made by fiat, the director dictating to all, by joint decision of the staff, or by the entire community sharing equally in voting? These decisions must be made in relation to some ideological model. In the hospital, the locus of decision-making was preordained; not so in the community residence.

Ultimately, the program will have to address itself to questions regarding the care and relationships of the individual residents. How should the staff and other residents relate to the isolated,

withdrawn resident? to the hyperactive resident? to the disorganized resident? to the untruthful, difficult-to-pin-down resident?
to the depressed resident who will not get out of bed? to the shy
resident in his twenties who has never dated or worked? The
task of the staff will be to create a living environment where each
individual can thrive by enhancing his strengths and overcoming his
particular disability. At the same time, for the sake of the community residence and the community itself, the facility has to recognize
its own limitations in its capacity to tolerate aberrant behavior or
disorder.

Given this variety of issues, the adoption of a conceptual model is
essential. The model should facilitate effective rehabilitation of residents at their highest adaptive capacity, while fostering integration
of the program as a whole into the fabric of the community. Without
ongoing reference to a consistent conceptual model, the danger
persists that the special interests of differing groups may ultimately
impinge upon the community residence, weakening the program.

There will always be frank opponents of any new program, but
even leaving such opposition aside, there are other, less obvious
dangers. If a new ideology is not adopted and carefully implemented, the old bureaucracy could render the program sterile
and impersonal, making the residence institutional.

The conceptual model proposed here—the family viewed as a
social system—should be consulted when addressing any issue involving the psychiatric community residence. The family is considered here to be a complex social system that functions at three basic
levels: the nuclear family and other social systems; internal family
activities; and the family in its impact upon the individual member.
The psychiatric halfway house is in a strategic position to reproduce
many of the functions of the family as a social system. While attempts have been made to improve the rehabilitative potential of
the psychiatric hospital, as a long-term rehabilitative resource it
continues to suffer from a bad marriage to the medical-institutional
model. The upshot is that hospitals are often intrinsically anti-
rehabilitative.

The family as a potential model has been mentioned in previous halfway house literature, but it has never been addressed in a systematic way, nor espoused as a comprehensive framework. Morris and Charlotte Schwartz made an early reference to the family model in 1964, when they recommended changes within psychiatric institutions:

> In addition to the conventional model of the mental hospital with its range of treatment modalities, other institutions might be introduced. One, modeled on the home, might be composed of a group of small cottages with from eight to twelve "patient members," run by a male and female "staff member" in which the primary emphasis is on family living and on interpersonal processes of resocialization.[1]

This obscure recommendation was not implemented, certainly not within a "psychiatric institution."

In the first monograph on the halfway house, David Landy and Milton Greenblatt mourned the lack of a good theoretical model. Nevertheless, in their study of Rutland Corner House, a halfway house for women in Boston, they discussed the staff's own sense of the house as a family. They described the director as frequently alluding to the whole group as "our family" and described how she tried to create a "family-like atmosphere." The authors concluded with an equivocal statement:

> The family in the house is a very special type of organization.... Although the director and housekeeper may be perceived either in the sororal or maternal image, no fraternal or paternal image is present. The number of sibling figures, or what might be called the resident peer group, number considerably more than the average size family in the outside community. Furthermore, while many of the women may have been socialized in similar social and psychological environments, the intensity of relationships is apt to be much less than in the case of siblings who from the beginning must cooperate and compete in the family economy. Nevertheless, the concern and understanding of the house staff seldom is found outside a family-like setting.[2]

Although the concept is explored, it is both rejected and supported, especially by the last statement. Further, it is only thought of in relation to the internal activities of the social system.

Naomi Rothwell and Joan Doniger, in their detailed description of Woodley House, a coeducational halfway house in Washington, D.C., only mentioned the homelike quality of the halfway house when comparing the architecture, furnishings, and location to that of a hospital: "Physically a halfway house is a home with bedrooms rather than beds, parlors and living rooms rather than day rooms, studies rather than offices. Ideally, it is indistinguishable in architecture and furnishings from the kinds of homes in the community in which the residents might live."[3]

Harold and Charlotte Raush, in *The Halfway House Movement*, a 1968 survey of forty halfway houses in the United States, make the most comprehensive effort to define the halfway house in ideological terms. They strongly believe that any milieu that is in the medical setting suffers. They state that the reforms of Philippe Pinel in 1806 and William Tuke in 1792, resulting in moral treatment of patients, were but short interludes of rationality between the witches, demons, inquisitions, and tortures of the sixteenth century and the asylums of the nineteenth and twentieth centuries. Asylums were considered to be "distant dumping grounds for social rejects." With the impact of Darwinism, the mentally ill were regarded as "cast offs in man's evolutionary rise," doomed to "incurability and decline." The moral treatment of Pinel was given up. Although the concept of witches was abandoned, the concept of sickness and treatment was in practice "merely a euphemism," according to the Raushes. They reviewed Stanton and Schwartz's account of ward turmoil caused by covert disagreements among staff members. They also pointed out how the hospital worked against human interaction:

Functions must be organized for efficiency and so to enhance and in no way interfere with medical requirements. The system of wards, and stations, each for patients having similar illnesses, the centralization of cooking, laundry, and purchasing, the hierarchy of differentiated responsibility in physicians, nurses, and attendants, accomplishes this organization. So too do the professional training and the inculcated culture and lore which enter into creating and maintaining a hospital atmosphere. Thus, for example, efforts are made to project an anonymity onto the patient, and staff are warned of close personal involvement with patients. The patient is a "case," a collection of diseased organs, because of the lore that any other view would interfere with the primary task of cure.[4]

Two simultaneous events promoted a move toward making hospitals more therapeutic—the advent of the use of antipsychotic drugs, and the concepts of the therapeutic community. Both began the movement of patients back into the community. The new medications took into account and specifically treated the recognized physiologic component of the illness. The therapeutic community concept began the movement of the living situation away from the traditional medical model.

But not until the 1950s, through the work of Maxwell Jones at Belmont Hospital in England, was there a real expansion on the concepts of Pinel and Tuke. Jones discarded the notion that treatment was a "schedule of appointments with a white-coated doctor." He stated that "the treatment agency became the total environment and the total environment was the agency for treatment. Activities from morning til night were to help activate and prepare the patients for community living within two to four months. The milieu was described as the 'therapeutic community.'"[5]

Rapaport studied the Jones milieu and described six basic elements as characterizing the therapeutic community:

(1) The total social organization—not just the doctor-patient relation—is seen as affecting therapeutic outcome.
(2) The social organization is not simply a background, but "a vital force, useful for creating a milieu that will maximize therapeutic effects."
(3) The notion includes opportunities for patients to take an active part in the affairs of the institution—democratization in various forms.
(4) *All* relationships within the hospital are regarded as potentially therapeutic, including those among the patients themselves.
(5) The atmosphere or emotional climate is recognized as important.
(6) Communication *per se* is highly valued.[6]

This was a clear advance in the treatment concept, containing some elements sustained in the halfway house itself. But, as the Raushes point out, the hospital's dehumanizing trappings continued to dominate the setting. The hospital unit of Jones's milieu was still a one-hundred-bed ward; the patients had to get passes to leave; bedtime was fixed at 9:00 P.M.; doctors and nurses ate in the same dining room, but at different tables, apart from the patients. As the Raushes put it, "Whereas the medical model had broken down, a sociopsychological scheme of function and malfunction was grafted onto the medical model, but the graft did not quite take."[7]

In another work, *Ego and Milieu*, John and Elaine Cumming see the hospital as a milieu which can be highly manipulated and controlled. However, their orientation is clearly and fundamentally medical. As the Raushes state, "The assumptive context—that of a hospital, of wards, of physicians, nurses and attendants having clear role definitions, and of formal, explicit hospital rules and prescriptions . . . is questioned far less than in, for example, Jones' unit."[8]

The Raushes cite another model from France, which they regard as closer to their own halfway house concept, in the little-known work of Paul Sivadon, done in the late 1950s at Neuilly-sur-Marne and later near Paris at le Mesnil Saint-Denis. Sivadon, a psychiatrist, emphasizes total milieu, action, and attention to processes of communication. Foremost is his emphasis on developmental progression as opposed to the illness cure model. As he stated, "Each procedure is premised on notions of developmental stages—proceeding from simple to complex, from undifferentiated to differentiated, from unorganized to integrated." Sivadon also believed in the "utmost respect for the individuality of the person." He did not overtly reject the medical view, but in practice his model appeared to be closer to a school than a hospital. The developmental orientation, together with the individual concern and respect accorded the clientele, created, according to Raush, a "unique model." In regard to the notion of the family as our conceptual model, especially interesting is Raush's idea that Sivadon's conceptual basis was "particularly close to Piaget's ideas about cognitive and perceptual development in children . . . and compatible with psychoanalytic ways of looking at the genesis of relationships."[9]

We are entertaining here the concept that the "patient" is not just "sick," but that he has had a defective or arrested development owing to either his environment or his physiology. Once a therapeutic course of psychotropic medication is begun, the individual needs to return to the task of emotional growth. The milieu's role is to help the person grow beyond his point of arrest, or to correct areas of distortion that occurred in the initial faulty family or physiological experience.

In the treatment of children, the family model and the developmental model come together. Raush points out the necessity of providing "educational and social experiences relevant to their society . . . as the task and experiences of growing up cannot simply be postponed for the time required for a specific therapeutic procedure." In further reviewing the residential treatment of children, Raush states that "the new model often comes close to that of a very special boarding school or a very special children's camp. Seldom does it become that of a family home." He continues to contrast the family model with the hospital's limitations:

The claim of being modeled on the family is most often made by those in traditional hospital settings; its absurdity is apparent in the ward structure, in the number of children, in the three daily shifts of workers. There are some children's institutions in Norway and Sweden which come close to exemplifying a home model.[10]

They point out that the Scandinavian models have six "children," of heterogeneous age and sex, and are staffed by couples who live in the cottages. This model from the north of Europe is close to the halfway house; and the Raushes, aware of the similarities, state in the conclusion of their book that the halfway house "more closely resembles the child residential institutions which must be concerned not only with problems of personality but also with growth and development and with education and socialization. The diversity and breadth of functions of the halfway house have a similar rationale."[11]

Throughout, however, only fleeting reference is made to the family. The Raushes state that "the halfway house situation is somewhat like family life in its informal atmosphere and style of living, in its demand for participation, and in the promise of comfort and support in difficult times." But they go on to qualify the concept by stating, "Yet it is unlike a family in being free from associations with past happenings in the resident's life; emotional involvements are less intense and in many cases less pathological."[12] Their qualification may be taken to mean that the halfway house is unlike the *family of origin* of the resident—*not* that the halfway house departs from the family model. Indeed, the freedom from past family associations in the context of shared group living (the family model) is why the halfway house is potentially so therapeutic.

The Raushes' own lack of a conceptual model leads them into some apparent contradictions. On the one hand, they point out that the halfway house is unlike a hospital in the democratic, informal, and relaxed atmosphere it provides. They state: "In virtually every aspect of living, the resident assumes a far greater degree of autonomy than does the patient in a hospital. He is not forced into the fixed patterns required by a complex administrative hierarchy but can make decisions for himself." But on the other hand, the halfway house "retains the rehabilitative aims of the hospital and emphasis on therapeutic function."[13]

This raises another crucial issue: Does a rehabilitative aim wed a program to a hospital model? Using common sense, the answer should be certainly not. The socialization and education of the developing person are natural family functions. They are also functions of innumerable social-service agencies which do not function on a medical model.

The halfway house is also compared to a boarding house, and the Raushes conclude that "in contrast to the boarding house landlady, the professionally directed halfway house staff is committed to an interest in the resident and to encouragement and support of his social and vocational adaptation to the community."[14] Another important issue is contained in this reference: even in the family-modeled halfway house about to be discussed, the staff should be professionally trained. Is this staffing pattern contradictory to the theoretical model? For a familylike social system to operate in the best interest of its members, the "family" leaders should have health, self-knowledge, psychological sophistication, and a capacity and commitment to help others. They are intended to be the ideal family members. This degree of knowledge, commitment, and skill is unlikely to be found without professional training. However, training needs to be used in a new manner—without the caparisons of cult, guild, power, and the medical mystique which in this situation only distance staff from those very residents who need meaningful, real, human relationships the most.

Among other psychoanalytic investigators, Elizabeth Zetzel reported that the treatment of the borderline patient requires the establishment of a *real relationship* with the patient by the psychoanalytic therapist. This idea has direct relevance and meaning in the conceptualization of the halfway house herein described.[15]

The references to the family-modeled psychiatric halfway house mentioned above all refer to internal family activities exclusively. The Raush work, for example, surveys many different external interfaces of the halfway house without discussing these interfaces in terms of their ideological ramifications. In addition, the literature is almost devoid of material addressed to the manner of care of specific resident types, or specific behavioral problems.

The mere creation and development of a facility to house patients in the community rather than in a hospital does not automatically ensure that the halfway house will be rehabilitative. Conflicting reports on the effectiveness of community care for the mentally ill support this view. Milton Greenblatt and I recently summarized several works which yielded generally favorable results. At the same time, William Kohen and Gordon L. Paul have reviewed the work of others who report unfavorable results. For example, they quote Franklin Chu and Sharland Trotter as suggesting that "more of the same is simply occurring in new locations." Kohen and

Paul also point out that Myron Koltuv and Walter S. Neff warned in 1968 that without a new technology, "it is quite likely that our only accomplishment will be moving the locus in which the emotionally disturbed vegetates and experiences personal misery."[16]

A review of the literature shows that some community programs are rehabilitative and some are not. The use of so-called boarding homes without bona fide rehabilitation programs, implemented without the use of trained professionals, has generally been viewed as disastrous. Robert Reich and Lloyd Siegel reported in 1973 on the problems in New York, describing proprietary homes with as many as 285 beds which provided no day programs, rehabilitative services, or systematic psychiatric care.[17] H. Richard Lamb and Victor Goertzel, in comparing boarding homes to high-expectation halfway houses, concluded that the boarding homes assumed the "guest" would "remain regressed and dependent indefinitely," in contrast to the high-expectation halfway house, which facilitated a "process of delabeling—the residents [being] less segregated, less likely to be labeled as deviate, and experiencing less stigmatization— with the individuals seeing themselves as functioning members of the community."[18] The authors struggle for answers as to what really helps a person to become a bona fide member of the community.

Maxwell Jones recently suggested that there was a need "to examine the social organization of the system in which patients live." He questions the need to follow the medical tradition's concern with pathology, symptoms, and illness. He asks, "Should we not give at least equal importance to a social system that can give its members a feeling of identity and of belonging, along with as active and creative a role in the system as the potentialities will allow?"[19]

Indeed, a new system is needed, and one is already being implemented by a variety of clinicians and programs. However, there does not appear to be a clear, common ideology for the nonmedical component. The seeds of such an ideology can be found in the works of two groups of authors, Norman W. Bell and Ezra F. Vogel, and E. Mansell Pattison et al.

As noted at the beginning of this chapter, when the nuclear family is seen as a social system operating at three levels (external systems, internal activities, and the impact on the individual), it provides a rational, comprehensive model for the psychiatric halfway house. The model replicates the social system which, throughout man's history, has had the function of educating and socializing people. Bell and Vogel offer a description of the family in these terms. The family functions as defined by Bell and Vogel also characterize the psychiatric halfway house and provide a natural rationale for its functioning.[20]

In relating the halfway house to the nuclear family, it is recognized that the American family does not appear today to be in the same condition that it was in fifty years ago. Addressing this issue, Pattison et al. have recently suggested four types of family structure in contemporary America:

(1) *The traditional extended family,* an interdependent social and economic unit, with each nuclear subfamily living in geographic proximity and depending upon the extended kin for major affective and instrumental resources. (2) *The dissolving or weak family* in which most kin functions have been assumed by large-scale formal organizations leaving the nuclear family with few resources and few innate coping abilities. (3) *The isolated nuclear family,* a structure that retains fewer essential functions; these are concentrated in the family and are maintained with stability, although often at the expenditure of great effort to maintain family cohesion. (4) *The modified extended family* structure, which consists of a coalition of nuclear families in a state of partial dependence.[21]

Clearly, part of the problem in our society today is that the nuclear and extended families have both broken down to some extent. But the decay of the family in contemporary society is no argument against the family as a model of social organization. Plans for a nonmedical component of a social rehabilitative program would do well to follow an authentic societal organization which has worked well for thousands of years and which has been shown to correlate with health.

CHAPTER 3

The Halfway House as a Family-Modeled Social System

The family plays an extremely complex role in the maintenance of the stability of our society and in the growth and development of new members. The three primary functions the nuclear family serves with regard to the total society are defined by Bell and Vogel as "replacing members, primary socialization, and maintaining motivation for participation within the society" (p. 7).[1] If we substitute "returning members" or "maintaining members" for "replacing members," we are defining three primary functions of the psychiatric community residence.

The function of the community residence immediately contrasts with the functions of the traditional asylum: the community residence sustains people *in* society, whereas the asylum excludes them from it. There are, of course, persons dangerous to themselves or others for whom it is essential to provide protection, for their own sake as well as society's. These cases, however, represent a small minority of the mental-patient population. The entire system should not be defined and structured around a small minority. Yet this is what has occurred throughout the nation's state mental hospital system. It was not until June 26, 1975, that the U.S. Supreme Court ruled unanimously, in a case representative of widespread unnecessary incarceration, that a mentally ill person could not be held against his will if three criteria were met: the hospital was not offering treatment; the person was not dangerous to himself or others; the person was capable of living in the community with the help of friends or relatives.[2]

Primary socialization and maintaining motivation for participation within society have traditionally been severely lacking in the mental hospital. Instead, the geographic removal of the hospital from society, together with the caste separation of patients, contributed to the "social breakdown syndrome" of patients described by Erving Goffman in *Asylums*.[3] This sequence of removal and isolation is the antithesis of the family function of socialization. It is interesting that the courts have only recently begun to respond to this issue. In *Dixon* v. *Weinberger*, it was ruled that patients in the District of Columbia have a statutory right to confinement in the least restrictive facility. Responsibility was placed on the District of Columbia and the federal government to develop a plan to identify the population that should be transferred to community-based facilities and means for achieving this transfer, including the creation of alternative facilities if necessary.[4] Thus, the courts implicitly recognized the desocialization effects of the mental hospital.

The Halfway House and External Systems

What other essential characteristics of the family in society relate to the halfway house? "No society is indifferent to the quality and number of families in its population" (p. 1), state Bell and Vogel—a simple statement, but one pregnant with the notion that the family *relates as a system to the outside society as a whole.* Until recently, society has been indifferent to the quality and number of state hospitals as long as they were remote, "out of sight" and thus "out of mind." Only in the last few years have fiscal constraints and class-action suits led to the court decisions that for the first time are recognizing the plight of the hospitalized patient. The halfway house, being in the community, relates to the surrounding society, just as the nuclear family home does.

Society is naturally concerned about the family's quality; for similar reasons, it is also naturally concerned about the halfway house in its midst. Society's often critical concern about the quality of life in the halfway house and the maintenance of neighborhood property values should not be considered, prima facie, anti–mental health. Rather, the surrounding community of a halfway house is playing an intrinsic family-related function that should be recognized and related to accordingly. Granted, neighborhood concerns may threaten or impinge in a variety of ways upon the halfway house, but the problems are basically no different from those which any family feels upon moving into a new neighborhood. If there are boundaries and limits governing society's reaction to new neighbors, there are also legal standards which new arrivals must meet. This leads to another basic concept, namely, that the family naturally functions within certain legal constraints.

The Law

"The family is much more than a private arrangement. It is also a social unit which is regulated by custom and law" (p. 1). It is through these customs and laws that boundaries are established and modes of behavior are sanctioned. Thus, when a new family moves into a neighborhood, it may be customary for the neighbors on the street to initiate a welcoming social function such as a coffee get-together or a cocktail party. This activity promotes social integration of family members into the neighborhood. Alternatively, the neighborhood may be characteristically indifferent and not react to the newcomers. If for some reason the family is experienced as foreign or unacceptable, then the neighborhood may show its animosity, but limits to the ways in which this animosity can be expressed are specified by civil rights laws.

The halfway house should have the same protections as any family which may be experienced as different or foreign to the neighborhood. The current struggles in the courts in regard to this issue, usually fought over zoning regulations and restrictions, will be discussed in chapter 8. Of course, the zoning of the halfway house as a family—defined as a group of unrelated people living together in a single housekeeping unit as a family—is entirely consistent with this basic rationale of the community residence.

Internal family activities are also subject to the law and so are intimately related to the outside system. These laws are so rarely used that there is a low level of public awareness of these legal protections of the integrity and quality of family life. However, a variety of behaviors within the family are prohibited by law. These include keeping children home from school, incest, abusing children by beating or other means, and the distortion of the marital relationship by taking more than one spouse at a time. In all of these instances, legal intervention is explicitly sanctioned by society, which has empowered its elected officials to enact laws prohibiting such behavior. It is important to note that many of the laws are for the protection of developing children. Further, the government's orientation to the family is "evident in its decisions and policies, which protect the privacy of the home, refuse to compel spouses to testify against each other, distribute welfare benefits in relation to the family's condition, and act in various ways to inhibit the dissolution of marriages" (p. 16). Through laws, society attempts to protect those values which are essential to the preservation of the integrity of the family.

In a similar manner, laws and regulations can be adopted for the halfway house which apply to its internal activities in such a manner as to enhance its natural family functions. For example, halfway house regulations can, within the family tradition, ensure the education of residents, prohibit their abuse, and prescribe clearly qualified personnel.

The recognition of the interrelationship of society and the halfway house in these terms is essential so that the different parties participating in the establishment of halfway houses understand the legitimacy of their different roles. For example, a community residence program that remains aloof from the neighborhood and from community agencies or groups would be losing a part of its natural family function. In fact, the residence would potentially be repeating a pathological pattern of some patients, promoting distrust and alienation from the surrounding community. This attitude also repeats the isolation and insularity of the remote state hospital.

A halfway house which opposed all legitimating and quality-control legislation would be claiming a special station certainly not shared by the family. A community residence should recognize that society's legal interventions may well serve its interests by ensuring the preservation of its essential family functions. In turn, society's obligation is to write regulations and laws to this end. It is essential that the laws not be written by a legislative body preoccupied with increasing its bureaucratic power and authority at the expense of the programmatic quality of a halfway house.

In summary, like the family, the halfway house ensures that its inhabitants will live *in the community within the law*. Deviants who cannot stay within the law do not belong in halfway houses. In exchange for this guarantee, the halfway house no less than the family is entitled to certain safeguards, including a safe but homelike dwelling, the right to locate in areas beneficial to the program, protection against arbitrary exclusion from the community, and financial safeguards and back-ups similar to those of the nuclear family system.

Work

Bell and Vogel point out that a basic family function is for family members to contribute labor in exchange for rewards. The family of orientation must provide the individual with a minimum of basic skills to enable him to enter the job market. This is considered a major responsibility of the family; it should also be a major responsibility of the community residence. If the resident is not ready for competitive employment, then sheltered workshops and appropriate rehabilitation counseling are arranged. These efforts on the staff's part to assist the resident toward economic self-sufficiency do not separate the community residence from familylike functioning, but are another example of family functioning in action.

Work contributes to the emotional well-being of the resident at a variety of psychological levels. It enhances stability and satisfaction, often to the surprise of the previously unemployed resident. Work provides a regular schedule, autonomy of action through appropriate compensation, an increase in self-esteem, an opportunity for expressing competitiveness, and advancement into new areas of growth. Further, the satisfactions developed through a work experience are communicated to fellow residents—much like Tom Sawyer's whitewashing—so the working experience easily becomes the acceptable group mode in the community residence. Thus, group solidarity and increased group self-esteem are fostered. Ultimately work will be one of the keys enabling the resident to move into his own lodgings in the community. The staff is expected to assess skillfully the level of each resident's work potential and to guide him toward that goal, just as in any healthy home.

The basic structure of family activities, schedules, and location is related to the work schedule. The halfway house similarly adjusts to the lives of its members. It is located within easy reach of transportation. The house routine is adjusted to accommodate working residents, for example, making the dinner hour at 6:00 P.M. to allow them sufficient time to return to the house. Further, routine appointment times or meeting times of the house would occur after the working day, as in a normal family.

This is a distinct contrast to the usual mental hospital routine, where activities and working schedules of professionals within the hospital take precedence. These, of course, are in the regular working day and are, therefore, in direct conflict with the patient who has been rehabilitated to the point of being able to work outside the hospital environs. Thus, the patient loses supportive services just when he needs them most—when he ventures forth into the community to seek employment.

Arbitrarily designated "mental health catchment areas" should not dictate that a community residence must locate in a site remote from employment opportunities. Flexibility in selecting the site of a community residence is essential. Access to other mental health services is important, but so are employment opportunities and proximity to shopping districts. Thus, to locate a community residence in a rural village where employment is scarce, or in a bedroom suburb, would deprive the residence of a vital sphere of natural family activity. Breadwinners of homes in such areas generally commute by private automobiles, a resource unavailable to the typical halfway house resident.

The capacity to work requires that the worker not bring his family troubles to the job, and that he be able to set aside family concerns long enough to accomplish work tasks. This is crucial in the functioning of the community residence. The resident must not be so dependent upon the house as to prevent him from venturing into the community to work. Having accomplished this, however, he must develop the capacity to leave his troubles, his pathology, at home. The milieu should encourage an ethic that one does not always focus on one's problems—there is a time and place for everything. Daytime is the time to be at work, focusing one's attention on the task at hand. The evening, after supper and evening chores, is the time to turn to one's fellow residents and house managers for understanding and support in relation to the trials of the day.

Normal family functioning includes intermittent alterations of family routines in relation to work schedule changes—for instance, during the Christmas rush. This is feasible in the halfway house because it is small enough and administratively flexible.

In normal family functioning, unemployment creates a crisis centering on loss of wages, demoralization, and potentially strained family relations. So, too, the loss of a job is a personal crisis for the resident and the community residence as a whole. The task of the community residence here is to support the resident appropriately, ensuring that the loss does not precipitate a relapse, by helping the resident correct personal deficiencies at work (if they existed), and by facilitating the hunt for new employment.

Members of community residences are true consumers in a community, in contrast to hospital patients, whose consumer functions are assumed by a purchasing department. Shopping with the managers for the house food should be a regular activity for the residents. Orienting residents to stores for other goods is another function of the managers which supports the residents' capacity to meet their own needs.

The Community

The law is one force demanding that citizens comply with community standards, but there are less formal ones as well. According to Bell and Vogel, an entity called the "community" exerts a second level of social control. The community is not necessarily defined as a specific neighborhood but "as diffuse affective relationships of varying extensiveness" (p. 16). The exchange thought to be crucial here is that the family trades participation in community activities for support from the community. Ideally, the community residence, as a family, can eventually command community support. The residence provides specialized mental health services for members of the community in need of them. In addition, the residence can become a good neighbor by paying local taxes (or making payment in lieu of them if legally exempt) in exchange for the services of the local community; it can participate in neighborhood cleanups, neighborhood improvement associations, and street fairs; and it can contribute to local church functions or other neighborhood group affairs. The community is seen as giving the nuclear family an identity in exchange for adherence to community patterns. Bell and Vogel state that this identity "gives the family a feeling of belonging and prevents anomie" (p. 17).

In practice, however, the community residence often has great difficulty in its family-community relationships. This problem is largely one of public relations and political education, rather than a legal one. The community may resort to legal action if it experiences a community residence as violating the two essential requirements of the exchange, namely, that the residence be inhabited by authentic members of the community at large, and that the residence conform to community patterns. The community is often fearful on both counts. Solid community resistance to a residence can provoke energetic efforts to deny its legitimacy, usually on the basis of explicit disbelief in the residence's guarantees of conformity. Neighborhood meetings may be called and ad hoc organizations may form to oppose the community residence, and the struggle may make local headlines.

However, strategies can be planned to counteract opposition from the outset. Stress should be placed on the residence's capacity to support existing community patterns, and especially on the residence's capacity to provide a community service. The intrusion of previously isolated patients from remote state hospitals can be perceived as a foreign invasion. But if the residence prevents or limits hospitalization of members of the community in which it is located, the community becomes less negativistic. Even facilities serving the formerly chronic state hospital patient can reserve places for members of the immediate community.

It should be noted that seemingly insurmountable local community resistance can generate a defeatist attitude among planners, so that neighborhoods are sometimes selected specifically because they have a very low sense of community solidarity, such as urban fringe areas, where people are often transient. The opposition encountered in highly organized, integrated communities is thereby avoided—but so is the resident's chance of belonging to a cohesive community.

The Value System

Bell and Vogel emphasize that "the nuclear family is the smallest social unit responsible for the preservation of the value system" (p. 19). They conceive the nuclear family's duty to be the socialization of new members into the basic value system. The religious and educational systems embody the ultimate values of society and communicate these values to society. The nuclear family aids in the preservation of these values by communicating them to its members, who internalize them.

In relation to the educational system, the rehabilitative psychiatric halfway house works at helping the residents to understand and gain knowledge about their psychological reality so they can communicate about it, deal with others in relation to it, and thereby cope with increasing effectiveness. In the most direct sense, they learn how to value themselves instead of regarding themselves as stigmatized outcasts. In addition, the psychiatric halfway house has the opportunity to communicate and propagate an altruistic value system as the residents learn to care and look after one another's well-being. These two values contribute to the residents' capacity to move into the community, knowledgeable about themselves and caring for one another.

The hospital system has supported a value system which communicates to the patient that he is totally sick and is there only to receive care and treatment. In contrast, the psychiatric halfway house prepares a person for living in the community through its communication of self-knowledge, the ability to cope, and altruism.

The Halfway House and Internal Family Activities

Task Performance

"Task performance within the nuclear family always occurs in the context of the family's relationship with external systems." This includes working in the external economy in order to provide the money to purchase goods and bring them into the family. Internal task performance is related to solidarity and integration of the relationships within the family. As Bell and Vogel put it, there must be "motivational commitment of the family members for the performance of the tasks." They note that "this can only be done as they are related to other family goals" (p. 21).

Thus, goods obtained from external systems are cared for and maintained as family possessions. Goods are maintained by cleaning, repairing, or improving. There are other tasks that can be referred to as "finishing" of goods, such as "cleaning and cooking food, installing equipment, sewing, 'do-it-yourself' operations, and the like" (p. 21). Tasks also include transportation and selection.

Bell and Vogel suggest, "To some extent, the relationships within the family develop as a result of the nature of task activity. For example, if productive activities performed within the family require close interaction between family members, then one would expect family bonds to be very strong." They go on to say that "if there are dependent members of the family, then other members of the family are expected to perform various tasks in connection with their welfare" (p. 21). In many cases the family is responsible for the care of the sick and aged.

Another major issue is the division of labor within the family. The distribution of tasks within the family has traditionally been based on certain biological factors. "The mother-child bond ordinarily leads the mother to perform tasks connected with the child . . . and the father to perform . . . activities that, directly or indirectly, will produce the needed goods and services" (p. 22). These sexual distinctions are becoming increasingly blurred, with parents sharing tasks more equally—the father more involved in child-rearing, and the mother often working for wages in the community.

In normal family development, the ability to perform tasks

evolves on a timetable appropriate to the development of the family member. Whereas the child is initially in the dependent role, he soon assists in the home by helping with the laundry, cooking and cleaning up, and setting the dinner table. Ultimately, he moves into the external system, first by working in part-time jobs after school, and then through full-time summer employment, contributing increasingly to the economy of the family. These experiences provide capacities and skills in preparation for moving out of the family home into independent living.

Unlike the family home, the hospital defines all tasks as the exclusive province of the staff, with the patients in the role of defectives and dependents. In the hospital system the responsibility for preservation of hard goods falls to one department, the cleanliness of the building to another, the cutting of lawns to a third, and the distribution of medication to a fourth. From the perspective of normal development, the hospital deprives the patient of stimulation, potential reward, and a sense of increasing mastery.

Task performance in the halfway house, however, is much like that in the family. Many of the residents work, significantly contributing to the income of the residence. They share in the finishing and maintenance of the goods in the community residence. Shopping, cooking, and cleaning are regular house chores, usually done in rotation. The residents participate in decisions affecting the purchase of major goods for the house. In contrast to the hospital, where the nurses and doctors are expected to perform the caring task, when one of the residents of the halfway house is in crisis, all members of the community, staff and residents alike, share the task of trying to relieve it.

Leadership

In a normal, functioning family, because we have a "stable group with the same membership over a relatively long period of time, its division of leadership is ordinarily rather clearly structured. For example, parents have clear-cut leadership over children" (p. 23). Within the family social system the basic exchanges occur, namely, loyalty of the family in relation to leadership and compliance in relation to decisions. The leadership and decisions will be greeted with loyalty and compliance if three conditions exist: that the decisions make sense; that the leadership is clear and not conflicted; and that the leadership is benevolent and clearly in the interests of the rest of the family. Leadership can emanate from a point above with sequential delegation of power and authority. If this flows from parents to older siblings to younger siblings consistently, benevolently, accurately, and without conflict, then harmony will likely exist within the family. If, on the other hand, there is abdication of leadership, confusion of roles, or dissension among the parental authorities, such that alliances of siblings with various leaders are formed, chaos ensues. Coalition patterns and manipulation are the response to this conflict, and other functions of the family are undermined, interfered with, and diluted. Harmony and growth will occur only under the right conditions.

Just as the multiple service systems of the hospital usurp task performance from patients, competing clinical systems tend to interfere with and dilute leadership, rendering it ambiguous and inconsistent. Whenever an institutional system with multiple arbitrary divisions affects the social milieu, that system by its very structure fosters conflict. At the simplest level we have a changing eight-hour nursing shift which may subject the ward to three very different expectations of patient conduct. Inconsistency creates conflict and anxiety in the patient as he tries to learn appropriate behavior. Confusion in this regard can reinforce social withdrawal. Alternatively, the more action-oriented patient could enter into destructive alliances with other patients, diminishing further the likelihood of productive reentry into society.

Within the clinical grouping assigned to a hospital ward, there are mental health workers, nurses, social workers, and physicians, each of whom is responsible to one of three departments—nursing, social work, or medicine. Each department commonly brings different approaches to the patients and their milieu. In addition, the different service departments may perform in a way that is potentially undermining to certain milieu plans or priorities of clinical care.

Critical issues in the internal system of the ward include the problems of hiring and firing personnel. Who has the power—the personnel department? the medical department? Does a physician in charge have control over the staff he supervises and directs? Can he fire an incompetent or uncooperative nurse? If not, then the establishment of a cohesive ward milieu can be extremely difficult. In the state hospital system, the hospital is often controlled by an area director, who is controlled by a regional administrator, who is controlled by the commissioner, who is controlled by the executive above him. Beyond that, a local legislator can block a ward staff move in the interest of an employee who also happens to be a constituent. The patient on the ward, in need of care, is potentially a victim of all this diffusion in the lines of power and authority, because clear leadership is almost impossible.

In contrast to the state hospital, the primary care givers in a halfway house are a live-in couple who provide leadership around the clock, much as the parents do in the conventional nuclear family. The administrative hierarchy above them is small and unified. The board of directors of a nonprofit corporation representing the community where the halfway house is located usually hires the administrative director, who then hires the manager or houseparents. This three-tiered administrative structure should operate smoothly and with cooperation, each staff member having been hired on the basis of qualifications and compatibilities. It should be entirely free of the trappings of patronage. House meetings can accommodate the managers, relief managers and the director, who work together as the total power system. This design minimizes structurally the potential for dissension and disagreement among staff. Ultimately, the consistency of leadership should permeate the residence and provide a feeling of security and trust among the residents. Under such conditions, they feel more comfortable risking new steps toward active community and social involvement. Further, the simplicity and openness of the staffing at the house meetings foster a sense of collaborative community decision-making that includes the input of the residents. This contributes to preparation for outside living, in contrast to the helplessness the patient often feels on the state hospital ward.

Integration and Solidarity

Bell and Vogel point out that "for a group to maintain close relationships between members over a long period of time requires some commitment and feelings of solidarity. . . . If there is little solidarity within the family, the obligations imposed by the group may seem oppressive, but if there is a great deal of solidarity, the obligations may be accepted as natural and not even felt as obligations. In addition, feelings of solidarity are very important in dealing with individual tensions and personality problems" (p. 25). Group solidarity is a key issue not only in the family, but in the halfway house as well. Harmonious leadership contributes to the establishment of this integration and solidarity. With leadership, and subsequent integration and solidarity, members of the family system are more comfortable and able to deal with outside obligations to society. They are relating from the strong base of a unified family that has meaningful values. Bell and Vogel suggest that "to some extent, the mere process of interaction, even when frustrating to the individuals involved, is related to solidarity; over a long period of time, the meeting of expectations leads to a feeling of faithfulness which adds to solidarity." They continue:

Furthermore, there are certain activities particularly significant for family solidarity. One obvious case is the family ritual or the family celebration. The performance of specific routines at mealtime, in which the family unites as a whole, gives the family a feeling of solidarity; special family holidays, such as birthdays and special occasions, also serve to give the family a feeling of solidarity. It is true that some of these larger celebrations, such as weddings, christenings, funerals, and the like, serve to unite the entire extended family as well as the nuclear family. But there are many occasions, for example, a Sunday dinner, family prayers, or family television-viewing, which can reinforce the solidarity of the nuclear family. (pp. 25–26)

A major difference between the halfway house and the hospital is that the halfway house routinely has family meals together and has group meetings together. When eating, all members of the community—including the managers—eat together family style. Like a family, the halfway house has rituals, including house meetings for the entire community, staff and residents. In contrast, the hospital usually *forbids* staff and patients to eat together. This is an example of a hospital practice which is explicitly opposed to family functioning and solidarity. Any community domiciliary program which perpetuates this kind of patient-staff splitting is antitherapeutic in regard to this ideological model.

Like the family, the halfway house has birthday parties, parties for departing residents or staff, graduation parties, and often special annual reunions such as a Christmas party. This last sort of event brings in the entire extended family, in this instance, the ex-resident group.

In addition to ritual activities that function to provide family solidarity there are also symbols of family solidarity, according to Bell and Vogel. These include common experiences such as family vacations, family secrets, family histories, and special memories of hard times. These memories are treasured in large part because of their significance in maintaining family unity and solidarity. The authors state that "it has long been recognized that family furnishings are symbols of social-class membership; it has been less common to note the extent to which certain family possessions, hope chests, heirlooms, and even the family house or car can serve as concrete symbols of family solidarity" (p. 26).

So, too, the halfway house over time develops its history and memories. Hard times are the starting up, the lack of furniture, the argument with the obstreporous neighbor. The common experiences of having emotional problems, having been in the hospital, and having had difficulties with one's original family also foster group cohesion and solidarity. The support of other house members is a distinct contrast to the environment of the hospital which subtly shames the patient. Often his wish is to leave a humiliating situation, rather than relate closely to it.

The furnishings of the halfway house are important components of family pride and togetherness, a fact which should not be lost on the developers of new programs. Self-esteem is also enhanced by a sense of pride in the comfortable, pleasing home setting.

Bell and Vogel state that family members who are considered to be behaving inappropriately are met with various sanctions in order to attempt to renew their participation within the family, its activities, and modes of behavior. "Any lack of motivation is always a potential threat to the entire group, and the family cannot let deviance from family norms occur without attempting to supply motivation to correct this deviance or at least making clear that such behavior is unacceptable" (p. 26). A staff member of the halfway house, in applying whatever sanctions he can muster in dealing with the unacceptable behavior of a resident, should not backslide into the medical model. Rather, there are legitimate techniques to be used in preserving family unity, integration, and solidarity that do not label the person "sick." Such modes rely on group pressure and household sanctions, and are built upon respect and trust instead of exclusion to remote institutions or seclusion rooms. As in the family, exclusion is used to deal with unacceptable behavior only as a last resort.

The Value System

Through their relationships with each other, family members come to have certain expectations about how other members should behave; these expectations are associated with feelings of rightness or wrongness. Specific expectations are related to more general standards, and together they constitute a system of values for organizing and giving direction to various family activities. This value system provides a hierarchy of goals and a body of rules for their attainment. These are valued far beyond their mere utility in solving specific problems. The family attempts to maintain this value system because it gives meaning and purpose to specific family activities. (p. 28)

An example of this value system in the halfway house would be the expectation that residents altruistically look after and care for each other. Similarly, verbal communication is emphasized, and destructive acting out is forbidden. An example of the distinction between the external value system and the internal value system is seen in relation to drugs and alcohol. The external value system dictates that smoking marijuana is a crime, although drinking alcohol is not, but both may occur socially without sanction. However, within the family system of the halfway house, both drugs and alcohol work against the value system, which is to enhance self-awareness and to gain the ability to tolerate painful feelings. The house at the same time is judicious in its sanctions when one of the residents violates the value system. Alcohol used in moderation either outside or inside might, for a given facility, be within the limits of the value system.

The highest value that permeates both the home and the halfway house should be love and care for one another. This is sustained through the value system within the halfway house family. In turn, the group's cohesion and solidarity are enhanced by this value.

Bell and Vogel point out that "the values of a family are not entirely, or even necessarily, conscious, except when there is conflict or when they are made explicit in the socialization process. Even in the socialization process, values are often taught through relationships and examples rather than by explicit precept" (p. 29). This concept directly relates to the fact that the house managers live in the halfway house with the residents and participate in the milieu as natural role models. It is therefore obvious that their selection by the hiring agent is critical to the operation of any halfway house program. The resident will learn a value system through the subtle process of identification with the house managers. In contrast to the traditional hospital professional, who remains aloof in relating his personal feelings and life-style, the halfway house managers should be open and relate as whole people to the residents, living beside them and exemplifying their values through their way of life. Often a married couple implicitly demonstrates to a young adult population that such arrangements as marriage actually can work out happily and productively. This may be in contrast to both the earlier family experience of the resident and more recent peer cynicism about marriage in general. That expression of a wide range of feelings is acceptable is another value which may be acquired by the resident through observation of the managers' interactions.

The house meeting is another activity characteristic of the halfway house. It may be a forum in which the group exerts its pressure on members who violate the value system. Issues that ultimately may be developed into house policies—for example, those regarding privacy, nudity, noise, house-cleaning, jobs, promiscuity, personal cleanliness, and social isolation—might be discussed.

The Halfway House Family and the Individual Personality

Bell and Vogel are "very tentative" in formulating "some relationships between personality, as a system, and the family, as a system" (p. 30). Their approach is distinct from the conventional one, and this section will comment briefly on some of their concepts.

Bell and Vogel describe three major interactions between the family system and personality development. First, they note that if the family social system "is to operate successfully, the members must have . . . similar orientations to the group and activities within it, to themselves, and to each other member, and they must have motivational commitments sufficient to maintain the system and to meet its functional requirements." Second, they suggest that "personality develops not entirely, but to a considerable extent, within the matrix of the family system and is maintained by the family." Third, they conceive of the personality itself as a "system of activities, orientations, motivations, etc., which has some internal cohesion, as well as a tendency to have and maintain boundaries" (p. 30).

In short, the family system in which the individual thrives and grows must have individual members who are committed to it. In terms of the family model discussed here, the hospital appears as a closed system to which the patient commits himself only to the degree necessary to win release. The halfway house, by contrast, requires a commitment equal to that of the natural family, and offers in return a supportive home base from which residents can participate in the core family system. An individual may choose not to move out, in which case he may remain as long as he preserves the common orientation and demonstrates a commitment both to the family and to his own personal growth.

Task Performance

As Bell and Vogel point out, the crucial issue here is that "the family, if it is to develop its members' personalities adequate for them to advance into the 'outside world,' must then give individuals the opportunity for graded involvement in, or identification with, task activities, and insure that learning takes place. This assignment of tasks must be appropriate to, and not above or below, the intellectual, physical, and attitudinal capacities of the individual" (p. 31). The responsibility for planning appropriate activities and chores also characterizes the family-modeled halfway house. Too often, these functions are seen as the responsibility of medical, social rehabilitative, or educational institutions; in fact, they devolve from the primary social institution, the family. This model is not a regressive one, for as Bell and Vogel point out, "even the most mature adult personalities require some support and recognition, if they are to preserve the proper orientations to work and maintain the appropriate flow of motivational energy" (p. 32).

Family Leadership

Bell and Vogel briefly comment in regard to the issue of family leadership that "the modes of meeting the leadership problems of co-ordination and authority which the family develops... have wide-ranging effects upon the developing and the developed personality" (p. 32). Healthy leadership will promote healthy development of the child, whereas pathological parental leadership will include inappropriate sexual acting out, uneven limit-setting, covert sanction of overtly unacceptable behavior, overprotective infantilization, or rigid demands for achievement. These are pathological parental modes frequently identified in the histories of incoming halfway house residents. The house managers should be alert to these patterns so they can be sensitive to the resident's early development and help counteract them through effective modeling.

Family Integration and Solidarity

Some degree of integration is essential in the family if socialization of new members is to take place. But as Bell and Vogel wisely point out, "both too much and too little integration can have deleterious effects." They also note that "the family is always faced with particular problems of this nature since personalities change over time." Intense solidarity, they continue, "may be effective when the child is a dependent infant [but] may be incapacitating when the child is old enough to be breaking away from the family and forming emotional ties to outsiders" (p. 33).

This is a crucial issue in the psychiatric halfway house. Staff who act as surrogate parents in relation to these issues must strike a delicate balance between meeting the dependent needs of the new resident while fostering his increased capacity for socialization. Over time, the resident should acquire broader social and task skills, and (in the secure context of the community residence and its aftercare programs) move toward greater capacity for autonomous living. Appropriate programs will be described fully in chapter 11.

Family Value System

The individual constructs his value system by internalizing family values, thereby developing a consistent superego. Bell and Vogel believe that "much of the process of acquiring values goes on unconsciously, and thus there tends to be a good deal of continuity from one generation to the next" (p. 33).

This is a very problematic area for the functioning of the psychiatric halfway house. At the beginning of this book I noted that dangerous people require a confined setting, for their own sake as well as society's. Clinical experience suggests that an adult who lacks an internalized value system, whatever his other problems, is difficult to alter in this regard. Sociopathic or psychopathic personality types who habitually lie, steal, and commit other antisocial offenses have no place in the psychiatric halfway house. They properly fall within the clinical and programmatic purview of a rehabilitative correctional system.

Thus, the psychiatric halfway house replicates the nuclear family's natural functions, and the traditional psychiatric hospital ward system does not. Given this family model, the psychiatric halfway house provides an environment in which to facilitate an individual's psychological development.

An individual moves out of the family nest in the natural course of events, but retains certain connections to it; nor are the important relationships confined to the nuclear family. The following chapter explores means of developing a psychosocial network which will enhance the individual's capacity for independent survival in the community.

CHAPTER 4

Beyond the Halfway House: The Extended Psychosocial Kinship System

The halfway house must relate to the larger social network if it is to be truly rehabilitative. The extended family kinship system provides two major resources for individual and family sustenance. One resource has been described as affective support, "that is, emotional involvement, personal interest, and psychological support." The other resource has been described as "instrumental support, in the form of money, food, clothes, and assistance in living and work tasks." More recently the extended family has been conceived of as including not just the extended kinship system, but also the "psychosocial network of neighbors, friends, and family associates."[1] The working together of these two groups, the extended family kinship system and the psychosocial network of nonrelations, has been called by Pattison and his co-workers the "extended psychosocial kinship system." The richness of this psychosocial system has been shown to correlate positively with health in families, and negatively with family pathology.[2]

The psychiatric halfway house, both during and after a resident's stay, can progressively foster the development of a psychosocial network that replicates many of the psychosocial kinship system functions. Helping the resident weave his life into this social fabric sustains progress made during his residency and increases his opportunities to live among significant others.

To define this function of the community residence is an important task, given some recent critiques of the concept of sheltered living. Some critics have warned that the conditions of the state hospital may simply recur in new places, and that large nonrehabilitative facilities could result.[3] Lamb and Goertzel demonstrated the vast distance between "board and care homes" and "high expectation halfway houses" in their rehabilitative capacity, and a more recent monograph examines the same issues in greater depth.[4] D. J. Rog and H. L. Raush reviewed twenty-six follow-up studies of halfway houses. In a composite picture of former halfway house residents, they found 20 percent rehospitalized, 58 percent living independently, and 55 percent employed or in school.[5]

Nevertheless, the reader should be aware that serious investigators have not been in agreement at all times about the value of halfway houses. As recently as 1976, M. A. Test and L. I. Stein, in describing their own nonresidential program (which is itself a significant contribution), suggested "serious consideration of *non-sheltered facilities*" across the board. That is, they recommended no special housing for discharged mental patients. They suggested that "managers of sheltered facilities" give tacit license to behave in "sick" ways. They further suggested that sheltered facilities, by providing so many services, share many characteristics of the "total institution" and can actually "atrophy" the resident's skills. In support of their contention, they quoted works by H. B. M. Murphy et al. and B. Weinman et al.[6] Yet the Weinman study does not describe a halfway house program. Rather, two different hospital-based pre-discharge programs and more rapid discharge to an apartment are described. Test and Stein concluded, "Community treatment is far more advantageous than residential treatment"—but the residential treatment to which they refer in both instances is hospital-based.

The study by Murphy et al. of foster home care in Canada is explicit in its exclusion of halfway houses. In a 1973 article, I responded to the potential of applying results of the Murphy study to halfway houses conceptually. After outlining the basic differences between the halfway house and the hospital and the need for a daily program outside the house, I suggested:

It is interesting to note that many of the above principles were not followed in the establishment of foster homes in Canada that have been recently described by Murphy et al. as repeating the conditions of the back ward of the large mental hospital. These foster homes were located generally in rural areas or small towns, not close to rehabilitative services. They were run by landlord supervisors and had no daily program. There was separation between the landlord and the residents even during the daily functions of eating and social gathering. The authors felt that the most critical factor was the landlord's attitude. The residents in these houses were regarded by the landlord as *patients* who were *infantile* and helpless. Thus, this was a facility which was isolated physically, had no daily program, approached the tenant as patient, and was run by landlords who had no training or commitment to rehabilitation. It is important that the entire community residence program not receive a general black eye as a result of a program such as this.[7]

The isolated, infantilizing, authoritarian program studied by Murphy is the antithesis of the family-modeled halfway house set in a community conceived of as an extended family. In fact, Leonard Stein, in November 1976, told me that his group no longer believes that sheltered living is antitherapeutic for all groups.

Pattison et al. define the extended family as an "extended psychosocial kinship system, comprised of nuclear family, some blood relatives, relatives by marriage, friends, neighbors, and close associates from church, work or recreational activities. This collage of relationships forms the functional primary psychosocial group of the individual." Pattison's group feels that "the affective and instrumental resources of this psychosocial system have been seriously underestimated."[8] They quote a variety of studies, including that of K. C. W. Kammeyer and C. D. Bolton, supporting the view that "sick" families have "fewer memberships in voluntary associations, fewer friendships with relatives, and fewer relatives living in the same community."[9] They support A. S. Alissi's findings of "psychosocial system impoverishment in families applying to group service agencies."[10]

Pattison's group developed an empirical instrument, the Pattison Psychosocial Kinship Inventory, to determine the structure of psychosocial systems. They found that the relationships in such systems (1) have a relatively high degree of interaction, whether face to face, by telephone, or by letter; (2) have a strong emotional intensity; (3) are generally positive; (4) have an instrumental base (people can be counted on to provide concrete assistance); and (5) are symmetrically reciprocal.

Studies based on the Pattison Psychosocial Kinship Inventory have produced the following conclusions: First, a healthy person has twenty to thirty people in his intimate psychosocial network. This would include five to six people in each of the following subgroups: family, relatives, friends, neighbors, co-workers, or social contacts. Second, in the neurotic population there are ten to twelve people in the psychosocial network. These people tend to relate less to each other—"as if the neurotic person is at the hub of a wheel, with individual relationships like spokes that have no interrelationship." They state, "In sum, the neurotic individual has an impoverished psychosocial network that does not provide a supportive psychosocial matrix." Third, the studies describe a pattern among the psychotic population where the psychosocial network consists of only four or five people, usually nuclear family. The interpersonal ratings are uniformly ambivalent and nonreciprocal. In this instance the social connectedness of the four or five people is very high. As Pattison et al. put it, "The psychotic is caught in an exclusive, small, social matrix that binds him and fails to provide a healthy interpersonal matrix." Finally, Pattison's group suggests that an impoverished psychosocial system can be aided by "repopulating" it with real people and resolving negativistic relationships. In the case of the psychotic, for example, "it may be important to open up the totally closed system and to establish interpersonal relationships with other social subsystems *so that an effective psychosocial system can be created.*"[11]

The common element in successful community programs may be that the psychosocial kinship system was introduced where it did not exist before, and was aided and assisted where it was weak.[12] In Stein and Test's work, the staff "was dispersed throughout the community working with the patients in such settings as their homes, their places of work, supermarkets, and recreational facilities" twenty-four hours a day. P. R. Polak and M. W. Kirby state that clearly "clinical work took place in the real life setting of the client and his family," and that "a crisis oriented social systems approach promoted growth within families." In both these projects, staff have apparently joined the extended psychosocial kinship system of the patient, which represents an important shift away from the medical treatment model. They have moved from a conception of themselves as remote, professional, singular bestowers of health treating the stigmatized sick, to skilled and caring people who have joined the world of these individuals to assist them in healthy living.

If *some* patients can be treated successfully this way, *which* are likely to benefit from halfway house programs? I would propose that patients who have no psychosocial system or only a very impoverished one fall into this category. These patients are totally isolated because of either living circumstances or pathology. In circumstances where nonresidential therapeutic work aimed at restoring an existing psychosocial network proves impractical, the halfway house can provide two essential services: a core nuclear family system, and an off-premises activity program that contributes to an extended psychosocial family system in the community. The requirement of a daily program off the premises reinforces health, fosters progression, and ultimately provides the resident with an opportunity to enter into a true psychosocial system in which he is sustained.

In general, two kinds of clients are likely to benefit from halfway house programs. One is the chronic patient who has been in the hospital so long that his family, as well as his friends, have abandoned him. His particular predicament is carefully and sensitively seen in the recent work of Lamb et al.[13] A second, and increasingly important, patient type is the young, isolated adult, who has suffered from a chronic psychotic illness perhaps for a number of years. He may well have led an isolated life during his development and had his first psychotic episode—usually schizophrenic, but perhaps manic-depressive—in the late teens. After a brief hospitalization, this patient cannot return home, as the home through the years may have sustained his isolation and may have become increasingly noxious to him. Home is a place where he is likely to regress into a previously held dependent, nonfunctioning position. This young adult needs in his first post-psychotic period a milieu where he can be with peers, at a time when it is natural to move out of the home of the family of origin. In the context of peer living, he can address himself more easily to the task of socialization and all the tasks of late adolescence. These include a capacity to deidealize the parents, separate from the parental home, develop vocational aims and skills, establish a comfortable sexual identity, and ultimately to develop a healthy heterosexual adjustment.

How does the halfway house bring all this about? First of all, the milieu itself should be egalitarian, bringing out the best in each member. It should encourage people to learn how to relate to one another, to get to know one another—including their vulnerabilities. Over time, certain residents will seek each other out because of affinities of interest and temperament. The speed with which this occurs, and the depth of relationships formed, depends of course on the size and clientele of the facility. However, in the modal group residence of fifteen or so residents, it is natural for clusters of three to four residents to become somewhat closer— especially if the program is designated as transitional and the residents know far in advance that they will need roommates with whom to live on the outside.

After a number of months, caring and knowledgeable house managers, like fellow residents, become significant others for the resident. Ideally, the resident can turn to them for another level of care if he feels that he needs a response of a different quality than he knows he can expect from a fellow resident. A little extra reassurance, or advice, or someone to intervene with a difficult outside situation of some sort—these are commonly sought from the house manager whom the resident has grown to trust. After a while, relief managers are also regarded in this manner, adding another two people to the resident's array of positively held, dependable people. There may be in addition one professional or another—a psychotherapist, an administrative psychiatrist, a social worker, a rehabilitation counselor—to whom the resident has over the months grown close and trusting.

The requirement of a program outside the halfway house adds further social contacts in a variety of potential roles—fellow workers in a sheltered workshop or competitive employment, or companions at a day center or a social club; supervisors at work, or counselors at the day center. All of these provide potentially meaningful relationships the resident may develop while living at the halfway house.

Depending upon the openness of the halfway house to the surrounding community, relationships with neighbors are also possible. In some instances neighboring families are friendly to the house and participate in occasional social functions, with the residents and and neighbors ultimately becoming friends. The resident may in addition be affiliated with a local church or other community organization and become attached to a particular pastor or priest.

If the family of origin lives in the vicinity, one of the tasks of the halfway house would be to help the resident relate to that significant group more effectively. Often this means that the resident is able to learn over time to deal with the difficulties that his biological family presents to him. Situations and interactions which in the past may have been extremely disrupting can be "detoxified" through discussion and insight gained in the halfway house milieu. The end result of this process may be that one or two significant family members may become less ambivalently regarded and actually become assets to the resident.

The sum of all these relationships acquired during a stay at the halfway house suggests that the milieu maximizes a resident's chances of acquiring a significant psychosocial network through a wealth of relationships. The resident who is prepared to move out should ideally have ongoing relationships not only with his apartment mates (say, three) but also with two other residents remaining in the community residence, the two house managers, two relief managers, the psychiatric consultant to the community residence or his therapist if he is in psychotherapy, two friends he has developed at work or at school, possibly a neighbor, someone from church or synagogue, and two or more family members with whom he may have developed a better relationship while at the halfway house. This adds up to sixteen people whom our hypothetical modal resident is in a position to call friend. Thus, if the halfway house nuclear family system has not isolated itself from the community, and has done its job within its own interactional milieu, the resident preparing to move out can do so with the support of a healthy psychosocial network of relationships. This matrix is composed of a variety of people from different settings with whom frequent contact occurs. He can expect instrumental help in a variety of ways—in finding an apartment, securing a proper lease, acquiring a job, or learning about social security benefits to which he may be entitled. There is a range of reciprocity in these relationships, with the professionals having somewhat less need of the resident than the resident has of them, but otherwise the network of friends potentially approaches symmetrical reciprocity. The psychosocial network is sustained through the practice of group movement out of the residence, so that clusters of friends tend to "graduate" together, and through the implementation of a regular ex-resident program that formalizes continuity of relationships. It creates structure and rituals that promote the retention of the extended psychosocial kinship system, as occurs in any family system.

Moving out with a group of friends has the advantage of ensuring continuity of relationships and mutual support. The moving process requires ex-residents to use newly developed skills and to acquire new knowledge. These include shopping for food and preparing it, and hunting for an appropriately spacious apartment with easy access to transportation and jobs in a relatively secure neighborhood. Negotiating with the landlord—not only about rent, but also about repairs needed before occupancy and about what services and utilities go with it—may be seen as an art in itself.

The halfway house should have an ex-resident program which provides a range of activities and social contacts supporting the viability and continuity of the psychosocial matrix. The halfway house should clearly be home base for the ex-resident so that he knows he is welcome to return to visit at any time free of charge. Nothing makes a residence feel like a "treatment" so much as the patient's knowledge that just setting foot in the place causes a cash register to ring. Thus, dropping in informally after work, in the evenings, and on weekends is encouraged, as it would be in conventional nuclear families where a member has recently moved out. By arrangement with the managers or the evening's cook, an ex-resident might, for a nominal charge, stay for dinner with former housemates. Through these informal encounters, the ex-resident renews closeness, shares new experiences, and simultaneously provides a model for the residents.

Sometimes a ritual develops among residents and ex-residents that has special significance—a housewarming that the new ex-residents give for current residents and other ex-residents. This is a subtle and pleasant way to counter fears of isolation and loss, since everyone knows where they live, how to get there, and how to reach them by phone. It also helps the resident left behind to venture out, in the company of his fellow residents, to the new dwelling of his former housemate. The managers, who have already helped in the selection of the apartment, are naturally invited, too. Similarly, the house invites ex-residents to continue attending house meetings.

After a few years of operation, a halfway house can establish a separate meeting for ex-residents, focusing on the problems of independent community living. A weekly meeting of ex-residents provides a forum for sharing problems and solutions and nurtures the ex-resident's social matrix. Regular weekly meetings with either the psychiatric consultant or the house managers, especially in the beginning months, can help to head off problems.

The house should always keep an extra bed—a sofa or hide-a-bed will do—so that the ex-resident may stay over for a few days in times of crisis. A variety of issues may generate a crisis in the ex-resident's life. These include loss of a friendship because of stress at work, or a love relationship gone awry. Loss can temporarily leave the ex-resident feeling devastated, and acute support can be instrumental in preventing hospitalization, especially in the young adult schizophrenic patient. Interpersonal problems in the apartment of the ex-resident can most properly be worked out in the ex-resident group, especially if all members of the apartment are in attendance. Problems at work are also crucial, and the loss of a job, like the loss of a friend or lover, can strike at the ex-resident's fragile self-esteem.

Mobilization of the best effort of the halfway house and its ancillary vocational counseling services can prevent relapse in this situation as well.

Other issues that commonly arise in the life of the ex-resident are generated by his family of origin. These include, for example, the serious illness of a parent, or the father's sudden loss of a job. If the family of origin has to move to another locale, the ex-resident may be thrown into a real-life crisis. Further, psychological turmoil in the family is a common effect of the resident's marked improvement; that is, the former resident may have served as a "reservoir of pathology" for the whole family. When he improves, someone else (a sibling or one of the parents) may be drafted to fill this role, suddenly becoming sick or dysfunctional. The halfway house staff can help prevent the ex-resident's tendency to slip back into previously held pathological patterns, a tendency reinforced by the family's crisis. Backsliding into old patterns may be seen as the ex-resident's attempt to reestablish the family status quo. By lending support and insight, the house staff can help make this effort unnecessary.

Planning vacations can also be important in helping the ex-resident to compensate for his own vulnerabilities. Generally, first vacations ought to be with friends, not too far from home base, with phone calls scheduled at intervals to ensure that alienation and panic do not occur.

Psychotropic medication is another issue to which the halfway house management must be alert. The ex-resident should be thoroughly educated about his need for certain medications and the managers should be sophisticated enough to know when a hyperactive ex-resident needs a lithium level checked and when an increasingly isolated, paranoid, delusional ex-resident needs a review of phenothiazine dosage.

Finally, the physical health of the ex-resident may require acute attention. He may have an illness that the managers recognize as requiring expert consultation, and they can help direct the resident to appropriate help. There are times when the ex-resident may need the intense support of the house—including sleeping over for a while. This may be due to physical necessity, such as a broken leg, in which case the ex-resident is put up on the first floor, next to a door, so he can be tended until the cast comes off. Or the occasion may demand emotional support after a traumatic event, such as an automobile accident or a mugging.

The interworkings of a social matrix, with a variety of available interactional patterns, plus alertness of the staff to typical crisis situations, will enhance the community tenure of the ex-resident. These are natural functions typical of any extended psychosocial kinship system.

PART II

The Halfway House, the Community, and the Law

CHAPTER 5

Government-Community Interaction in a Statewide Program

Although community residences are ultimately based in the local community and created in relation to it, each new group sponsoring a community residence should not have to research the state requirements and basic prerequisites for its program. Instead, the state government should form a special office to provide expert leadership and guidance and to facilitate the development of the highest-quality programs. Not only is such an office needed to help developing new programs, but it is essential as an ongoing "watchdog," to monitor constantly all state and federal legislative actions which ultimately affect *any* individual program. Issues likely to be affected would include federal and state funding, civil rights, judicial decisions, zoning issues, and building codes. Any one of these issues could prove critical to the life and existence of either a developing or an ongoing program.

The functions of such an office might include: offering programmatic, legal, and financial expertise in consultation with community residence groups; assisting in community preparation for entry of new programs; establishing quality control of existing programs through appropriate regulatory mechanisms; collecting and disseminating information for citizen referral and status reports for other bodies, including the executive department to which the agency is responsible; attempting to obtain needed financial aid for the program; ensuring that the appropriate local branch of the state office be prepared, informed, and consulted with regard to implementation of the program; and fostering enabling legislation and preventing potentially detrimental legislation.

The successful fulfillment of these functions depends upon recognition of two key facts of institutional and political life. First, the interactional system involved in a program of this scope is exceedingly complex. Second, the components of this system are in constant evolution and relate to each other differently over time.

The Interactional System

A community residence office is part of an intricate and often conflicting government-community system. The public, the executive branch, the legislature, and the judiciary are the major participants—and each, to some extent, is made up of conflicting factions.

The Public

An administrator who believes he is serving a "public" that is uniform and unconflicting in its needs, aspirations, and fears is in for a series of unpleasant surprises. In terms of establishing and maintaining a community residence program, the "public" is best seen as a combination of nine component parts: (1) the clients in need of services; (2) the provider of programs who delivers services; (3) the advocacy groups supporting the interests of the clients; (4) the professionals who provide direct service to the client or advisory service to the providers; (5) the citizen mental health area board representing the overall needs of the community; (6) the voters at large; (7) governmental bodies—such as town councils, planning boards, and the selectmen or aldermen; (8) the immediate neighbors of a new program; and (9) influential members of the community such as the clergy and groups like the Chamber of Commerce or the League of Women Voters.

Any action initiated by any one of these groups may arouse a variety of reactions from the other components of the system. For example, if a town planning board tries to adopt a new zoning ordinance designed to distribute community residences equally throughout the town, this plan might be opposed by the town council that has authority over the planning board and is sensitive to the whims of the electorate. The council may encounter stiff opposition from the citizen mental health area board, which in turn may be opposed by neighborhood organizations. The conflict can split the ranks of the professionals, who differ in their assessment of the value of the program itself. The upshot may be that the providers of the program look to other communities for residence sites. In this instance, the clients in need of service become the ultimate losers, as they remain cloistered in remote institutions or ghettoized in disorganized neighborhoods. This is the kind of struggle in which the community residence office must engage to meet its responsibilities to each component of the "public."

The Executive

Stresses, strains, and conflicts are not limited to relations between the agency and the public. There are two qualitatively different kinds of conflict with which the office must deal: the *administrative-hierarchical*, regarded as normal in any large organization; and the *programmatic-political*, which is more specific to this type of agency.

Administrative-hierarchical issues are a product of interagency conflicts within the executive branch organization. The agency must respond to both dictates and criticisms from above and needs and complaints from below. In Massachusetts, for example, there are two levels above the agency responsible for community residence programs. The Office of the Secretary of the Executive Office of Human Services functions much like the U.S. Department of Health, Education, and Welfare, coordinating all human-service agencies. In addition to mental health, the office handles public health, public welfare, youth services, corrections, and an office for children. The executive office reports directly to the governor's office. Below the office for community residences is a largely decentralized department, including seven regional offices and thirty-eight area offices, in addition to several state hospitals.

As in any organization, the upper levels of the hierarchy depend on the lower levels to implement policy. The lower levels depend on the upper levels to formulate policy. Disagreement may arise owing to intransigence at either end. The upper level may want to implement a new policy that is too radical for the tastes of the implementers; on the other hand, the local offices may be calling for revolutionary policy which is stymied by a traditional, entrenched upper echelon.

If there is disagreement over a policy or the method of its implementation, tension arises which may be expressed at the lower levels by foot-dragging ineffectiveness. Alternatively, when the lower levels feel things are too staid, they may form alliances with outside advocacy groups, giving them ammunition to attack the higher administration. The upper levels may express their dissatisfaction by under- or overreacting—either by further isolating the lower levels from knowledge and influence, or by arbitrarily ordering readjustments in their work situation.

Programmatic-political conflict is the second major area of potential stress within the community residence agency. Two distinct motivational forces tend to dictate the priorities of the state. One is a professionally based concern for the programmatic needs of the clients. The other is a politically based concern for the desires of the electorate. Sometimes these two concerns are in harmony with respect to a particular matter; at other times they are not. Too often, as decisions are made from the top down, the community residence office is the recipient of priorities set at a more political level. This can take the form of programs being funded and pushed ahead on a crash basis even though a more orderly, systematic approach, with preparation of the various components, would do the job more effectively. This kind of crash program can be successful in the short run but counterproductive in the long run. The community, after an initial experience of relief that "something is finally being done," may react with hostility when they begin to think they are being intruded upon. A backlash of community resentment at the state-implemented program may result.

Another form of the political unduly influencing the programmatic occurs when needed programs are politically blocked because there is no noticeable clamor from the electorate for them, in spite of the need. It appears that programs can be funded by virtue of executive political support if they deal with problems which frighten the community, such as drugs and crime; or if they attract intense support, as in the case of mental retardation. Other clienteles—the blind, the mentally ill, the aged—get less support in spite of their obvious need.

The Legislature

The community residence office is subject to conflict, not only from the executive office above it, but also from a horizontal struggle between the executive and legislative branches. This battle was especially obvious in Massachusetts, where the struggle was in part a legacy of the long history of Republican governors and Democratic legislatures. Proposals in Massachusetts were evaluated not so much on their merits as according to who was sponsoring them. "Massachusetts politics has come to resemble a bullfight, with the Governor as the dazzling matador, and the Legislature as the tormented bull."[1]

Another aspect of the interbranch battle is an intense dispute over what kind of people should run the state government. More and more in recent years the executive branch has given top policy appointments to a new class of professional problem solvers. Whether specialists or skilled generalists, these professionals are adept in new techniques of budgeting and management. Almost all of them are highly educated in the formal sense and are committed to vertical mobility in their careers, rather than to the state in which they are working. This in itself engenders the distrust of the legislators, who see these administrators as taking what they can and running to the next higher position in whatever state makes the best offer. The ascendancy of this group is, in addition, intensely resented by the bulk of public employees. The legislators identify culturally and ethnically far more with the "native" employees than with their new supervisors. As a result, conflicts over policy debated in the legislature tend to be solved not so much in terms of the policies themselves, but over whether the new people are administering them in the best interests of the employees—as distinguished from the interests of the clients in need of service.

The two critical areas of interest to the community residence office in relation to the legislature are enabling or constraining legislation, and enabling or constraining appropriations. Law and money are the two critical components which can make or break the program as a whole. The relevant legislation relates primarily to building codes, zoning, licensing, and regulatory mechanisms. The legislature may, at times, favor local control, which in an extreme form has a shattering effect on groups attempting to start several programs in different areas, with different standards in each locality making administration confusing and inhibitory. Further, excessive local control in the wrong hands can open the door to local harassment and exclusion.

Appropriations may be viewed in terms of the type of funding and locus of control. The legislature jealously guards its traditional methods—such as block positions in Massachusetts with each employee's salary and job description under its total control through legislated line-item appropriations. Increasingly, this tendency has conflicted with the executive's desire to let private contracts for service, with the public program-developing agency maintaining supervisory responsibility.

The Judiciary

The judicial branch of the government has recently become intensely involved in mental health, significantly influencing community residence programs and other community rehabilitative resources for discharged patients. Two opposing pressures have developed in society to which the courts have had to turn their attention. First are civil rights cases, which have resulted in patients being discharged into the community. Second are community-generated legal actions to exclude the community treatment facilities for these discharged patients on the basis of zoning laws.

Both individual and class-action suits have compelled the judiciary for the first time to address itself in earnest to the issue of the basic rights of mental patients. These decisions relate to a broad spectrum of issues, including the right to treatment, institutional conditions, commitment procedures, the right to wages, the right to education, and freedom from discrimination in housing. Any state mental health agency must now address itself to these cases and be familiar with them.[2]

A sequence of judicial decisions is having an increasing impact on the need for halfway houses and other community rehabilitative facilities. *Wyatt* v. *Stickney,* now known as *Wyatt* v. *Aderholt,* "represents the first class action suit successfully brought against a state's entire mental health system." In this case, a U.S. District Court "affirmed the constitutional right to treatment for those mentally disordered persons who are involuntarily civilly committed."[3] As a result of this decision, a federal court dictated for the first time to a state government the specific standards to be met, down to the last detail of staffing patterns and staff-patient ratios. This has an enormous impact on the state's budget, because compliance is mandatory, irrespective of cost. The courts could be viewed as beginning to be involved in the direct management of the delivery of mental health services in the interest of patients' rights, in the same way they are taking over the educational systems in some municipalities in the interest of minority children's rights.

Wyatt v. *Stickney* in 1971 began to sensitize the states to potential attack on the grounds of inadequate staff-patient ratios in their institutions. This worry, compounded by increasing state insolvency in much of the nation, resulted in the widespread discharge of patients into the community. This maneuver was designed to avoid the threat of state fiscal chaos. With the number of patients in a hospital reduced drastically, potential added expense goes down as the staff-patient ratio improves.

A second historically important case was *O'Connor* v. *Donaldson.*[4] It appears that this case, in and of itself, will not lead to the massive discharges initially anticipated. Nevertheless, it is a highly significant precedent. The decision stated that a mentally ill person could not be held in a state hospital against his will if he was not dangerous to himself or others; was not being offered treatment; and *was able to survive on his own in the community.* This decision did not address itself to the possible alternative of release to a halfway house if the patient was *not* able to survive on his own in the community. This omission is ironic, because denying the plaintiff the right to move to a halfway house had been a crucial precipitating factor in the case.

A decision that did address itself to community treatment was the judgment of a District Court case in Washington, D.C. (*Dixon* v. *Weinberger*).[5] In this class-action suit against the federally operated St. Elizabeth's Hospital, the court ruled that mental patients were guaranteed "suitable care and treatment under the least restrictive conditions," including placement of patients in community-based facilities. This decision may open the hospitals' gates and establish a precedent for the courts to dictate treatment—in this instance, in community care—just as *Wyatt* v. *Stickney* led the courts to dictate institutional standards.

The community's response to the influx of mental patients has led to another series of important court decisions in regard to zoning (this will be discussed in greater detail in chapter 8). A brief review indicates that whereas a growing body of lower court decisions had established that the community residence could be defined as a family—being a group of people sleeping, cooking, and eating on a premises used as a single housekeeping unit, irrespective of blood relations—a Supreme Court decision has challenged that. The Supreme Court decision in the *Belle Terre* case, written by Justice William O. Douglas, ruled that a group of unrelated adults could legitimately be zoned out of a residential neighborhood that specified its zoning requirement to be one-family dwellings, defining the word "family" to mean "one or more persons related by blood, adoption, or marriage or not more than two unrelated persons living and cooking together in a single housekeeping unit."[6]

In a post-*Belle Terre* decision, however, the New York State Court of Appeals allowed a group home in a single-family zone despite a restrictive definition of family.[7] In this case the court differentiated a group home from a "temporary living arrangement" of college students, the defendants in the *Belle Terre* decision. This case yields hope that the *Belle Terre* decision will not be treated as applicable to community residences for the mentally ill.

In conclusion, the fate of a community residence program is inextricably bound up with the outcome of judicial decisions past and to come. A state agency for community residences must approach the courts as an active participant to ensure that justice is done for all parties—the community as well as its less fortunate mental patients.

The Massachusetts System in Evolution

When first being developed in Massachusetts in the mid-1960s, the halfway house or community residence for the mentally ill and retarded was at an opposite ideological pole from the state Department of Mental Health. The community residence was born out of disenchantment with the medical model, which was seen as rigid and irrevocably committed to the large institution. Opponents cited the Department of Mental Health as the perpetrator of this system. The sprawling and cumbersome department, employing more people than any agency in the commonwealth, was represented by many of the old guard who initially viewed the community residence as "suspect" and "unprofessional." Clearly, the interaction between the two systems was potentially fraught with distrust and tension.

The initial technical problem of the community residence office was twofold. First, the office had to avoid a negative confrontation with the halfway house managerial group that would only confirm their suspicions and heighten already hostile notions. Second, the office had to convince the old guard within the department itself that, although nonprofessionals were involved, the community residence was a sound, valuable, and progressive step in service delivery. In time, the community residence office also recognized that its responsibilities involved far more than just dealing with various departmental echelons and the community residences themselves. The program grew in six years from ten to more than one hundred facilities for the mentally ill and retarded.[8] Through this period the office came into contact with an increasing number of different public sectors as its functions became more diverse.

The experience of the Massachusetts community residence office is presented here, not as a model for development, but as a summary of actual experience that may be useful to others. It is by no means inevitable that others follow this pattern.

The Massachusetts community residence office developed in discernible stages of evolution over a six-year period.

Benevolent but uninvolved consultation with a detached independent community residence (1969).   In the initial year there was no binding link between the department and the halfway houses themselves. There were no regulations or licensing, nor was there an official funding program. There were only ten psychiatric halfway houses in the entire state and two for the retarded. Certainly, there was no conception of a formal state program.

The community residence office at this time tried to help new groups get started by contributing its knowledge about programs and budgets. It met with groups already running programs and listened to their fears of external state control. They were assured that the state office was committed to facilitating the program, not harassing it. These existing halfway houses were accustomed to functioning very independently. They operated without legal constraint, and they generally did not suffer from financial constraints, as many were receiving demonstration grants from philanthropic foundations. The office played a similar role for regional and area mental health administrators. They seemed relieved that there was an official central office to deal with the "questionable" new programs. The office assured them that the programs would be observed and assisted where appropriate and that, at a minimum, it would ensure the programs were doing no harm.

The halfway house management teams were both aware of the widespread skepticism confronting their new programs and keenly sensitive to the fact that the commissioner himself was generally more receptive to their innovative spirit than were the lower echelons of his own department. The more resourceful of those in need of financial help made sweeping end runs—bypassing the entire department hierarchy to gain access to a few vacant state institutional attendant job blocks under the commissioner's control. The jobs helped pay for halfway house operations. On the face of it, this tactic circumvented the will of the legislature, as the job description for these positions had little relation to the halfway house function to which they were put. However, the legislature had not yet considered, or perhaps even heard of, the halfway house phenomenon.

In the first year, then, halfway houses were operating (with but one exception) quite independently of the department and of the legislature. In addition, there was very little impact on local communities, as the program was too small and nonthreatening.

Recognition and legitimation (1970). With twenty programs in operation and another ten attempting to start, there began to be scattered episodes of community reaction against the establishment of community residences. Some towns had turned down initiating groups, saying the program would be a nursing home, requiring around-the-clock care and grade-one institutional construction—neither of which was available to these groups. In response, the halfway house program providers asked the state office to intervene. They wanted and needed recognition and legitimation from a higher authority to assist them in their struggle with the community.

Coincidentally, a new mental health law established the authority of the department to draft regulations for these facilities. The office organized a task force for this purpose, composed of representatives of ten community residence management teams, as well as officials of the Department of Mental Health. In this forum, it was discovered that a suitable body of regulations could be agreed upon by both sides—the department and the community residence providers. The Department of Mental Health conceded the legitimacy of private groups working in the community in a fairly autonomous fashion, providing needed services to the emotionally troubled. The groups showed themselves to be reliable, sensible, ethical, and as desirous as the department officials of having checks and quality assurances in the program. This task force went a long way toward dispelling the distrust which had been present on both sides. Suspicious strangers had become allies in the face of a common enemy, community resistance, which although spotty and unorganized was beginning to affect the programs.

This bond led to further consolidation of the community residence advocates through the addition of agencies serving other groups developing community residences. An Interdepartmental Rehabilitation Facilities Board (IRFB) was formed including agency representatives for drug rehabilitation, alcoholism, youthful offenders, and adult offenders. Through the board, they represented the overall interests of a new modality in its struggle for support and recognition.

Limited financial allocation and support (1971).   By 1971 there were thirty community residences for the mentally ill and retarded. Not only had they come to the department for legitimation, but now, since private demonstration grants began to run out, community residence programs were forced to come to the department for funding assistance as well. In response to increasing awareness of the need for these programs, the commissioner made it state policy that at least 50 percent of all new positions were to go to community-based services. However, funds for new positions were difficult to obtain as the state increasingly moved into an austerity budget. Therefore, a policy of reallocating existing resources wherever possible was instituted. Seventeen programs were assisted in this way— usually a community residence received funds for one or two state hospital attendant positions. The reallocation of these funds represented the limited but important support for the program of the state hospital superintendents. They saw its value and were willing to relinquish positions from their hospitals, risking criticism for lessening their staff-patient ratios. This certainly undercut those critical of what they saw as the state hospital superintendents' propensity to be interested only in strengthening their "empire."

At this time, neither the legislature nor the general public was aware of or interested in the program. So far, the participants had been able to work together in a constructive, positive manner. The program itself was still initiated and basically rooted in the private sector, with no direct governmental funds committed.

Total partnership—the adoption of part of the program by the state (1972).   There were now forty community residences for the mentally ill and the retarded. A class-action suit by citizen advocates attacking the deplorable conditions in the state schools for the mentally retarded led to a remarkable demonstration of the swiftness with which the executive can move when it is politically necessary. There was very high awareness of *Wyatt* v. *Stickney* and a determined effort to head off the courts from dictating standards as they had done in Alabama. The entire state budget was at stake. This clarity of purpose was augmented by the reorganization of the state government, establishing the Executive Office of Human Services. Deinstitutionalization was suddenly the word of the day. All institutions were to be emptied as much as, and as soon as, possible. Suddenly, the halfway house was the cornerstone of the governor's program. The journey from obscure stepchild to mature program with state authorization took just four years.

A crash program for halving the population of six thousand in state schools for the retarded included provisions for funding forty new community residences on private contracts. But to the consternation of the department, the program was attacked by the Massachusetts Association for Retarded Children. They claimed that the program was ill conceived and hurriedly assembled. Some critics believed the attack stemmed from a hidden desire to discredit the department, so that under reorganization, the retardation program could itself attain independent departmental status. The association's letter ended up in a gold frame over the desk of the Secretary of Human Services, because one of his goals was to have such an active administration that the community would start complaining about too much action as opposed to too little.

At the same time, funding for programs for the mentally ill was stalled. In this case the clamor of a class-action suit had not been raised. Some citizens, recognizing the efficacy of that route, began to plan just such a suit, attacking the conditions in a state hospital for the mentally ill. The plan was never fully carried out.

Similar crash programs, however, were being initiated during this stage for juvenile offenders (the commissioner somewhat precipitously closed all but one of the state training schools) and for drug rehabilitation. The legislature made new monies available for these programs in an attempt to protect the community from drugs and crime among youth.

Community reaction (1973). By 1973, there were over 225

community residences in the Commonwealth of Massachusetts, including more than 80 for the mentally ill and retarded. New legislation authorized community residences for the adult offender. With this additional prompting, the previously dormant communities came alive. Twelve cities and towns simultaneously held hearings on local zoning ordinances with regard to these facilities. They took up the following issues: (1) putting quotas on the total number of citizens served in each city and in each community residence; (2) controlling the distribution of community residences within the municipality; (3) specifying minimum amounts of land to be held by each community residence—especially in suburban locations; (4) requiring mandatory public hearings prior to the establishment of any community residence, with special permits required in some cases; (5) establishing mechanisms for handling community grievances; and (6) specifying periodic reviews of the community residence's standing in the community.

At the same time, five bills were filed in the 1972–1973 legislative session calling for either outright curtailment of the community residence program or state authorization of greater community control over the establishment of community residences. More than ever, the program became politicized. One critical issue at stake was the equal protection clause of the Constitution, that is, former mental patients, or any other troubled persons, could not be discriminated against if they decided to live together in a community residence. If no greater town services were required for such a group than for any other group, it should be unconstitutional to restrict them. At the same time, the principle of local control was paramount in Massachusetts.

The Office of Community Residence Programs and the Interdepartmental Board took an active role in these community struggles. They testified at public hearings, assisted the legislature in gathering data, brought legal expertise to bear to protect the civil rights of the needy, and proposed legislation of their own to further the programmatic goals.

Crisis of the state hospitals (1974).   In 1974, a newly appointed mental health commissioner vigorously called for phasing out state mental hospitals altogether; state reports also called for their demise. Concern arose as to the adequacy of community treatment resources. The final report of the United Community Services of Metropolitan Boston–Massachusetts Department of Mental Health Mental Hospital Planning Project, completed in November 1973, stated:

We have learned during the past decade that the mental hospital is not the optimal residential facility for chronically ill people, including those who through the years of institutional living no longer possess meaningful links to the community. A variety of community-based residences . . . successfully meet the needs of these people. When properly funded through public welfare and social security payments mechanisms, and appropriately staffed by houseparents supported with relevant human services consultants, community-based residences offer clinical, social, and economic advantages which only now are coming to be realized.

For the first time, in 1974, Department of Mental Health budget instructions declared the community residence one of the essential services to be made available in all areas. In response to a sometimes errant community, the state legislature was considering a bill drafted jointly by the Governor's Commission on Citizen Participation and the IRFB, creating an appeals committee in the Department of Community Affairs to provide recourse from unreasonable and arbitrary prohibition of community residences by local communities. At the same time, a new building code for community residences was drafted by the IRFB and a new Uniform Building Code Commission.

From obscurity in the 1960s, the community residence had become not only a legitimate state program with high state priority but also an emerging national issue. The numbers of patients discharged from state institutions in New York and California, and the rapidity with which the discharges took place, had created heated controversy. The State of New York in 1973, for example, discharged 35,960 patients into the community. This resulted in community attacks on the State Department of Mental Hygiene. State officials said they were caught in a squeeze. "We are accused of dumping patients into neighborhoods. And we are accused of imprisoning patients in violation of their civil rights," lamented a beleaguered assistant commissioner.[9]

The ninety-third Congress was alert to all these issues. Community residences were included among the essential services of the community mental health center in a Senate bill, and it was hoped that national health insurance, if enacted, would also include flexible benefits so that care could be provided in a community residence in the first year of treatment.

Fiscal crisis (1975). In 1975, a new Democratic governor recognized a full state economic recession. This resulted in a 10 percent across-the-board budgetary cut for all state agencies, including essential services such as health programs, and a freeze on hiring of all state personnel so that no vacant positions could be filled. This led to a dramatic slowdown in the expansion of community facilities. Preserving the status quo was the best the office could hope for. In the meantime, other sources of funding, especially the federal government, were looked to as a solution to the fiscal crisis for community residences.

Planning for the future (1976). In Massachusetts, the Office of Community Residences was fortunate in that severe cutbacks did not imperil what had already been accomplished. Primarily, 1976 was a year of planning for the future. Needs for a comprehensive community program were carefully assessed, including the needs for community residences with ancillary services and daily programs for residents. The department planned to go more fully into contracting with private nonprofit agencies for services, including training and research. The need for a broad spectrum of residential services (including the long-term group home, the transitional facility and cooperative apartments) was also emphasized.

Conclusion

Given an understanding of the complexity of the "public" and the political system, a community residence office can more effectively promote its community-based program. Periodic reanalysis of conflicting forces as they alter and realign enables the office to respond with greater understanding, accuracy, and fairness. In this manner, unnecessary and counterproductive confrontation, alienation, and consequent polarization can be avoided. Thus, such an office, instead of becoming merely one more adversary in a dynamic system, can function as a continuous mediator and facilitator for all parties. The programmatic goal is ultimately best served by an administrative style that is not limited to the establishment of the community residence alone. The aim is collaborative development in the government-community matrix which affects all of us.

CHAPTER 6

Legal Issues, Standards, and Regulations

The first halfway houses were developed explicitly for ex-patients, a fact which raises basic questions as to the legitimacy of any form of special regulation. One question is, If patients discharged from psychiatric hospitals choose to live together in a social living arrangement, don't they have a right to do so without special regulations? The definition of the residence as a "family" living together in a single housekeeping unit poses a related question: Why is the state entitled to treat this family differently than any other?

Events have effectively answered both questions. In the space of only a few years, the community residence has been transformed from an aftercare facility only to the preferred site for almost all alternative domiciliary care. Thus, an alternative to institutionalization has become a crucial additional entity. Furthermore, the "special" character of the community residence has been formally recognized by government subsidization of many programs through instruments such as National Institute of Mental Health construction and program grants. Finally, community residences are usually established by nonprofit corporations representing themselves to the public as providing care for needy people. For all these reasons, the group living arrangements of residents can no longer be conceived of as just a group of ex-patients living together for social reasons.

As halfway houses become more numerous, a clear legal status for them becomes increasingly essential. Three key areas require delineation: first, quality control through reasonable but rigorous implementation of regulatory guidelines and statutes; second, standards for safe, suitable structures to house community residences, as determined by building codes; and third, beneficial location and equitable geographical distribution of these facilities, through local and statewide zoning ordinances and enabling laws.

These three issues do not, of course, exist in isolation. Rather, they are closely interrelated. Good state regulatory standards reassure local communities and set the stage for more lenient and open zoning ordinances. Similarly, public safety officials are reassured by programmatic standards guaranteeing that the residents will be capable of self-preservation, which eases the way for adoption of noninstitutional building codes. Finally, quality programs, integrated within the community and housed in safe dwellings, will help ensure accreditation by such national bodies as the Joint Commission on Accreditation of Hospitals and the National Institute of Mental Health, which are currently struggling to draft national standards.

It is essential that standards not be so stringent as to compromise the essential programmatic characteristics of the community residence, and mental health professionals have a special responsibility in this area. The community residence must continue to be a relatively small, familylike living arrangement, functioning as an open social system within the community; it should have a flexible program and assist the resident's attainment of his highest level of independent functioning.

The entire program is at stake during the evolution of these standards, for unnecessarily strict standards can ticket the program for oblivion. For example, quality control that requires excess numbers of around-the-clock staff can make the program unmanageably expensive. Further, such controls would perpetuate the old system by encouraging dependency on staff and arbitrarily denying residents the opportunity to learn that they can live successfully together by pooling their own strengths. Strict building codes, likewise, can make large capital outlays mandatory and, by mandating such accoutrements as steel doors, obliterate the family home atmosphere. Zoning ordinances can be designed to harass and to make community entry difficult. Even when entry is accomplished, such ordinances subject the community residence to a seemingly endless series of annual reviews and special conditions. These defeat the residence's rehabilitative goals of natural integration within the community.

As I have noted repeatedly, carefully thought-out standards pose no threat to the community residence. On the contrary, they can become a distinct asset to all interested parties—the client, the provider of services, the community, the state and federal legislatures, and national standard-setting bodies. As an aid to the formation of such standards, this chapter explores the development of regulations in Massachusetts (a pioneering state), surveys the status of regulation in other states, and comments on early efforts toward establishing national standards. The rationale for writing special building codes for community residences, strategies for community entry, and the legal status of zoning laws are explored in chapters 7 and 8.

Massachusetts Regulations

A Note on Drafting and Implementation

While the authority to write regulations usually devolves upon the executive branch (in Massachusetts the agency is the Department of Mental Health), it would be futile for one department to try to draft in isolation. In Massachusetts, a special task force drafted the regulations, representing the views of providers and selected government personnel. The department provided programmatic expertise, legal counsel, and general consultation in liaison with related programs, both in the department and outside it. Providers on the task force represented directors and managers of halfway house programs. Personnel from mental health centers joined in the drafting as well, representing the interests of the day care, vocational, medical, and social rehabilitative components of the program. This group ensured that nothing would be written to hamper an integrated approach. As more programs come into existence, it is increasingly feasible and often helpful to have consumers themselves represented. This might include current residents of halfway houses or "graduates" who have gained some perspective on the impact of halfway house living in the course of their own life crises. Through the combined efforts of all these people, then, the regulations are drafted, presented at a public hearing, and adopted.

Too often, however, the people crucially concerned with adopting regulations are divorced from their implementation. The programmatic creativity achieved by this special drafting process is delivered into the hands of an inspection office. If the inspectors are the only interpreters of the regulations and enforce them in a strict, military fashion, the regulations can hinder both the development of new programs and the conduct of existing ones. We therefore felt in Massachusetts that the community residence program office itself ought to retain the inspection function. Thus, each inspection became a consultation session in which the halfway house was given suggestions and the benefit of experience elsewhere in the state. At the same time, the inspection team was educated by local residence staffs. Each program had its own contribution to offer, and feedback and integration were crucial. The inspection team included personnel from the central office of the department, as well as from the regional and area offices. This group then met with the management and executive directorship of the community residence, and sometimes with members of the corporate board as well. In this setting, significant misunderstandings about such issues as budgetary policy and departmental planning could be clarified. Support of the area office needed in the next budget and priorities for staffing could be discussed. Neighborhood or community issues could also be reviewed. Frequently, inspections gave key area and regional staff a chance to visit a halfway house for the first time. The general spirit of these occasions is stated in the introduction to *Developing a Community Residence for the Mentally Ill:*

The Office for Mental Health Services is interested in the development of a wide variety of innovative programs. Toward this end, neither the regulations nor the information communicated in this statement ought to be regarded as fixed, final, or unchangeable. Rather, this Office considers the development of these programs to be in a continual process of evolution, such that review of any issue at any point in time is welcomed. We believe that this continued openness of mind, readiness to exchange in communication, and flexibility in regard to official policy and regulations together will contribute to a higher quality program for the emotionally troubled citizens in the Commonwealth.[1]

It ought to be noted that a few unscrupulous or misinformed operators may mistake this openness for a license to exploit the vulnerable and unaware. When confronted with outright violations and defiance, the department must be prepared to close down a program. This is an essential protective function. In addition to harming its own clients, an unscrupulous, destructive program can wreak havoc upon a good public image and a solid record of achievement. Without swift enforcement, the department can be discredited as an effective purveyor of standards, the community's trust can be lost, and the attempts of residences to enter the community can be made extremely difficult.

The regulations adopted in Massachusetts include general provisions and provisions for physical structure, personnel, program, records, and inspection. The complete text is provided in Appendix 1.

General Provisions

This section houses a variety of distinct issues. The first is a definition of facilities affected by the regulations:

A halfway house, group home, group residence, cooperative apartment, or any similar residence offering to the public and representing itself as providing care but not treatment shall be subject to this [regulation], and for purposes of this [regulation] shall be referred to as a "community residence."

This statement specifies that any facility which "represents itself to the public as providing care" is accountable to the public through this regulation. The language is identical to the authorizing legislation and places all kinds of community residences, transitional or long-term group homes, and cooperative apartments under its jurisdiction.

The regulations then specify that "individuals receiving care in a community residence shall be certified as capable of self-preservation . . . and for purposes of this [regulation] shall be referred to as 'residents.'" All persons living within a community residence must be able to sense physical danger through sight, sound, or smell; judge when such danger requires immediate egress from the dwelling; learn a route of egress; and implement that egress. A uniform test is to be given by referring agencies (if any), or by the community residence management (if the client came from home), verifying the client's capacities. Limited certification can be given, for example, to a retarded person who could learn a route of egress from his or her room in a particular community residence. This set of regulations (Appendix 3) also assures the communities and the public safety agencies that any person who is sufficiently impaired—owing to psychosis, acute alcohol or drug intoxication, retardation, or temporary incapacitating physical injury—will not be allowed to live in the community residence for the duration of the impairment. This also permits the management of halfway houses to make clear to any resident that if he arrives in the evening in an inebriated state, or high on illicit drugs, he will have to sleep elsewhere that night, often in the emergency room of a nearby hospital, or on night care at the referring psychiatric hospital.

Another important part of this section relates to the legal status of operators of community residences. The decision was made in Massachusetts to allow every conceivable kind of business organization to operate a community residence. The regulations state: "A community residence may be legally organized as a corporation (business or non-profit charitable), a partnership, an individual proprietorship, an unincorporated association, or a public agency." Some states have felt that all community residences should be operated by nonprofit corporations. However, we felt that the first priority was to facilitate the development of the greatest number of programs with the highest degree of flexibility, creativity, and innovation. To rule out business corporations was to rule out a potentially important source of capital investment in noninstitutional care. The principle was followed that profit realized from a population which could afford it did not necessarily compromise quality. It was felt that other components of the regulations adequately address themselves to programmatic aspects. In addition, this provision recognizes that some developers of fine community residences, especially in rural regions, are recently transformed paraprofessionals who had used their own meager savings to initiate these facilities on a proprietary basis. The legal fees of incorporation would contitute, at least initially, a financial hardship. However, the majority of community residences in Massachusetts were nonprofit corporations, as this status was required to receive state funds (see chapter 9).

Physical Structure

This section added some specific programmatic items, including the requirement that the building inspector's certificate of compliance with the group residence code be posted and a copy sent to the Mental Health Department (chapter 7). Further, no more than four persons were permitted to sleep in any one bedroom. This apparently minor provision was designed to prevent dormitorylike living arrangements. Other provisions included: access to a telephone for all residents; conspicuous posting of a fire procedure (including location of the local fire box); the name of the medical facility or physician available in case of a medical emergency; easy staff access to fire extinguishers; quarterly fire drills; and a requirement that all fires be reported to the Mental Health Department within forty-eight hours.

Personnel

To avoid the hazards of rigid staffing patterns, the following regulation was adopted:

Personnel: No uniform staffing pattern shall be required for any community residence. Each community residence shall maintain the following personnel functions: residence directorship; in-residence management; professional consultation; and medical coverage. In the discretion of the residence director, and with the approval of the Department, the function of in-residence management may not be required. Personnel functions may be performed by one or more persons.

This is an example of a regulation allowing the greatest freedom for innovation and creativity. Cooperative apartments, included under the regulations, do not require live-in personnel; adequate visiting staff at reasonable intervals is more appropriate. Separate staffs for various functions are not mandated, so that a psychiatrist who is well-trained in general practice can provide both emergency medical availability and consultation. Similarly, the residence director could also serve as the live-in manager.

Following this general statement, the regulations define the duties and responsibilities of each function. The residence directorship includes the overall implementation of all policies, practices, and procedures of the community residence including: reports to the department; formulation of the budget and financial management; overall supervision of the medical health, nutrition, education, and general welfare of the residents; maintenance of all records relating to both residents and finances; and supervision of the residence manager.

The in-residence manager must "have demonstrated qualities of ability to relate effectively to all residents" and is required to handle all daily matters in the residence, including assisting residents in problems relating to work or school adjustment and carrying out duties delegated by the residence director.

Neither the director nor the manager is required to have specific academic degrees. This departure from convention was designed to facilitate the hiring of persons committed to the rehabilitation of residents through their capacity to establish warm personal relationships. Unfortunately, this quality is not conferred with a degree. At the same time, the department recognized that a minimum level of professional guidance was needed. Hence, it was specifically required in the definition of the consultant that "a community residence shall have a written affiliation with one or more professional consultants in one or more of the following fields: psychiatry, psychology, social work, special education, vocational rehabilitation or any other field which is directly related and pertinent to the needs of the residents." The broadness of this definition of the specialty is intended to recognize the authentic abilities of the whole range of rehabilitative professions. Again, no professional hierarchy is to develop in these new programs like that which stultified the hospital setting. This is an example of the regulations specifically facilitating the ideology outlined in part I of this book.

Moreover, even in this provision, recognition is given to expertise and experience. The professional consultant definition continues:

The professional consultant shall have earned a graduate degree or degrees in an acknowledged specialty and a license or certification where required under Massachusetts statute. However, upon application of the community residence and in the discretion of the Department, experience and expertise may be considered in lieu of academic degrees or licensure.

The regulation further stipulates that the "consultant or consultants shall consult with the program at least once per month." This provides professional input to ensure that a sound rehabilitative program, appropriate for each resident, is implemented.

Twenty-four-hour availability of a physician or a medical facility for medical emergencies rounds out the mandatory personnel requirements of the Massachusetts regulations.

Program

Program regulations have become increasingly important as concern mounts about the dumping of patients into nonrehabilitative facilities. In the initial drafting of this section in Massachusetts there was only a requirement that the community residence submit a general statement to the department which denoted its program:

The community residence shall develop a written statement of its program, policies and practices. Such statement shall describe the program goals; the services, training and care offered by the community residence; the kinds of activities and facilities offered; the group or groups of persons to be served including any sex or age characteristics; admission and discharge policies, including parameters of length of stay; and limitations, if any, on sources of referral. The community residence shall develop rules regarding safety and health and these shall be communicated to the residents by the community residence staff.

It was required that this statement be in the hands of the department prior to the inspection for certification, in addition to an extensive reporting form. Subsequently, it has been felt that this section needs to be more specific, and a proposed addition was drafted by the Committee on Community Residences, Social Rehabilitation and Vocational Rehabilitation:

Goal development: a major emphasis should be placed on the resident's participation in the definition of goals while in residence. Goal definition coupled with the delineation of expectations of the resident and the staff in meeting these goals should be pursued. A written program plan should be developed as soon as possible, and not longer than a week after each resident's entry to the program, and reviewed at least once a month, and in the case of short-term residents every two days. This plan should emphasize:

Life skills improvement including personal hygiene, cooking skills, ability to get around in the community, using public transportation, ability to handle money and a checking account, capacity to shop in local stores, and acquiring knowledge in apartment selection;

Vocational planning so as to ensure that each resident participates in a daily program at maximum potential;

Education planning either for elementary, high school, or college levels. An educational consultant should participate where necessary in planning goals, in application and entry, curriculum selection, and academic load-level judgments;

Social programs in the house assisting the development of interpersonal relations that are free from pathological patterns such as isolation and withdrawal, grandiose hypomanic intrusiveness, paranoid suspiciousness;

Avocational interests in the house such as developing a capacity to be aware of the world about and to engage in social activities such as card playing, Monopoly, ping-pong, etc. Outside the house, the capacity to seek and enjoy such social and avocational activities as tennis, swimming, boating, skiing, hiking, and entertainment such as movies, concerts, and art museums;

House and staff milieu planning involving anticipatory consideration of requirements for staff and group to provide support, limit setting, reality testing, confrontation, etc. in individual cases as appropriate;

Family Relations. Planning for crucial relationships with close family members, parents, spouses, children, etc.;

Physical health care management including general medical care, dental care, exercise, diet, and birth control;

Psychiatric care and therapy. The client's needs, resources, and problems should determine his/her treatment plan. Relevant therapies may include chemotherapy; individual counseling; family, group, and couples therapy; problem-solving in a social network; day support; types of behavior therapy; short-term and long-term psychotherapy; and crisis intervention.[2]

With hindsight, we can recommend additions to this programmatic section. For example, reference to the aftercare program and to special "alumni" functions at the residence ought to be included.

Records

The residence is required to maintain records on both the individual resident and the entire program. Confidentiality of such records is also stipulated.

The regulations state: "The community residence shall keep a record on each resident. Such record shall be confidential and not open to public inspection without the consent of the resident." The department policy is that the record must contain at least the name, birth date, address immediately prior to entry into the program, next of kin, their addresses and telephone numbers, dates of entry and departure from the program, and address to which the resident moved upon departure. Recommendations also include the written program plan with monthly reviews, as noted above.

It is further required that the residence submit to the department an initial description of itself, including "its program, facilities, organizational structure, staffing patterns; and an annual report relating to residents, budget, and personnel."

Confidentiality is prescribed as follows:

Reports and records required by and submitted to the Department shall be confidential and not open to public inspection except in the discretion of the

Commissioner for the purposes of research approved by the Department. . . . No studies disseminated to the public based on these records shall identify the community residence by name without its consent or any resident by name without his consent.

This section is intended to protect the privacy of both the individual resident and the community residence. It was strongly felt that there should be no opportunity for "witch hunters" to dig up unfavorable data to use in an effort to oust the community residence.

Inspection

Finally, the regulations call for at least one inspection annually. The most effective means of conducting this inspection is the consultation process described at the beginning of this section.

A National Survey

A national survey of state regulations on halfway houses, taken in the fall of 1976, showed a broad disparity in their accomplishments. Only six states—Massachusetts, New York, Rhode Island, South Carolina, California, and Wisconsin—had bona fide regulations authorized by state law; six states—Alabama, Florida, Kansas, Pennsylvania, Texas, and Utah—had guidelines written as general information; and two—Indiana and Maryland—had guidelines for state funding. Twelve more states—Arizona, Connecticut, Hawaii, Minnesota, Missouri, New Hampshire, North Carolina, Oregon, South Dakota, Vermont, Virginia, and West Virginia—were reportedly drafting regulations. Of the twenty-five remaining states (including the District of Columbia), twenty reported that they had no regulations or guidelines and were not in the process of drafting. Five states did not reply to the survey. The states without any regulations at all include both populous ones and others with established halfway houses. Some of these have proposed regulations but have been unable to get them adopted by responsible governing bodies. This was the case, for instance, in the District of Columbia and Illinois.

Notably, all the regulations so far adopted or drafted bear strong resemblances to the Massachusetts regulations. Notwithstanding the variety of drafting language, the general goals and ideology remain the same throughout the states. Halfway houses for the mentally ill are to provide a homelike environment and skills to cope in the outside world. Whereas the goal of all programs is to socialize the resident for life in the outside world, some states specifically separate long-term facilities from short-stay, transitional residences.

The states address themselves to a variety of issues, but there is overall consensus on a need for a structured program, daily integration with outside rehabilitative services, and conformity to the community's health, building, zoning, and fire requirements. Many states emphasize that the physical structure of the building should conform to the neighborhood and not be recognizable as a halfway house. Staffing requirements emphasize the ability of the in-house managers to relate to the residents. Records of the residents and of the house are generally required and protected under laws about privacy and confidentiality.

Because the potential regulation drafter will be assisted by specific knowledge of some of the significant differences among the various states' regulations, a summary follows.[3]

Definitions and General Issues

The formal definitions of halfway houses vary slightly from state to state but are similar in overall intent and goals. In Rhode Island, "Group Residence means a place, however named, which is established, offered, maintained, conducted, managed, or operated by any person for a period of more than twenty-four hours, for the purpose of providing accommodations for two or more persons who are mental health clients." The Indiana Department of Mental Health states: "For the purposes of this program, a halfway house is defined as a domicile in an Indiana community providing a therapeutic environment, and temporary transitional residence, for mentally ill or mentally retarded persons who need the benefits of intermediate group living arrangements which either follow mental hospitalization or are alternatives to hospitalization."

Pennsylvania's definition of services includes the following: "Domiciliary Care Services for Adults arranged by State approved agencies provide a safe, supportive substitute home, in the community, for adults whose marginal social adjustment prevents independent living." The service goals of Pennsylvania explicitly state that domiciliary care service should "provide homelike, community based living arrangements for adults who cannot live independently in the community, encourage and assist adults in developing and maintaining maximum initiative and self-determination, in a homelike setting, prevent unnecessary institutionalization, and help adults in the institution to return to their own community and ultimately, if possible, to their homes."

In Wisconsin, there is explicit regulatory separation of residential care facilities for the aged from halfway houses for the young adult. Residential care facilities, for residents who are over sixty-five, "provide social service and activity therapy, as distinguished from nursing care." The halfway house is defined as providing domiciliary care for younger adults "who are capable of being employed in a full time or part time basis or are capable to be involved in a work adjustment training or vocational training." Alternatively, it is defined as providing "services for mental and emotional disability."

New York similarly states that "community residences for the mentally disabled are facilities for mentally disabled persons who are unable to live independently at a particular time. Community residences are specifically designed and operated to assist disabled persons to live as independently as possible through the provision of training and assistance in the skills of daily living, and by serving as an integrating focus for the mentally disabled person's overall rehabilitation." The New York regulations are unique in stating that the community residences are "to implement the principle of the least restrictive alternative." Thus, the individual "must be served in the community residence which is the least restrictive of the civil and human rights consistent with his or her need for services." This wording clearly emanates from *Dixon* v. *Weinberger*.

The New York regulations also introduce the concept of a system of services for the residences' clientele. The regulations state that "the community residence must exist in a system of services for its clientele. It cannot be an independently functioning facility without ties to other service providers." There is a strong emphasis on the need for the resident to move on to a less restrictive setting as soon as he attains skills to warrant such a move.

Finally, New York is unique in requiring the governing board to relate to the community. That is, "unless the governing body is broadly representative of the community in which the community residence is located, the community residence shall have a community advisory board composed of at least residents of the neighborhood in which the residence is located and residents of the community residence." This board is strictly advisory, without specific powers.

Residents' Rights

Some states have sections in their regulations to protect the rights of residents which take a variety of forms. The right to leave at any time is stated by New York: "No overt or covert physical or psychological pressure shall be applied to prevent a resident who desires to leave from doing so." The right to spend money is also covered: "Fees shall be established for any resident who receives income from the Supplemental Security Income Program to ensure that such a person retains at least $37 per month for personal expenditures from his or her income from SSI benefits and other sources of unearned income."

Alabama addresses some very specific rights: "to receive and send unopened mail; to visit and counsel with a minister in privacy; to visit with immediate family at reasonable times; to be free from mechanical restraint and seclusion." These seem more relevant to the hospital than to a community residence; however, the past abuses of the hospital may have induced these explicit requirements.

Rhode Island makes a general statement that "there shall be great care to protect the rights of the resident, and to maintain the confidentiality of his participation in the program."

Physical Structure

The importance of a homelike physical structure was noted in many regulations, including drafts by New York, Minnesota, Texas,

Florida, and Pennsylvania. The general expectation of the guidelines and regulations was for a homelike building, fitting into the neighborhood, with sufficient living, sleeping, dining, and bathroom facilities for the occupants served. Size is defined as not exceeding twenty-four beds in New York. If the facility is larger, it has to be organized so the residents are served in groups of no more than fifteen. It should be noted that in Massachusetts the law calls for from four to twenty-five residents in defining the community residence for building-code purposes.

Other space aspects are also covered by state regulations. For example, the square-footage per resident in bedrooms varies from sixty square feet to one hundred (Wisconsin, South Carolina, and New York), with a maximum of four residents per bedroom often the limit (Wisconsin, Massachusetts, New York, and Rhode Island). New York also required fifty-five square feet of living space per resident, with other states requiring similar space. Both Maryland and Texas require that the dining areas be large enough to accommodate all the residents and staff for at least one meal per day together. Texas adds, "There should be one or more living rooms and day rooms. Each activity room should be large enough to seat ten people comfortably with sufficient space allowed for such articles as television, radio, and reading literature." These provisions for living space are an attempt to ensure the homelike atmosphere of the community residence, and to facilitate group living through adequate space.

Some states become idiosyncratically particular about very detailed items. Rhode Island, for instance, states that "no resident shall be placed in a room for sleeping that does not have an exterior window." They even specify that "no bed shall be placed so that a resident might experience discomfort because of a proximity to radiators, air conditioner, heat or light glare." Wisconsin has specific regulations with regard to furnishings such as beds, pillows, chairs, reading lights, dresser and drawer space, linen and bedding, and window coverings as well as specific items involving food preparation.

The states' intent to help the community residence to become an integral and unobtrusive part of the community is noted in regulations such as Maryland's: "Community residences should be similar in appearance to other buildings in the area." Florida's proposed guidelines further recommend that "evidence to the general public that the home is being maintained as a rehabilitation unit shall not be apparent."

Personnel

There is general agreement that there should be no specific educational requirement of personnel, and that natural caring ability is more important. Also there is a somewhat flexible approach to staffing patterns, with a premium on live-in personnel. Typical of a state's regulations in this respect are Maryland's, which emphasize "previous demonstration of ability to establish and maintain warm, supportive relationships with persons in need as well as with fellow workers and ability to accept and benefit from supervisory and professional consultation."

New York states: "There shall be sufficient numbers of competent personnel to supervise, operate, and maintain the premises of the facility to provide assistance to the residents at all times." In its draft of guidelines Florida states that "at least one responsible member of staff should be on duty or residing at the house and available for emergencies."

Two other issues not always specified are resident-staff ratios and employment histories and physicals for staff members. South Carolina requires a minimum staffing level of one employee for every ten adults. Alabama requires one full-time employee for each five residents. Rhode Island requires a personnel record that shows personal data, physical exam, references, and employment data. Wisconsin also requires an employment record.

Program

Both a general statement of the community residence's overall program and a specific individualized program for each resident are often required. Wisconsin requires that

the halfway house administrator shall provide a written program of plan of services for residents which shall be reviewed by the department. This program shall be a statement of specific services and staff personnel assignments to accomplish and justify the goals to be attained by the facility. Service for residents, and staff assignments should be clearly expressed and justified in program terms. Such a program should include admission policy, program goals, program elements including relationships, contracted services and arrangements with other health and social service agencies and programs.

New York requires "the governing body to adopt a written functions program which shall set forth the specific type, purposes, goals and objectives and operating procedures of each community residence." California simply requires "a defined program of goal directed activity for all residents either in the facility itself, with cooperating agencies, or a combination of these."

Rhode Island requires, in addition to a clear definition of "philosophy, purpose, objective, and functions of the group residence," that "there shall be established a comprehensive individual program plan for each resident." Alabama's standards recommend "within the first week after admission, a written individualized treatment plan shall be developed through interdisciplinary collaboration based upon pre-admission and post-admission diagnosis, and recommendations from various medical areas." Monthly evaluation of treatment shall include "the appropriateness of treatment plans, and goals, client progress, family and/or collateral involvement, efficiency and need for any medication or medical treatment, treatment plans and recommendations." South Carolina suggests a patient activities plan be developed that includes "socialization, daily living activities, and recreation," but there is an apparent neglect of the vocational rehabilitative or educational modes. Minnesota's pending Rule 36 requires a "Treatment Rehabilitation Plan" for each resident written within thirty days of admission: "The plan shall define the specific problem to be overcome, the specific measures to be used in the solution or mediation of the problems, and the specific goals to be achieved."

Other Issues

There is unevenness in regard to the requirement for entering residents' prior medical examinations and diagnostic tests. There is an obvious economic implication in the degree of medical evaluation to be required. Rhode Island, for instance, requires a complete neurologic and physical exam, as well as a mental health evaluation. New York, Wisconsin, and Rhode Island require a chest X-ray within sixty days of admission, in addition to a physical exam.

Rhode Island is specific about financial responsibilities, requiring an annual audit, receipted bills for all cash payments, and receipts for all monies collected, as well as a periodic review of the per capita cost of care. They also require adequate insurance to cover damages due to injury or loss of life by accident, fire, or other cause. Alabama also requires liability insurance.

New York requires the review of all untoward incidents, including "assaults, injuries, sudden deaths, or unauthorized absences."

National Standards

On July 29, 1975, the Congress passed Public Law 94–63, which expanded the federal support of the community mental health center. In this legislation, for the first time, the community residence was included as one of the essential services of the community mental health center. It stated that there shall be, in the community mental health center, "a program of transitional half-way house services for mentally ill individuals who are residents of its catchment area who have been discharged from a mental health facility or would without such services require inpatient care in such a facility."

Section 304(b) of Public Law 94–63 required that the secretary of the Department of Health, Education, and Welfare submit to the Congress within eighteen months "a report setting forth (1) national standards for care provided by Community Mental Health Centers and (2) criteria for evaluation of Community Mental Health Centers and the quality of the services provided by the centers." A draft of such standards was completed and circulated on November 19, 1976, by the Office of Program Development and Analysis (OPDA), National Institute of Mental Health (NIMH), Alcohol, Drug Abuse, and Mental Health Administration. The standards draw heavily on proposed accreditation standards for community mental health centers developed by the Joint Commission on Accreditation of Hospitals (JCAH) under NIMH contract.

The NIMH standards were influenced by the JCAH position that separate standards for separate services were not desirable. The JCAH concluded:

To write separate standards for different facility types, age groups, and disability groups would not only be unwieldy but inconsistent and incompatible with the intent and functions of a community mental health center. In addition, as work on the standards progressed, it evolved that they be able to accommodate the new and expanded federal legislation. Therefore, it became apparent that a theoretical model was needed that would conceptualize the delivery of mental health services. The model had to be capable of being applicable to all age and disability groups served by community mental health programs and at the same time cover all the service environments and possible facility types. The Balanced Service System, the conceptual model used to generate principles, indicators, and standards for the accreditation of community mental health service programs, represents this effort and is applicable to all mental health programs and functions they perform.[4]

Thus, the NIMH standards address two major headings from a general point of view: first, program administration and second, "various standards related to all services." These are followed by only a few specific standards for specific services.

In the program administration section, the standards require items such as organizational charts, comprehensive plans of services, descriptions of the community to be served, as well as identification of target populations. They also address the issues of personnel administration, program evaluation, staff development, and fiscal administration.

Under the general guidelines for services they cite the need for availability and accessibility of services, protection of patient's rights, and continuity of services. All service facilities are required to meet federal, state, and local requirements, including building, health, and fire codes. They are to be "kept clean and maintained in good repair" and are to have "adequate lighting, ventilation, and temperature control." Service records are to be "organized and complete," and "the center shall provide a full range of services to meet community mental health needs for all ages."

Follow-up care is addressed somewhat more specifically:

The center shall establish procedures to ensure that all catchment area residents discharged from inpatient care in a mental health facility have access to follow-up services which provide continuing mental health treatment as needed, and which assure the availability of other health, residential, rehabilitative and/or supportive services which may be required to enhance or sustain the capacity of the clients to function in the community.

The standards then take up transitional residential services:

The center shall arrange for or provide a program of transitional residential services for catchment area residents who have been discharged from a mental health facility or who would without such services require inpatient care in such a facility. Through this program, the center provides or makes available appropriate community-based living arrangements and the mental health and rehabilitative services necessary to: (a) prevent inappropriate or unnecessary admission or readmission to inpatient care; and (b) assist individuals in their transition from one level of care (such as inpatient, nursing home, or other institutional care) to more independent functioning.

The standards address five additional issues in greater detail:

1. The center shall identify needs and existing resources within the catchment area for provision of transitional residential services to persons with mental disabilities.

2. The center shall provide consultation and education to existing transitional residential facilities in order to upgrade the quality.

3. The center shall directly provide or arrange for development of new transitional residential facilities and programs as necessary to fill unmet needs in the catchment area.

4. All transitional residential services must be provided in accordance with an Individualized Services Plan, which includes attention to health, mental health, social and vocational needs of the client.

5. If transitional residential services are provided through affiliations with one or more community agencies, the authorities and responsibilities of the center vis-à-vis the affiliating agency must be clearly spelled out in writing.

Conclusion

This review of the nation's current approach to the community residence presents a generally optimistic picture. In general, our priorities are withstanding the tests of the political process. Increasingly, then, it is being recognized that there should be a program focused on helping residents to attain their highest potential as functioning members of society. They should be trained in the basic skills necessary for independent living, in the context of a continuum of residential alternatives, and with access to other social and medical services. The resident's rights to dignity, privacy, and a comfortable environment are also being recognized.

The attainment of these ideals in written and adopted regulations is a goal of the highest priority.

CHAPTER 7

A Group Residence Fire Safety Code

with Raymond Caravaty

Like any other building, the halfway house must conform to the building code of its community. This is necessary to protect both the health and safety of the residents, as well as to ensure that the residence acts as a responsible member of its community. However, the building code should not require the community residence to sacrifice its ideology and goals.

The need for a specific building code for community residences is based on the fact that community residences are neither institutions nor lodging houses. Strict institutional codes inhibit creation of a homelike milieu, and the safety regulations required for lodging houses are often inappropriate to the community residence, where people know and care for each other, live in a more organized manner, eat together, and share chores. The state or local community should therefore develop a building code that takes into consideration both the programmatic ideology of a community residence and safety factors relating directly to halfway houses.

Massachusetts was the first state to take this step, and its code is discussed here as an example of how life safety can be incorporated into the halfway house concept. The Massachusetts building code for community residences deals exclusively with fire safety and emphasizes preserving lives rather than property. In some structural aspects, the Massachusetts code for community residences is less strict than the lodging house code; in three areas, however, it is

---

Raymond Caravaty is Professor of Architecture at Rensselaer Polytechnic Institute and Chairman of the Massachusetts State Building Code Commission.

more stringent. It requires an extensive fire detection and alarm system; guaranteed, adequate, dual egress ways; and mandatory self-preservation guarantees of the occupants. The code eliminates many of the structural changes required in stricter codes that not only are expensive, but tend to turn homelike dwellings into institutionlike buildings.

An institution implicitly assumes responsibility for the safety of its occupants. On the other hand, the common-law dictum that a man's home is his castle has, until recently, allowed the family home to exist outside the law. The community residence falls into a gray area between home and institution, requiring special code formulations that take account of the residents' psychiatric needs, their safety requirements, and the economic limitations of the program. Massachusetts defines group residences in section 424.0 of the Uniform Building Code (see Appendix 2) and deals specifically with the certification of a resident's ability to preserve his life in section 9.1 of Title 9 in the Code of Human Services Regulations (see Appendix 3). These laws allow the community residence to retain a homelike interior while instituting strict life-safety procedures.

In general, the Massachusetts code comes down on the side of the halfway house as family home and conforms to the basic spirit of the halfway house movement. The central concept is individual independence and natural self-determination as preparation for a return to normalcy. While the institution serves *in loco parentis* and fosters dependence through elaborate regulations, the individual in a private residence assumes full responsibility for himself and moral responsibility for others. Thus, the Massachusetts code recognizes the close affinity between halfway house and nuclear family living by returning responsibility for personal and peer safety to the residents themselves.

To accomplish its goals, the halfway house must be absorbed and accepted into the surrounding residential neighborhood. Friendship, work, play, and social exchange and amenities are most easily accomplished in an environment of similarity, not difference; so the community residence must be the counterpart of its neighbors. Pull boxes, sprinklers, wire glass, extinguishers, and automatic closers are the paraphernalia of institutions, not of homes. An institutional residence is a contradiction in terms, and no cosmetic label—for example "group residence"—can gloss over the fact that institutions are usually considered out of place in the neighborhood.

If safety is achieved at the expense of either self-reliance or acceptance, then the concept of the halfway house has been lost.

Self-Preservation and Customized Codes

Building codes define institutional buildings as those "providing sleeping facilities for the occupants and . . . occupied by persons who are mostly incapable of self-preservation because of age, physical or mental disability, or because of security measures not under the occupant's control." In contrast, a residential building "is one in which sleeping accommodations are provided for normal residential purposes."[1] The basic difference is in the words *incapable of self-preservation*. Safety from fire in the group residence, then, can be predicted on the basis of the individual's demonstrated capability of self-preservation. This can be achieved through building codes, regulations, and statutes that are customized to the needs of the specific individual in a specific building.

The Life-Safety Matrix

Since the building designer establishes the parameters for life safety by his decisions, there should be some simple way to understand his design logic. The factors which should determine the basic logic are grouped and related in figure 1. Before explaining the use of this matrix, I will provide a brief explanation of its elements.

The vertical axis describes the occupant as an individual, not as a member of an occupancy type. It ranks this individual qualitatively in terms of his capability of self-preservation as determined by his mental capacity, physical mobility, and degree of confinement. *Mental capacity* in this respect has two important aspects: the desire to live, and judgment. *Physical mobility* is relative. How much time does it take to react to an alarm? How long does it take to cover a

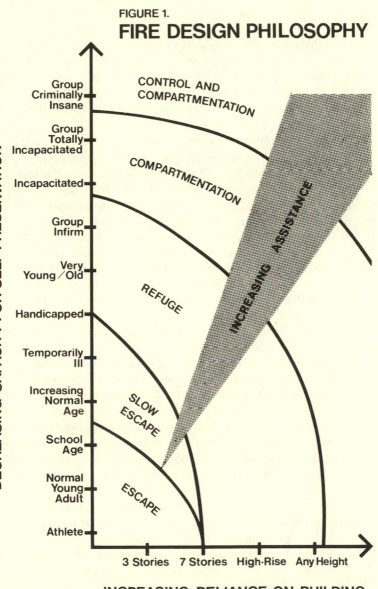

FIGURE 1.
FIRE DESIGN PHILOSOPHY

specified distance? How much effort can the individual expend before tiring? How far can he travel on one breath, in the presence of
heavy smoke? Will all mobility be temporarily lost because of illness? alcohol? drugs? Finally, what is the normal *degree of confinement?* A strait jacket in a cell? a locked room? a locked building? an
enclosed compound?

The lower horizontal axis in figure 1 represents the factors related
to the building, on which the occupant depends increasingly in the
various design philosophies. The occupant's location in the building
is important, as are four aspects of the building itself. *Design* is
responsible for determining the occupant's escape routes, distance
to exits, distance to refuge, time to assistance, and rescue time. The
length of a fire ladder and the throw of a fire hose are realistic limits
for quick rescue and extinguishment from the ground, so the *height*
of the building is relevant. Three stories is about the limit for fast
escape from a building; seven stories is the limit for practical escape
and intervention. *Area,* too, relates to the throw of a fire hose,
distance to safety, and fire load. *Fire resistance* will determine time
to building involvement, time to building collapse, degree of refuge,
and degree of compartmentation.

As a fire burns, its dangerous by-products build to higher and
higher levels. At some point these levels become intolerable to the
human occupant, and his life is lost. The elapsed time from the start
of the fire to the attainment of these intolerable levels is called
critical time. While these levels are increasing, the occupant is
either escaping or being rescued. The time it takes to achieve life
safety is called *reaction time.* Obviously, if the occupant's *reaction
time* exceeds the fire's *critical time,* intolerable conditions will be
reached and the occupant's life will be lost.

In terms of life safety, then, we must consider the person, the
building, and the planning logic which relates the two. There are at
best only five fire design philosophies available:

Escape.   As used here, the term *escape* means total separation of
the individual from the building. Whether escape is achieved alone
or with assistance is immaterial.

Slow Escape.   Various techniques can increase the protection of egress routes and so improve critical time. This in turn increases the time available for less mobile individuals to escape.

Refuge. When it is not possible to provide total escape from a building, the building can be safely divided into two completely separate fire areas by the use of fire walls. In effect, the individual is asked to escape from the fire by moving through a horizontal exit (fire door) into the building "next door." There he is safe until the fire is extinguished or burns itself out.

Compartmentation. The idea that fire can be enclosed in each room which acts as a fireproof container until it burns itself out is analogous to the use of a potbellied stove. The fire and its products are isolated and it is not a hazard to life around it. The concept may be visualized as a number of such stoves, only one of which contains a fire. As a design logic, this provides a life-safety tool for dealing with individuals who are incapable of self-preservation. By moving the endangered persons from the compartment in which the fire originates to a compartment with no fire, life safety is accomplished with a minimum of disruption to other occupants in other compartments.

Control and Compartmentation. The most complex problem is dealing with the occupant who, for the safety of others, must be restrained during rescue. If maintaining security means increasing reaction time, then it also increases risk. An appropriate design logic would suggest compartmentation with a connecting fire door, which is also a security door. Added to this would be the logic of the earliest possible extinguishment of the fire, as with sprinklers.

Thus figure 1 is simply a visual statement of the elements a designer must consider in developing a life-safety strategy for any combination of conditions. It is also a closed decision system, in that the designer can begin with any fixed element and easily see the relationship of the remaining elements—the individual, the building, the assistance, the time, and the logic. For example, it is irrational to build a wooden nursing home for thirty bedridden patients with only one night nurse and a volunteer fire department, even if the building is only one story high and has an outside exit from each patient's room.

The matrix also requires consideration of three other inherent considerations:

Expendability.   It is obvious that any attempt to reduce loss of life to zero would be extremely expensive, even if it were possible; but by tacit agreement, the expendability of certain occupants is never discussed, or even understood. Statistics suggest that one out of four people who die in a fire die from entrapment. This one person in four is part of an "acceptable minimum," simply because he is not given an alternative escape route. An analysis of any building plan, when related to the design logic, will quickly identify the number and location of possible expendables for the worst conditions of fire. These may then be accepted, or something may be done to improve their chances of survival.

Reinforcement.   The designer can strengthen the logic in all his related decisions if they are based on a rational code. If, for example, the strategy for life safety is escape, the designer can verify each occupant's capability; provide detectors to decrease reaction time; provide alarms which suit the occupant's needs (sight, sound, vibration, and so on); provide short, direct, protected egress routes; provide back-up escape routes in the event that the principal means of egress is lost; provide alternative locations for individuals with temporary loss or reduction of mobility; and eliminate the possibility of hazardous areas or flashover dangers in exit paths.

Percentages.   In most fires in which many lives are lost, some link in the life-safety procedure broke down or was bypassed. The fire department was delayed; the attendant assumed that someone else called the fire department; someone wedged a fire door which interfered with function; water pressure was lost; and so on. When all else fails, survival is determined by the occupant, the building, and the fire design premise which links the two. Everything else merely increases or decreases this baseline chance of safety. Only the building and the logic of its design are not, in the broadest sense, susceptible to chance; egress routes, refuge, and compartmentation are relative constants. Assistance, whether from the fire department, staff, another occupant, or a passerby has an element of fortune, as do detectors and alarms. The chances of a fire department or sprinklers always extinguishing the fire are statistically less than perfect.

Thus, one can play the percentages by following recipes, or consider the statistics of custom design and increase the probability of survival.

The Massachusetts Code

A life-safety rationale has been developed in Massachusetts for psychiatric halfway houses. The Massachusetts Group Residence Code is an example of a custom design (see Appendix 2).

When the Massachusetts Department of Mental Health began to implement the concept of the halfway house, it immediately faced the familiar roadblocks of codes and zoning. The central idea of recycling sprawling old Gothic and Victorian houses as community residences was saddled with the institutional requirements for life safety. Then a third major roadblock emerged: economic limitations.

The code was directed at health, safety, and public welfare and was a state concern. Zoning focused on the nebulous area of public welfare, specifically, protection of invested capital, and was determined locally. The code viewed the halfway house as institutional and required that these standards be met. Zoning would not permit "institutions" in exclusively residential neighborhoods. Also, the irrationality of piecemeal fireproofing of a combustible building negated the concepts of self-reliance and acceptance of the halfway house. Instead of viewing these as three distinct problems to be solved separately, the Department of Mental Health adopted the capability of self-preservation concept as its approach.

The Department of Mental Health reasoned that the Gothic and Victorian houses to be used as community residences were all combustible, so that no refuge or compartmentation could be planned. Almost everything in the layout of many of the houses violated current institutional standards—for example, the corridor and door widths, stair construction and enclosure, and flame-spreading ratings. But these were residences, no better or worse than their neighbors. The only strategy for life safety would have to be a quick escape, because the old wood was probably very combustible. Thus, the occupant's ability to escape was essential and would have to be tested.

Capability of self-preservation is normally difficult to pretest. How fast can the occupant move? How ingenious is he? How self-reliant? The following solution to this problem was developed. The individual is first pretested orally by the Department of Mental Health. A uniform test is given by referring agencies or by the community residence management if the client comes from home, verifying four capacities: (1) the capacity to sense physical danger through sight, sound, or smell; (2) the capacity to judge when such danger requires immediate egress from the dwelling; (3) the capacity to learn a route of egress; and (4) the capacity to implement that egress (see Appendix 3). Then the potential occupant is taken to the residence and briefly instructed in life-safety procedure. During the first test period, the individual is told there is a fire drill and to make his escape. Two noncrossing means of exit are provided in each group residence. Whichever route the individual takes first is blocked near the exit, so that the person being tested must use the second route. All this, from start to escape, must take less than two and a half minutes. This tests not only the individual, but his proper location in the building, egress routes, door and corridor widths—in fact, the entire system.

If the elapsed time is more than two and a half minutes, then either the building or the occupant has failed. This is a true "performance test" and leaves no room for subjective interpretation. The two-and-a-half-minute test applies to the group as well as to the individual. It also determines the maximum number of occupants that can safely occupy a given building.

For group residences, no assistance in any form is assumed. Any assistance provided under actual fire conditions will then improve the percentages.

The two and a half minutes assigned to escape is, of course, reaction time. It is based on the best current information derived from time to achieve critical levels in residential fire tests. A safety margin is included even though it is recognized that some fires are faster (explosions, flashovers) and some are slower (smoldering). The time is acceptable, in the code sense of the word.

A number of additional factors are included to increase the occupants' percentage chances of survival: a smoke- and fire-detection system is mandatory; a tailored alarm system is required; an "escape route" must be provided to prevent entrapment; no individual with temporary loss of mobility is permitted to remain in the building overnight; a fire-prevention list is provided for the surrogate parents as a check on fuel-loading; and, finally, flame and flame-spread resistance on surface materials in exits must be assured.

It should not be difficult to appreciate that the individual who is capable of self-preservation is safer in a community residence than in his own home. The normal single-family residence has an open central stairway from the upper levels—one means of escape. Even the so-called ranch house normally locates bedrooms off a single central corridor, and windows are screened or storm-sealed and do not constitute an exit for a person incapable of self-preservation— again, a single means of escape.

In traditional institutional buildings, life safety is equated with noncombustible buildings with "separate" exits. In almost every case, the two exits are at opposite ends of a common corridor, and if the corridor is filled with smoke or fire, both exits are unusable. The two crossing paths constitute essentially a single, blocked exit. Security in institutional buildings has frequently led to locked exits and total reliance on the staff or outsiders for assistance in surviving.

In a combustible building the only planning logic available is escape. It should be clear, too, that refuge and compartmentation are the only fire-safety philosophies that can be justified for a group of people who are incapable of self-preservation. By extrapolation, the difference between refuge and compartmentation is the amount of assistance immediately available to the helpless occupants. For example, reference was made earlier to the irrationality of the combustible nursing home. If the nurse can move only one patient from the fire area to the area of refuge before critical levels are reached, then all the other patients are expendable—unless they are safely enclosed in compartments beyond the fire's reach.

In halfway houses which are incorporated in high-rise, noncombustible buildings, the concept of self-reliance and community acceptance remains the same. In this case, refuge replaces escape as the design logic. All reinforcement is directed to enhancing the concept, without jeopardizing the psychiatric principles.

Thus, if a building code is adopted that emphasizes life safety through the concept of the capability of self-preservation, there should be no problem in protecting the residents of halfway houses, which the community has a responsibility to do. At the same time, there is no need to sacrifice a homelike atmosphere or the economies of using existing buildings.

CHAPTER 8

Community Entry and Zoning Requirements

The manner in which a community residence can best enter a community involves a number of issues and principles. Some of these have been discussed in previous chapters, so that the reader is already familiar with them. But the crucial question of how these issues and principles relate to the legal and social realities in the community remains to be considered.

Setting the Stage

The entrance of a community residence program into a local community is a drama whose outcome depends on the interaction of four separate elements: the residents and their degree of deviance from "community standards"; the "public" and its constituent groups; the site and its proximity to rehabilitative resources; and the selection of the building in which the residence is to be housed.

Community Standards

In chapter 3 I discussed in some detail the natural interaction between the family-modeled halfway house and the community. The halfway house trades compliance with community norms for status in the community. In practice, however, this involves a delicate ethical problem. On the one hand, it can be argued that society should be more tolerant of deviance within its midst, assuming that the deviance does not include acts destructive to the self or others. On the other hand, it can be argued that to accept deviance is to accept pathology and therefore to perpetuate it. As a general rule, the resident ought to be able to live in the community without calling undue attention to himself because of his appearance or behavior. In fact, one important part of the community residence's program is teaching residents what is acceptable behavior in the community, and what is not. There are, of course, exceptions—for instance, a person with irreversible tardive dyskinesia, who makes continuous involuntary movements with his extremities. For the sake of the residence as a whole, such exceptions ought not to be commonplace.

The Public

When a community residence is in the planning stage, the complexity of the community setting must be recognized. Otherwise, the initiating group may find itself at odds with a community group that it did not even know existed. As outlined in chapter 5, the "community" is likely to consist of the following groups: the client in need of services; the service provider; advocacy groups supporting the interests of the clients; professionals who provide direct service to the client, advisory services to the program providers, or both; groups representing the overall mental health service needs of the community; citizens of the town or city who make up the electorate; governmental bodies, such as the town council and the planning board; the immediate neighbors of a new program; and particularly influential members of the community, such as the clergy, politicians, officers of the Chamber of Commerce, the League of Women Voters, or other community organizations.

The Site and Building

Once the service population and general locale have been identified, the exact location should be chosen. To facilitate daily outside activities for residents, the site should offer easy access to the following outside services: public transportation; competitive employment or sheltered workshops; shops for food and other sundries, preferably within walking distance; educational facilities appropriate to the ages of the residents; mental health agencies, especially an outpatient clinic for medication, counseling, and crisis intervention;

social-service agencies to assist in acquiring future housing, proper social security benefits, and family and vocational counseling; and emergency medical services, preferably a hospital emergency room.

The selection of location is also dictated by the availability of suitable buildings. Decisive architectural requirements include space properly distributed, with enough bedrooms of adequate size, space for a manager's suite (if necessary), adequately sized common rooms, and a dining room that can seat all house members at once. There should also be one room large enough for the house meeting, which all members attend. (A more detailed description of space requirements is provided in Chapter 10.)

Political and Legal Factors

The drama of entry will be played out in two distinct arenas. One is political, the other is legal. There are, of course, connections and similarities between the two, but it is important that their separateness be acknowledged by residence planners and sponsors.

Some planners believe the community residence should announce its entry and seek the community's blessing right from the start. They envision the community welcoming them with open arms. Without such community knowledge (the argument goes) the community residence is destined to remain isolated, and everyone agrees that strong ties with the surrounding community are an essential goal of residence programs.

On the other hand, it can be argued that the ex-patient is entitled to privacy in reestablishing himself in the community, a right apparently violated by labeling the residence as a facility for the mentally ill. Labels help establish community expectations (this argument runs), and lowered expectations would replicate the antitherapeutic conditions of the state hospital. The result would inevitably be "special" status for the residence in the community, with one of two equally undesirable reactions projected: either the community would be overly accepting of deviance, and the residents would lose the opportunity to be just plain neighbors; or the residence could become the scapegoat for any untoward event occurring in the neighborhood. According to this logic, the community residence should enter the community quietly, with a low profile.

To some extent, zoning laws will dictate which of the two arguments wins out with a sponsoring group. The key questions are: Is a public hearing required? Does a special permit have to be granted by an official body? Low-profile entry is *only* feasible when no hearing or permit is required. For example, if the group is starting a cooperative apartment program, for which they are acquiring a small apartment building in a location zoned for such an occupancy, then there may be no legal requirement for either a hearing or a permit. If, however, the community or state has specifically written a zoning category of community residence into its zoning bylaws, then a low-profile approach may be precluded. Such laws invariably require both hearings and special permits.

The most common community entry problem is location in a single-residence zone. Generally the town or municipality will consider the facility to be a multiple dwelling and require a public hearing to entertain the application for a special use permit or a variance. And it is in just such a situation that the distinction between the legal and the political becomes most important. The political task is to convince the governing body to grant the permit. If this fails, the question becomes a legal one: Is it lawful to deny such a permit?

Political Strategies

The sponsoring group must assess the factors that influence the governing body. If the agency is composed of elected, paid officials, then it will be very responsive to the electorate, so acquiring the electorate's support becomes the primary political goal. Several general principles are helpful in this context.

First, never appear to be a foreign intruder. The program should be seen as offering a service, not imposing a burden. This means making it clear that the residence will be available to members of the immediate community, either directly, as an alternative to hospitalization, or as a transition from the hospital back to the community. The community may deny that any of its citizens have problems. In anticipation of such claims, the sponsoring group should prepare both family members of likely residents and professionals from the community to speak to the real state of affairs. Both groups should be recruited from the community. Besides, it is good practice to pay local real-estate taxes rather than to claim exemption.

Second, establish explicit standards for both the behavior of residents and the maintenance of the property. This will reassure the community that its norms will not be violated in either area. Educational materials can help document the nature and record of similar programs. The issue of property values should be taken up directly, with the sponsoring group spelling out the budget and plans for *improving* the property. This can be done without undue expense by using resident labor to improve landscaping, do painting and repairs, and generally turn what is often a neighborhood eyesore into an acceptable residence.

Third, utilize influential community leaders—such as the clergy, members of the Chamber of Commerce and League of Women Voters, local politicians, shopkeepers, and articulate neighbors—to support the contention that the program will be an asset in the community. Their participation on the board of the sponsoring group can be an additional sign of both personal support and community involvement.

Fourth, consider the immediate neighbors as a very special group. They will feel most threatened about property values and personal safety, and they are likely to become the best-organized opponents of the community residence. Recruiting respected immediate neighbors as allies can therefore do a great deal to ensure successful entry. If a neighbor of the residence stands up before his fellows and bluntly states that the "buck stops here," or "our community needs this service," then the likelihood of success is greatly enhanced. In no event should the power of immediate neighbors be overlooked.

The timing and sequence of communications are also crucial. Premature disclosure of group plans can lead to rumors and half-truths, creating irrationally organized opposition before the facts are known. The community residence sponsoring group must therefore be organized and disciplined in its program exposition and timetable. An example of a successful sequence would be:

1. Developing a program, with clear definition of the population to be served by a core initiating group that has the support of organized mental health agencies in the community and of a local mental health professional who knows the community's needs and who acts as consultant and supporter.

2. Appointing a board of local citizens who support the program and enhance its integrity. This group contributes expertise in the following areas: mental health; accounting and other fiscal matters; the law, as it pertains to contracts, leases, and regulations and standards affecting the residence; and architecture, as it pertains to fire safety, building code acceptance and implementation, and building and landscaping esthetics. The advisory group might also include members of the clergy, the business community, a respected politician, and a realtor who speaks to the issue of property values.

3. Inviting the immediate neighbors to meet with the board to review the proposal before the hearing. This is the time that neighbors' fears should be heard and (ideally) allayed through the point-by-point presentation of all of the protective and service aspects of the program. This is also an appropriate time to announce the participation of respected community members to ensure that these plans will be realized. If the neighbors arrive in a hostile mood, with some budding organized resistance, the sponsoring group should be ready for this and not meet it in a combative, adversary way. Rather, a thorough hearing of the community's fears followed by a careful presentation can sway and move such a hostile group—especially if some of them are already predisposed to favor the project.

4. The last item is applying for a hearing before the community's governing body.

If, after all this preparation and work, the sponsors fail to win approval from the governing body, then legal recourse may be sought. The sponsoring group can bring its case before the district court in its county and proceed as necessary through the court system. However, the legal route is complicated by the expenses involved and by the lack of consistency in recent court decisions on community residence programs.

Legal Strategies and Precedents

In general, sponsoring groups can take comfort in the growing legal precedent defining the family as a group of people sleeping, cooking, and eating on a single premises, rather than as a group of people related by blood or marriage.[1] According to this definition, community residences would universally qualify as families for zoning purposes. Courts in Wisconsin, Florida, Kentucky, and New York have been unanimous in refusing to include in the definition of a family the requirement that individuals be related by blood or marriage where this has not been stipulated in the zoning code.[2] Even where a zoning code does explicitly define a family in terms of blood or marriage, the courts have sometimes not enforced that definition. A New Jersey court ignored the requirements of an ordinance that individuals had to be related on the grounds that to give it effect might render the ordinance unconstitutional, in violation of the Fourteenth Amendment.[3] But the law, as determined by precedents, is far from a sure refuge for sponsoring groups. Conflict and inconsistency seem more the rule than the exception.

In Massachusetts, one community residence has won a case which is potentially of national importance. Downey Side, a charitable corporation, was attempting to operate a group home for troubled youths in the town of Holyoke. Residents in the general vicinity of the home complained that the use being made of the premises was in violation of the zoning ordinance relating to that district, which permitted only detached, one-family dwellings. The court ruled that a "family in context of the zoning ordinance of the city of Holyoke in the absence of precise definition would include a group of people who live together in one housing unit under the management or control of a directing head." It further stated that "the use of the premises contemplated by the respondent, Downey Side Inc., would come within that definition since the premises would be occupied by a group of persons sharing the benefits and responsibilities of living together and under the direction, management, discipline, and control of parental authority."[4]

The Belle Terre Decision

One Supreme Court decision, in the case of *Belle Terre* v. *Boraas*, has generated great concern within the entire community residence movement. Whether or not the ruling does put community residences at risk, sponsoring groups must give it serious attention. This decision, written by Justice William O. Douglas, was announced on April 1, 1974.[5] The case centered on six unrelated college students at the Stony Brook campus of the State University of New York who desired to live in a home together in the village of Belle Terre, on Long Island. The village restricted land use to one-family dwellings and excluded more than two unrelated persons from the definition of a family. Upon the village's attempt to evict the students, they and the landlord brought suit on the grounds that the village's definition of "family" was unconstitutional. The lower courts held that the definition did indeed violate the equal protection clause of the Fourteenth Amendment. But the Supreme Court found otherwise. Justice Douglas wrote that a group of unrelated adults *could* be zoned out of a residential neighborhood restricted to one-family dwellings, because the word *family* was defined to mean "one or more persons related by blood, adoption, or marriage or not more than two unrelated persons living and cooking together in a single housekeeping unit." Justice Douglas reasoned that "the regimes of boarding houses, fraternity houses, and the like present urban problems. More people occupy a given space; more cars rather continuously pass by; more cars are parked; noise travels with crowds." He added that "a quiet place where yards are wide, the people are few and the motor vehicles are restricted are legitimate guidelines in a land use project addressed to family needs." Justice Brennan's dissenting opinion took the position that where population density is the issue, the proper concern of zoning laws might be the number of persons (or automobiles or decibels) per household, not blood relatedness or the lack of it. The concern persists that *Belle Terre* could be used to support the argument that any single residential zone can exclude community residences made up of a number of unrelated persons.

A crucial question that relates to the impact of the *Belle Terre* decision on the community residence is whether the special needs of potential residents change the balance of deciding factors. If this proves to be so, a community residence might be permitted in a one-family dwelling zone, whereas an ordinary group of unrelated persons would not. This argument would be strengthened if the potential residents came from the same community in which they desired to live together as a family.

The White Plains Decision

This question has been answered without challenge in one court decision thus far. In a post–*Belle Terre* decision, *City of White Plains* v. *Ferriaioli*, the New York State Court of Appeals allowed a group home for dependent and neglected children in a single-family zone despite a locally restrictive definition of "family."[6] In this important case, the court differentiated the group home from a "temporary living arrangement as would be a group of college students sharing a house and commuting to a nearby school":

So long as the group home bears the generic character of a family unit as a relatively permanent household, and is not a framework for transients or transient living, it conforms to the purpose of the ordinance. . . . In short, an ordinance may restrict a residential zone to occupancy by stable families occupying single-family homes, but neither by express provision nor construction may it limit the definition of family to exclude a household which in every but a biological sense is a single family.

This later court ruling gives some precedent and hope that community residences will not be excluded arbitrarily from local communities. There are two factors in this decision, however, that do not apply to most of the halfway houses of concern here. First, this decision relates to a facility for *children*. Second, the population in this case is *not transient*. This leaves the transitional halfway house for adults in a legal limbo, as no court has yet ruled on the appropriate definition of family in relation to this type of facility. It could be argued that such facilities fall more under the star of *Belle Terre* than *White Plains*.

Finally, if legal issues do arise, the Mental Health Law Project in Washington, D.C., is willing to assist community residences with particular legal difficulties in regard to zoning.[7]

Citizen Rights and Zoning Laws

Beyond the question of what constitutes a family, there are two other important fronts in the battle to ease community entry. One is the influence of official state policy; and the second is the influence of federal court rulings on the civil rights of mental patients. Both affect the issue of zoning.

Given the unstable mass of current court rulings on zoning, successful community entry for a statewide program would be facilitated if state governments adopted a policy for community rehabilitative housing for handicapped citizens, along with enabling legislation to help bring this policy to realization. The policy would ideally give handicapped citizens the right to live together in group residences which enhance their development into more useful and independent persons. The issues that must be addressed in a state zoning law include: defining state policy objectives on rehabilitative housing for handicapped citizens; defining the community's needs for such housing; establishing distribution on the basis of local needs for such housing, as opposed to encouraging ghettos in any one community; affirming the residence's right to protection from arbitrary exclusion by the community; and finally ensuring compliance with preexisting state standards of care in ongoing residential programs.

In answer to many of these needs, the Mental Health Law Project has proposed a uniform zoning code allowing community residences of up to eight persons in any residential zone, and proposing dispersion and density controls to prevent the excessive concentration of facilities and facility residents in any one area.[8] Several states have either adopted or are actively considering such zoning legislation. California's Lanterman-Petris Short Act in 1970, providing for community care of the mentally and physically handicapped, was amended to address the exclusionary zoning issue:

Pursuant to the policy stated in section 5115, a state's authorized, certified, or licensed family care home, foster home, or group home serving six or fewer mentally disordered or otherwise handicapped persons or dependent or neglected children shall be considered a residential use of property for the purposes of zoning, if such homes provide care on a 24 hour basis.[9]

In a case challenging the law, San Francisco "argued that the state law could not control in a chartered locality. The court held that local zoning in conflict with the statute was unenforceable."[10] Minnesota allows state-licensed community residences of up to six residents in single-family zones, with larger facilities of seven to sixteen residents permitted in multifamily areas, but a local conditional use permit may be required.[11] However, the Minnesota statute calls for licensure of new facilities to be denied where issuance "would substantively contribute to an excessive concentration of community residential facilities within any town, municipality, or county of the state."[12] Wisconsin considered similar legislation, which unfortunately was rejected. Under the proposed Wisconsin legislation, "state licensed community residences accommodating up to 8 persons with social, physical, or mental disabilities can locate in single family use zones without obtaining zoning variances or exceptions. Larger facilities (up to 16) can locate in other zones without applying for a variance, and can apply for a variance in single family use zones."[13]

A Model Law

Massachusetts addressed this issue in 1972, when the Governor's Commission on Citizen Participation, in conjunction with other executive agencies, drafted and submitted community residence zoning legislation. The commission report succinctly identified the problem:

The Commission has found that where communities have blocked group residences, the balance between the desires of local citizens and the responsibility of the Commonwealth to protect minorities has been upset. Acting in what they see as their self-interest, these communities have blocked programs which could give citizens of the Commonwealth the means to stay out of, or make a transition from, a large institution.

The report also suggested a solution: "To redress the imbalance, the Commission strongly urges legislation which will change the route which group residences have to follow in order to enter a community. At present, the incipient residence must first run a gauntlet of town and city boards in order to obtain the necessary permits."[14]

The proposed legislation, in my view, represents a national model law, and it is worth quoting here at length. The full text is provided in Appendix 4.

First, it defines policy objectives of the commonwealth relative to group residences in the following terms:

Mentally, physically, and socially handicapped persons should to the maximum extent possible, have the opportunity to receive care in group residences where they can live in normal residential surroundings rather than in large impersonal institutions. County and municipal zoning ordinances and building codes, and other ordinances and administrative interpretations thereof, should not unreasonably obstruct the creation and operation of group residences. Each city and town in the commonwealth should be prepared to assume some responsibility in the placement of group residences; however, no city or town should bear a disproportionate share.

Second, it provides simpler entry procedures: "Any person proposing to build or to operate a group residence may submit to the board of appeals . . . a single application to build or operate such group residence in lieu of separate applications to the applicable local boards."

Third, it specifies a minimum obligation for each community, stating that the numbers of all types of community residences could be limited only after they were "in excess of five per cent of the housing units reported in the latest decennial census of the city, town, or ward."

Fourth, it provides sponsors with an appeals process should a community arbitrarily exclude a group residence:

Whenever an application . . . is denied or is granted with such conditions and requirements as to make the building or operation of such group residence infeasible, the applicant shall have the right to appeal to the group residence appeals committee in the department of community affairs for a review of the same. . . . If the group residence appeals committee finds, in the case of a denial, that the decision of the board of appeals was unreasonable and not consistent with community needs and the policy objectives of the commonwealth relative to group residences, it shall vacate such decision and shall direct the board to issue a comprehensive permit or approval to the applicant.

Finally it protects the community by requiring that community residences comply with both the community residence building code (see chapter 7) and licensing standards of the mental health agency (see chapter 6):

The committee shall not issue any order which would permit the establishment or operation of a group residence unless the applicant is able to substantially comply with the building code applicable to group residences and is licensed or operated by or under contract to a department or agency or the commonwealth, or can show that such license will issue or such contract be signed upon granting of such comprehensive permit or approval.

This last phrase was included to prevent a "catch-22" situation in which the appeals board makes licensing a precondition for obtaining a building permit, and the state agency makes the building permit a precondition for licensing.

Legislation on the Massachusetts model can be extremely helpful

in developing a balanced statewide program of community residences. It should be noted, however, that this law failed to pass the
Massachusetts legislature. The failure was due to a strong sentiment
that local communities should maintain their prerogatives on zoning
matters, without state interference. But the matter is hardly settled.
The growing need for community programs and their obvious worth
makes passage of such legislation a live political issue.[15]

Recent court decisions have added fuel to the flame by ordering
community placement of patients in settings of minimum constraint
(*Dixon* v. *Weinberger;* see chapter 5). At the same time, *Belle Terre*
sets a precedent for potential community exclusion of these same
patients. Thus, two federal court orders effectively double-bind the
mental health professional. This resulting "conceptual conflict" may
some day be settled by the Supreme Court. The situation illustrates
the very heart of the problem of conflicting rights of citizens with
different needs. With proper safeguards, education, and participation of all the parties involved, the ultimate result must be that
there is room for citizens with differing needs within the same
community.

CHAPTER 9

Profile of a Statewide Community Residence Program

Because I have used the Massachusetts program as an example of regulations, building code, and community entry strategies, it seems worthwhile to review the actual results of that statewide program. I view Massachusetts as a test of whether our ideology and administrative structure are practical for statewide implementation.

This evaluation proceeds from several vantage points: the adequacy of the total number of beds and facilities; the quality of the program in terms of internal milieu, outside daily program, and destination on discharge; community acceptance or resistance; and integration of the community residence into a network of services.

The first question, then, relates to size of the program. As of May 1976, there were eighty-one alternative residential programs for the mentally ill in Massachusetts, with a capacity to house 758 residents: forty-six community residences serving 586 residents, or 12.73 per residence, and thirty-five cooperative apartments housing 172 residents, or 4.9 per apartment. Ten new community residences in various stages of planning and certification are not included in these figures. Figure 2 shows the growth of community residences in the state since 1967, when there were only six such residential programs. Figure 3 shows the development over time of the cooperative apartment programs. The apparent leveling-off in the numbers of programs in 1975 and 1976 reflects the acute state fiscal crisis during these two years, which required severe cutbacks in state mental health funding. As noted in chapter 5, the program has been stalled and is in an uncertain state largely because of a lack of fiscal support from the commonwealth.

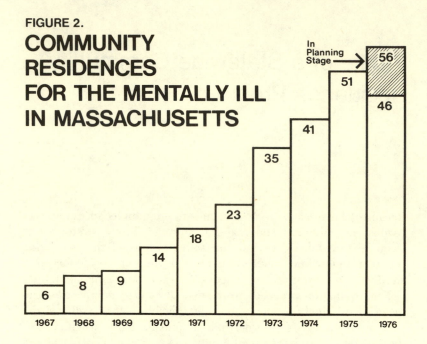

FIGURE 2.

COMMUNITY RESIDENCES FOR THE MENTALLY ILL IN MASSACHUSETTS

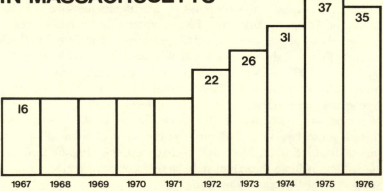

FIGURE 3.

COOPERATIVE APARTMENTS FOR THE MENTALLY ILL IN MASSACHUSETTS

In 1976 the Division of Mental Health Services in the Department of Mental Health assessed basic service needs. It concluded that in the community residence program, at least 10 community residences housing annually about 200 residents were needed in each catchment area population of 200,000 throughout the commonwealth. This adds up to 400 community residences housing a total of 8,000 people annually, out of a total state population of 8 million. This is about one bed per thousand population. This appears to be a very generous estimate, but it nevertheless highlights the fact that while there has been a significant start in Massachusetts, with almost 800 beds available, a considerable need continues to go unmet.

Concern about the second area of evaluation, quality control, has revolved around the fears that the halfway houses would become too large, have inadequate programs, and act as a dead end for patients, who would be lost here as surely as they were in the state hospitals. Quality in community residential programs is determined by the adequacy of state regulatory standards and the resources and integrity of the particular provider. The rationale and details of state standards are outlined in chapter 6, and chapter 12 documents the fact that a well-motivated and advantaged program can have impressive results. More broadly, Rog and Raush's review of follow-up studies on twenty-six halfway houses paints a fairly optimistic picture: overall, only 20 percent of the ex-residents had been hospitalized, 58 percent were living independently, and 55 percent were employed or in school.[1] However, these evaluations are based on programs which conduct their own follow-up studies, so they may not be representative. More convincing evidence would come from a follow-up study of a statewide program. This chapter partially fills that bill, presenting an administrative profile and a limited clinical follow-up on thirty-seven halfway house programs in operation in Massachusetts throughout 1974.

A primary concern here is the sort of person who was likely to enter the residential system. In Massachusetts we have believed that there were primarily three groups of patients who could use community residential care. The first was individuals in crisis, coming directly from the community, who would require short-term, intensive, nonmedical supervision and support. The second group was composed of individuals ready to leave a psychiatric hospital after short-term care, but not yet ready to assume the full responsibilities of independent living. The third group consisted of individuals who after long periods of hospitalization are capable of personal care but lack social skills and competencies.[2] In response to the differing needs of each of these population groups, several types of community residences have evolved over the years. One model is embodied in the transitional halfway house which explicitly anticipates that residents will leave for independent living within a defined time period, usually one or two years after entry. Another is embodied in a group residence having no requirement that the residents leave for independent living within a specified time. Finally, the cooperative apartment model covers a group living independently without live-in staff or time limitations. Increasingly, the distinction between the transitional halfway house and the group residence has been blurred. This results from the recognition that length of stay is not always easily predictable. Further, it is increasingly felt that to categorize patients into long-term and short-term groups tends to re-create the destructive stratification of the state hospital. Accordingly, these two types will be treated here as one group and referred to as "community residences" for the remainder of the chapter.

Method

To provide both a profile of what exists and some ongoing clinical follow-up, the Massachusetts Department of Mental Health uses required annual reporting forms to collect specific information from each community residence regarding the previous operating year. Information is organized in two categories, administrative and clinical. Administrative information includes ownership of the facility; affiliations with other organizations; prior use of the building; the nature of the community (urban, suburban, small-town, or rural); resources available within one-half mile; and charges and costs per resident. Clinical data requested are: source of admissions; nature of eating arrangement (residents segregated from staff or entire community together); frequency of house meetings; leadership of meetings; daily activity patterns; length of stay; and destination on discharge.

The following data are taken from these reporting forms, which represent all 1974 reports for thirty-seven reporting facilities which were in operation during the entire reporting period. The remaining four of the total of forty-one either did not send in reports or went into operation some time during the reporting period.

Results

Among the thirty-seven community residences which reported, there were 471 beds, with a mean number of beds per house of 12.72 and a range of 4 to 38 beds, and a mean occupancy of 81 percent (or 381 beds filled at the time of reporting).

Administrative Profile

The review of the owners of the facilities in table 1 shows that a preponderance of them (68 percent) are nonprofit corporations. Certainly the profit-making sector is in a distinct minority (32 percent).

This reflects the Department of Mental Health's policy of getting the state out of the business of direct delivery of service by state

TABLE 1. Ownership of Facilities

Nonprofit organizations	
Churches	1
Corporations	18
Other	6
Total	25
Profit-making organizations	
Individuals	5
Partnerships	3
Corporations	4
Total	12

employees whenever possible. This policy is partly based on the fact that each state employee position is created through an act of the legislature and can only be removed by the legislature. Thus, attempting to alter the delivery of service in any way often becomes politically cumbersome at best, and impossible at worst. Community programs funded by the department but not directly staffed by department employees have been seen as a way out of these difficulties. The hope has been to contract with private nonprofit corporations to deliver services. This frees the department to assume its responsibilities of quality control and monitoring. If quality is deemed insufficient, the department can dictate the need for improvement or terminate the contract should deficiencies continue. In this event, funds are employed in a new contract to a better program. This change in the method of funding is not yet complete, since relinquishing state employee positions has its political problems as well; the legislature's loss of patronage is but one obstacle. Thus, as an interim procedure, some nonprofit corporations actually retain "their" employees by using a "borrowed" state position assigned to them by a cooperative state hospital superintendent or regional administrator.

A second advantage of this nonprofit corporate system is that the officers of the corporation are most often leaders of the community in which the facility is to be located. This facilitates community entry and true integration by assisting in job placement, establishing affiliations with local social agencies (such as community centers and churches), and involving the facility in community avocational activities. Table 2 documents the affiliation of community residences with local mental health facilities or agencies—twenty-five of

TABLE 2. Residence Affiliates

DMH Area Mental Health Center	17
Mental Health Association	2
State hospital	3
Private hospital	3
Total	25
Unaffiliated	12

TABLE 3. Prior Use of Building

Single-family house	9
Multifamily house	11
Lodging house	6
Built for this purpose	2
Small apartment house	1
Inn or hotel	2
Rest home	1
Other	3
Unknown	2

the thirty-seven have such affiliations. It is noteworthy that seventeen of these are closely affiliated with area mental health centers.

In Massachusetts, the community residence is closely related to its local community and service agencies; moreover, it is modeled on the family social system. Accordingly, each community residence usually looks for a big old family home in which to locate. Table 3 demonstrates that twenty of the thirty-seven community residences were single-family or multifamily homes immediately prior to their conversion to community residential use. The former lodging houses (of which there were six) were also usually single-family homes prior to their conversion to lodging houses. Thus, probably twenty-six of the thirty-seven in the sample were family homes at one time.

The paucity of rural locations is noted in table 4, with thirty-three of thirty-seven locations in urban, suburban, or small-town settings. This reflects not only the density of population centers and location of mental health facilities, but also the need to locate the residence

TABLE 4. Nature of Community
Where Residence Is Located

Urban	15
Suburban	10
Small-town	8
Rural	2
Hospital grounds	2

TABLE 5. Resources Available
Within One-Half Mile

Public transportation	26
Shopping	28
Recreational facilities	27
Mental health agencies	26
Social-service agencies	24
Educational facilities	24

near other resources, as seen in table 5. The availability of transportation, shopping, and recreational facilities is a necessity for a program seeking integration into the fabric of community life. It also advances the clinical goal of fostering the residents' capacity for work, play, and the ability to care for themselves in the community.

While there has been considerable concern about the problem of community entry, the record in Massachusetts tells a surprising story. The survey showed that only two of the thirty-seven community residences (5 percent) had to change communities from targeted entry because of community resistance. Of the thirty-seven neighborhoods in which the community residences ultimately located, only four (11 percent) developed organized community opposition. In each of these instances, the opposition was successfully met and resolved. Only one of the thirty-seven residences reported community problems during the last year of operation surveyed. This is a remarkable record of minimal community opposition.

Calculations based on table 6 demonstrate that 55 percent of the programs' costs are recovered by contributions from the residents themselves. Sources include work income, Supplemental Security Income, and other federal sources. The remaining 45 percent of the programs' budgets required state subsidization. The actual cost of the program—$11.60 daily average—is certainly less than that of private (over $100 a day) or public ($32 a day) hospitalization. It should be borne in mind that this is a direct paid cost reflecting the 1974 fiscal year. Considering inflationary trends, 1977 costs would be at least $14 per day. We do not yet have a complete cost analysis,

TABLE 6. Charges and Costs per Resident

Daily average charge	$ 6.36
Monthly average charge	189.76
Daily average cost	11.60
Monthly average cost	348.21
Monthly average deficit	158.45

Note: Based on 30 of 37 programs reporting.

one providing an estimate of the cost of all rehabilitative services being rendered to the resident.

In summary, the "average" residence in Massachusetts is operated by a nonprofit corporation that is affiliated with a community agency and performs a service for the community in which the residence is located. Its program is monitored by state regulatory standards. It would appear that these factors taken together have contributed to a relatively accepting community environment.

Clinical Profile

There were 681 admissions in the thirty-seven reporting community residences. There was a mean of 18.4 admissions per community residence and a median of 14. It is noteworthy that only 344, or 51 percent, of these admissions were from hospitals. Thirty-one percent came from homes in the community; 18 percent came from elsewhere (see table 7). These figures testify to the local community's use of the community residence as an important alternative to hospitalization and is another consequence of the administrative integration of the residence into the community.

Before turning to the crucial question of program quality, I should note some structural considerations. First, the size of the program—approximately thirteen residents per house—contributes to sustaining the family model of social living. In thirty-five of the thirty-seven residences, the group takes meals together family style. The residents participated in the cooking in thirty-two of the programs.

TABLE 7. Sources of Admissions

Source	Number	Percentage
Acute general medical hospital	26	4
State psychiatric hospital	217	32
Private psychiatric hospital	101	15
Total hospitals	344	51
Home of family of origin	136	20
Independent home or apartment	75	11
Total homes	211	31
Nursing home	16	2
Other community residence	28	4
Correctional institution	27	4
Other	34	5
State School for the Mentally Retarded	17	2.5
Unknown	4	0.5

All of the programs reported that they held house meetings. We feel that these meetings facilitate group solidarity, sustain a focus on growth and rehabilitation, and thus help keep residents from retreating into isolation. The meetings also keep the staff alert to the conditions of individuals and the morale of the whole group. Twenty-four of the thirty-seven programs reportedly held meetings weekly; three held them daily; two held them twice a week; and eight, with some other frequency. Table 8 shows who conducts the meetings. That residents were involved in conducting meetings in twenty-four of the thirty-seven residences reflects the high degree

TABLE 8. Leadership of Meetings

Staff	8
Residents	4
Staff and residents	16
Staff, residents, and consultant	4
Staff, consultant, and other	1
Other	2
Unknown	2

TABLE 9. Residents' Daily Activities

Activity	Number	Percentage
Work full time in sheltered workshop	61	14.5
Work part time in sheltered workshop	28	6.7
Work full time in competitive employment	42	10.0
Work part time in competitive employment	34	8.1
Work on cooperative farm program	35	8.3
Do volunteer work	24	5.7
Total working	224	53.3
Attend school	60	14.3
Attend day care	59	14.0
Attend intensive milieu group program	20	4.8
Other	13	3.1
Remain idle in the residence all day	44	10.5

of resident involvement in the management of the day-to-day affairs of the houses.

Crucial in our inquiry is how the residents spend their time during the day. The data collected show that the 381 residents in thirty-seven residences engaged in 420 activities (as shown in table 9). Nearly 90 percent of the activities were active daily program endeavors, 53.3 percent including some kind of work, 14.3 percent school activities, and 14 percent day care programs. It is especially noteworthy that of these 381 residents only 44 (or 10.5 percent) were reported to be idle and in the residence all day. Two community residences which had not yet developed programs for their residents accounted for 21 of this number. (Both of these were in the process of affiliating with their local community mental health center day programs.) This means that in the remaining thirty-five community residences there were only 23 idle residents (6 percent), or less than one idle resident per community residence. This is taken to be strong evidence that the community residence programs, integrated with the mental health agencies, have provided active rehabilitation for their residents. It counters the idea that a statewide community residence program can only offer "flophouses" or back wards off the grounds.

TABLE 10. Average Length of Stay

Length of Stay	Number	Percentage
One month or less	136	25
One month to six months	277	51
Six months to one year	96	18
One to two years	23	4
Over two years	9	2

There were 541 discharges in the entire group, with a mean annual discharge rate of 14.62 per facility. The average lengths of stay are noted in table 10. That 413, or 76 percent, have a stay not exceeding six months, and 509, or 94 percent, stayed no longer than one year, suggests that these facilities are largely providing a transitional living arrangement. Indeed, only 6 percent of the residents

TABLE 11. Destination Upon Discharge

Destination	Number	Percentage
Independent home or apartment	222	41
Home of family	140	26
Foster home	3	0.6
Total to homes	365	67.6
Other community residence	51	9
Nursing or rest home	6	1.2
Residential school treatment center	8	1.5
Detoxification center	1	0.2
Total to other community facilities	66	11.9
State psychiatric hospital	59	11
Private psychiatric hospital	13	2.4
Total to psychiatric hospitals	72	13.4
Acute general hospital	5	0.9
Chronic disease hospital	1	0.2
Total to other hospitals	6	1.1
Unknown	13	2.4
Death	3	0.6
Other	16	3.0

stayed over one year. This discounts the notion that these facilities are dead-end streets.

Table 11 shows the destinations of the 541 discharges. Whereas 344 residents (or 51 percent) were admitted from hospitals (47 percent from psychiatric hospitals), only 78 (or 14.5 percent) were discharged *to* hospitals (with only 72, or 13.4 percent, to psychiatric hospitals). This clearly represents a flow of patients to the community. Whereas only 31 percent came from a home, 67.6 percent returned to one.

Discussion

More rigorous research into the Massachusetts program and in-depth follow-up studies are needed. Longer follow-up of the patients' courses following their departure from halfway houses is essential in order to confirm the long-term rehabilitative result. Despite their limitations, however, preliminary findings suggest that the Massachusetts programs based on the principles described earlier are rehabilitative and are not repeating the institutional problems of the past.

PART III

The Halfway House in Practice

CHAPTER 10

Planning a New Community Residence Program

Planning and starting a community residence is a complicated and demanding job. But having examined the ideological and legal aspects of the community residence, we are now in a position to discuss its creation in concrete terms. This chapter offers a sequential approach to starting a program, broken down task by task, as follows:

1. Forming the operating organization.
2. Establishing the type of client who clearly needs community residential services.
3. Identifying the type and size of the facility that will meet the specific needs of this clientele.
4. Planning the program components of the facility.
5. Establishing the network of ancillary services to be made available to the client off the premises.
6. Establishing staff requirements, job descriptions, staffing patterns, and hiring procedures.
7. Finding a suitable location (described in chapter 8).
8. Finding a suitable building.
9. Planning and implementing a community entry strategy (described in chapter 8).
10. Developing a budget (capital and seed money) in relation to the building, initial staffing, and operating expenses.
11. Establishing sources of funds.
12. Monitoring these tasks to keep them in compliance with relevant laws and regulations (an ongoing task that is inherent in all the others).

13. Drafting a comprehensive program statement, suitable for public education, describing effective completion of all these tasks.

Forming the Operating Organization

First, there must be a core of dedicated persons who conceive, back, and pilot the project from its initial conceptualization to functional maturity. Starting a community residence requires commitment and preparation. False starts by poorly prepared sponsors who drop the project at the first difficulty, or seriously blunder in their public relations, create ill will in the community and make entry all the more difficult for groups who try to follow them.

Ideally, the core group should consist of members of the community in which the residence is to be located. They should have a variety of skills corresponding to the variety of tasks to be accomplished. The initiators may be members of local mental health associations, state local area boards, or others with an interest in mental health. This group usually forms a nonprofit corporation. A mental health professional should be on the corporate board to coordinate program planning and to maintain its clinical integrity in the face of a multitude of administrative decisions. Expertise is also required in the following areas: legal, to facilitate compliance with zoning and other regulations; fiscal, in the area of accounting (to assist in preparing a sound budget) and banking (to help in obtaining a loan for start-up costs); architectural, to assist with building-code compliance and structural renovations; and real estate, to inform the group of new listings of appropriate houses or apartments. Further, important community leaders such as a clergyman, a local politician, or a respected businessman can help with strategies for community entry by educating other community members, thus facilitating acceptance and support.

The fiscal survival of the community residence depends in part on the establishment of relationships with existing agencies in the community. Liaison with other elements of the mental health delivery system is important in this respect, as it ensures a balanced turnover of residents. This function may fall to members of the board itself, or solely to the director whom the board hires. In either case, liaison requires a thorough familiarity with referral sources in the community, including the private mental health sector and county or state agencies. Similarly, liaison with outside rehabilitative agencies helps develop the residents' social and vocational skills and eases their movement into the community. Liaison at both entry and departure helps the program sustain its rehabilitative function by minimizing concerns that when a resident moves out, he or she will leave behind an empty, nonpaying bed. This concern may especially affect private entrepreneurs, who might be tempted to keep community residents in residence more for the sake of income maintenance than for effective rehabilitation.

Primarily because of this hypothetical conflict between profit and rehabilitation, it is generally accepted that a nonprofit organization, preferably a corporation, ought to be the governing, sponsoring body of the community residence. Despite the limitations this dictum imposes (and it is not universally accepted; witness the case of Massachusetts), the nonprofit corporation *is* the organization of choice. It lends assurance that the rehabilitative aim will be primary, it facilitates government funding (which requires nonprofit status), and it eases acquisition of start-up and demonstration funds.

The sponsoring group, made up of representatives of the community, is rehabilitative in more senses than one. Beyond its obvious commitment to residence objectives, the board, through citizen participation, helps bring the whole residence into a closer relationship with the community. This is a vital normalizing function which the core group serves throughout the life of the community residence.

Selecting the Client Type

In recognizing that the characteristics of the clients to be served by a residence need to be established, we are not saying that a residence cannot be designed to rehabilitate a variety of diagnostic groups. It is axiomatic, however, that there must be a rehabilitative programmatic component for each resident's deficiency. The specifics of each program will therefore be dictated by the spectrum of problems presented by the residents.

Potential characteristics of the client population include the following:

Diagnostic group. This includes schizophrenias; manic-depressive disorders; other affective disorders, especially the depressions; personality disorders (including drug dependence, alcoholism, and antisocial personality); adolescent adjustment reaction; behavior disorders of adolescence; and mental impairment due to senile dementia, developmental disability (mental retardation), or other organic brain syndromes.

Time in history of illness. There are three categories here: acute (a new evolving illness); intermediate (after an initial episode has subsided); and chronic.

Source of residents. There are three referral sources to be considered: the community (home prior residence); the community mental health center (some acute inpatient or partial care having been rendered); a state hospital.

Age of residents. Residents may be adolescent, adult, or elderly.

Vocational level. This may be classified in terms of developed job skills; minimal job skills which can be enhanced; and no job skills, categorized as trainable, difficult to train, or untrainable.

Educational level. This may be categorized as further formal education inappropriate; college education a reasonable goal; high-school completion an appropriate goal.

Life skills development. This is rated along a continuum ranging from primary life skills attained to significant life skills to be developed.

Psychosocial network—community linkages. This is similarly considered along a continuum, ranging from intact, with significant positive objects, to impoverished, needing replenishment.

Programmatic Consequences of Resident Characteristics

The various diagnostic groups require distinct approaches and interventions. In general, when pathology is in a more active phase,

a staffed program is required, as opposed to an unstaffed, cooperative apartment arrangement.

Residents who have schizophrenia will generally need an environment which is very supportive and which fosters socialization.
Special alertness should be maintained to those issues and situations
injurious to the fragile self-esteem of such residents. These events
can initiate such reactions as social withdrawal, activation of a delusional system, or a paranoid episode. Patients in this group who are
on antipsychotic medication will usually need careful monitoring to
ensure they are following their prescriptions. Arrangements must
be made so that the clinic administering the medication notifies the
community residence management if the patient misses an injec-
tion. This can be one of the most crucial administrative interventions to prevent relapse.

The resident with a manic-depressive disorder will similarly need
to have his lithium level monitored. In this instance, however, there
are problems at both ends of the spectrum. If the level is too high
(above 1.3 mg%), toxic symptoms occur that ultimately can be serious. If the level is too low (less than 0.7 mg%), the medication is no
longer therapeutic and the patient may shortly revert to a manic
stage. Again, close liaison with the testing clinic must be maintained. Generally, the manic-depressive resident does best when
slightly depressed. A highly structured environment and program
are essential to help prevent hypomanic behavior that can progress
into frank mania.

The community residence's primary responsibility to the depressive resident is to be alert to those situations which historically have
precipitated suicidal feelings or acts. Further, a relationship must
be established with the depressed resident so that he will inform the
houseparents or other staff or residents when he is feeling self-
destructive.

The personality disorders require a strong peer group that is
committed to rehabilitating its fellow resident. (Fostering such solidarity among the residential group will be discussed more extensively in chapter 11). Residents with problems of drug dependence
must first be educated to the fact that the residence forbids the
further use of drugs. Second, unscheduled urine checks in the out-

side clinic define the program in the resident's eyes as neither gullible nor naive; rather, they suggest the program's understanding of
the difficulties of abstaining in times of stress. Enhancement of this
resident's confidence in his inner self and in his ability to form
relationships based on caring and feeling is a primary task. This
generally results in a decreasing need for illicit drugs as a source of
gratification.

Residents with histories of alcohol abuse are not dissimilar from
the drug dependent. Often the habits overlap. Management issues
are also similar, except for the potential use of Antabuse and Alcoholics Anonymous.

The antisocial or psychopathic personality, or any potential resident who has a major superego defect (such as the lack of an internalized conscience), presents a major problem for a community residence. One of the cornerstones of life in the community residence
is trust. For their own sake, as well as the program's, residents share
responsibility for the chores of everyday living, are trusted to abide
by house policies, and are encouraged to be caring toward one
another. Lying and stealing have no place in a community residence. Such behavior can be destructive and disruptive to the entire program, both internally and relative to the external community. Persons predisposed to such behavior and pathology must be
carefully monitored. The rules and expectations of the program
should be made most explicit to them, with the consequences resulting from violations clearly spelled out. All members of the community must be openly alerted to the dishonest propensities of this
potential resident. The entire milieu then helps to keep this resident "straight." Even so, admission of such an applicant must be
carefully considered.

The primary administrative feature of community residential care
of the young adolescent is that the facility must be small—not exceeding twelve youngsters and preferably numbering eight to ten.
These residents are characteristically action-oriented, with a propensity for rapid, intense mood swings and running away as a common form of acting out. The adolescent program must also be carefully structured, with a firm, cooperative high-school environment,

where appropriate. Skilled houseparents for this group foster positive cohesion as opposed to negativistic rebellion. A capacity for family intervention and liaison must also be included in such a program.

The organic impairments (senile dementia, mental retardation, and others) impose a special responsibility of ensuring that the residents are capable of self-preservation if the facility is a community residential one as opposed to a nursing home. (The nursing home would have around-the-clock, on-the-job, awake nursing personnel, as well as class-one institutional construction; see chapter 7.) In their early stages, patients suffering from the senile dementias can be housed in a community residence; even at this stage, however, they require increased staff, special safety precautions, and unique social and activity programs. Signs indicating the place and date also help orient these residents.

The community residence may also cater to residents who have some degree of mental retardation. Depending upon the degree of deficit, the staff needs to be alert to the safety of the residents, organize special life-skill programs, and provide vocational and day care programs carefully scaled to each resident's level. Special attention must be given to preserving the dignity and civil rights of these residents.

The resident who moves into a facility in the midst of, or shortly following, an acute illness usually has not yet incorporated the "sick" or "patient" role as part of his identity. This is an advantage. By being alert to the potential for intensification of the illness, analyzing the precipitating causes, and establishing a back-up inpatient resource for acute, short-term assistance, the staff creates a context in which the resident's intact psychological system can heal and grow. The optimal time to enter a community residence is generally at the termination of an acute episode when the patient no longer has unmanageable psychotic symptoms. At that time he is most ready for social, vocational, and avocational growth and rehabilitation. Such a resident is potentially a candidate for a high-expectation, transitional halfway house.

The chronic patient usually needs a very different type of facility.

These potential residents frequently demonstrate a loss of socialization and life skills, the absence of a functional psychosocial kinship system, considerable dependence on the program, and slow progress. They require a long-term group residence with staff who can maintain a therapeutic stance over the long haul. The program must be one of gradual increments—but nevertheless rehabilitative rather than custodial. Interactions with the "real world" through shopping, entertainment, and work (even if sheltered) should be maximized. Once essential life skills are attained, and the patient is stable and can reliably travel to his daily program, a cooperative apartment arrangement may be suitable.

Age is an important variable, as we have seen in the adolescent's need for a small facility, with skilled staff and a firm educational resource. An adult population can live in a larger facility, with or without staff (depending upon debility), with work as a primary rehabilitative aim. The elderly require a facility that is ideally one story, with or without staff, with a special day activity program and attention to physical infirmity.

The degree of vocational impairment will dictate the necessity for liaison with employment agencies and counseling (when the resident is capable of competitive employment); sheltered workshops (when the resident is deficient in work skills but is trainable); and a psychosocial rehabilitation center, day center, or social club (if he is unsuited for work).

Similarly, effective liaison with schools and colleges is essential if an educable population is being considered. Special arrangements for reduced course loads and open communication with the school counselors and advisors can be most helpful. When such a population composes a substantial portion of the residents, serious consideration should be given to including a part-time education counselor on the staff, if such a person is not available in a community resource.

When life-skill development is a major task, the idea of using community volunteers should be entertained. They can be very helpful in providing one-to-one community training in skills, including use of public transportation, use of money, shopping, use of community recreation and entertainment resources, working with community social-service agencies, and learning how to obtain emergency medical attention.

Generic Versus Specialized Community Residences

If the catchment area has resources for only one facility, it will of necessity be a generic one. Where resources permit, a more specialized community residence can be planned, though counterarguments may be raised against such specialization.

It can be argued that housing chronic schizophrenics with more recently upset people is just asking for trouble. Chronic and acute patients generally have very different levels of daily living skills; moreover, acute patients may be frightened by being included with long-term ones. On the other hand, grouping chronic patients in special facilities only perpetuates their identification as "sick." It also denies acute patients the chance to feel useful and adequate in helping others. Similarly, a good case can be made for housing a group of young adolescents together on the grounds that establishing a positively motivated peer group is a singularly important therapeutic goal. On the other hand, it can be argued that the young benefit from older residents in the program who represent natural alternative parental figures, thus providing a more natural family model.

Obvious conflicts between patient types pose a different problem. For example, the schizophrenic patient who generally has a problem with trust, and who can be pathologically gullible, can be particularly easy prey to the psychopathic character who takes secret delight in duping a fellow resident. Again, psychopaths constitute a special difficulty for the community residence, especially one of the generic type.

Viewing the resources and goals of a particular program in terms of these arguments may help the residence planner decide between a generic and a specialized program design. If the planner opts for a specialized facility, some prototypical ones are those for the adolescent, for the elderly, for the alcoholic, or for the drug dependent; a short-stay, transitional residence, long-term, group residence, unstaffed cooperative apartment, or landlord-supervised cooperative apartment. Alternatively, the groups served by all these residences could be handled in a single community residence if necessary.

Planning Program Components

There are five significant programmatic variables in planning a community residence:

Time in the history of the illness. The community residence can provide initial care at the onset of an acute psychologic disturbance; or aftercare, following a course of institutionalization. These can be provided exclusively or concurrently.

Length of stay in the residence. The community residence can be a short-stay transitional facility with a specific maximum length of stay; or a potentially long-term facility with no deadline or explicit expectation for the resident to move out.

Staffing. The community residence may have: a small live-in staff; an increased staffing pattern consistent with an increased degree of dependence and disability in the residents; live-in staff plus volunteers such as local residents or college students to serve as healthy role models; no live-in staff, but visiting staff from an affiliated community psychiatric program; or landlord supervisors.

Daily program. The community residence may be a high-expectation facility requiring residents to be in competitive employment or attending school; an intermediate-expectation facility in which the residents are engaged in a sheltered workshop, day care center, or social club; or a low-expectation facility in which the emphasis is on improving life skills both at the community residence and at a day activity center.

Meals. Meals are usually provided (evening meal and perhaps breakfast) but may not be in a cooperative apartment organization.

Various combinations of these programmatic aspects are possible. In table 12 three distinct types of residences are defined for illustrative purposes: a high-expectation transitional halfway house; a low-expectation, long-stay group residence; and a cooperative apartment.

TABLE 12. Possible Types of Community Residence

Program Component	High-Expectation, Transitional	Low-Expectation, Long-Stay	Cooperative Apartment
Time in history of illness			
Initial care	X		
Aftercare	X	X	X
Length of stay			
Transitional	X		
Long-term		X	X
Staffing			
Live-in houseparents	X	X	
Visiting staff			X
Daily program			
High-expectation	X		
Intermediate-expectation			X
Low-expectation		X	
Meals			
Provided	X	X	
Not provided			X

These are only three possibilities; there are many others. Furthermore, a community residence can change in time from one kind of facility to another, according to the needs of the particular population being served at that time. One example of this is an aftercare, long-term community residence which initially has houseparents who provide the meals. In about two years' time these houseparents could help the residents learn to live together successfully, negotiate effectively with the community, and shop and cook for one another. At the conclusion of this phase the houseparents, instead of the residents, move out. The residents are then in a cooperative living arrangement with visiting staff assuring that all continues to go well. The costs of the program decrease significantly, as the salaries of the house managers are no longer budgeted after the expiration of the two-year training period. These same houseparents could then begin the process with an entirely new group of chronic patients.

Cooperative apartments may be developed not only to provide

programmatic scope, but also to avoid various constraints: to minimize start-up costs; to lower operating costs; to avoid community opposition; and to circumvent special building codes. Such a program may be set up in an entire small apartment building, with a live-in couple in one apartment. It permits many of the programmatic functions of the halfway house, such as community meals and meetings. This is a compromise in response to limiting realities, but it is nevertheless based upon the principles of the traditional halfway house. Other cooperative apartments may be independent units of larger apartment buildings, with visiting staff only. A network of residential facilities should evolve providing gradations of care. In this manner, sheltered housing need provide no more care than is needed to sustain the resident in a productive, social life in the community. The traditional halfway house can function as the core facility to which affiliated cooperative apartments relate.

Ancillary Services

The community residence should have ongoing cooperative relationships with a variety of ancillary services to meet the residents' needs. These will be instrumental in assuring that residents have a range of additional psychiatric services available, that they have an off-the-premises rehabilitative program which helps them to function at their highest capacity, and that their basic health, dental, legal, and financial needs are met.

These can be summarized as follows:

Psychiatric services.   These include: an outpatient clinic with medication supervision; a day care center; a social club; night care; inpatient care; and family counseling.

Rehabilitative services.   These include: vocational counseling; sheltered workshops; employment agencies for competitive employment; educational counseling; and cooperative schools and colleges.

Other essential needs.   These include: health care, both routine and emergency; dental care; social service to assist with Supplemental Security Income payments; and a legal aid bureau.

Staffing the Community Residence

The greatest influence by far on the quality of the program will be the quality of the clinical staff—the executive director and the live-in house managers. They have the task of leading the entire program. The house managers' position is so important that a full job description is included here for reference. Because it is generally best that the house managers be a married couple, the position is so described here. However, if necessary, the job could be filled by one individual.

Position Description: House Managers

Title: House Managers.

Responsible to: Director of the program.

Clinical responsibilities: The house managers will be responsible for creatively establishing a therapeutic milieu to facilitate the growth and rehabilitation of the residents. They will participate in both formal and informal groups. They will be expected to have the attitudes, leisure-time skills, and interpersonal expertise to serve as both models for and trusted friends of the residents. They will have the responsibility of recognizing when residents are in trouble and require immediate psychiatric consultation. The house managers also will be responsible for obtaining immediate medical assistance, at the nearest general hospital emergency service when necessary. The house managers assist in planning for appropriate departure of residents, ensuring that they have found adequate housing.

Administrative patient responsibilities: The house managers will participate in admissions and in the selection of new residents. They will supervise the implementation of all house policies. They will collect the rent and maintain resident account files with secretarial assistance. They will oversee their component of the operating budget, including the foodstuffs, and oversee the quality of the food served in the house. They will supervise the heavy cleaning personnel, if any. They will be responsible for appropriately handling all inquiries from the community either by taking care of the matter themselves or by referring the inquirer to the director. The house managers are responsible for adequate communications with relief managers and, where necessary, training them, prior to taking time off. The house managers will be responsible for ensuring that all residents are capable of self-preservation, as certified by testing at assigned intervals and other times as well, as they deem fit.

Physical plant responsibilities: The house managers will be responsible for supervising the entire physical plant. They will report as soon as possible to the director or appropriate maintenance personnel the malfunction of any large appliance, including the furnace and heating plant, hot-water heater, stove, freezer, refrigerator, and other major kitchen appliances. Further, general interior repairs shall be overseen by the house managers. Any external deterioration will be reported to the director, as well as to appropriate maintenance personnel. The house managers will procure necessary equipment for overall house maintenance and will be expected to make suggestions for improving the physical plant.

Qualifications: The house managers must be able to manage the household, including the budgeting, meal-planning, and cooking. They must have a basic knowledge of math, simple record-keeping, and communication skills in English. They shall have sufficient familiarity with household appliances and general maintenance to supervise the upkeep of the physical plant. They will be expected to have skills in the use of leisure time (for example, in arts and crafts, recreation, cultural arts, or other activities that relate to a resident's leisure time) and will be expected to have interpersonal and social skills sufficient to serve as examples to residents of sound, healthy, trustworthy, and respected individuals (that is, to serve as "role models"). They should have both demonstrated leadership ability and a basic understanding of community resources. Screening of house manager applicants will include a psychiatric assessment conducted by the psychiatric consultant. Live-in house managers shall be legally married.

The scope of the house managers' job is clearly greater than that of most mental health positions. However, seen in the context of the family (see chapter 3), the position takes on the more human proportions (in terms of tasks and responsibilities) of the head of the family household.

The successful selection of capable house managers is of paramount importance. It can be the most difficult task of community residence administration.

The most successful way to ascertain the "human" capabilities of the managerial applicant is through the skillful use of a modified psychiatric interview. This should be conducted by the psychiatric consultant to the program or the director, if he or she has expertise in such interviewing skills. The interviewer should inquire into the applicant's early life to establish the character of his parental relationship and sibling position. Exploration of his family background and adjustment will help in assessing his readiness to lead a "family" of his own.

A second crucial issue is motivation. Generally one must view with hesitation a naive and inexperienced need to "rescue" the residents. This leads to overprotection and overinvolvement, and ultimately to disillusionment and resentment when difficult realities do not conform to expectations. Rather, seeking work as a growing and learning experience in an evolving mental health career is more likely to enhance success. When the job is a natural step in a manager's career development, it provides the residents with a natural role model of continuing effort at self-improvement.

Third, the stability and quality of the marriage is important. This can be ascertained most effectively during the interview from direct observation of the quality of the couple's interaction. When the interviewer asks direct questions about the marriage, he should be suspicious of a claim of "no problems." A healthier sign is when a couple can comfortably review the scope and nature of problems encountered and the manner of their resolution.

Prior academic and work performance need careful reviewing, as it will usually reflect future patterns. A review of satisfactions and frustrations in previous work situations will alert the interviewer to the work needs of the applicant.

Conscientious acquisition of references by phone as well as in writing ensures the validity of the picture obtained through direct interviewing.

Following this screening procedure, suitable applicants should be seen by the director (if he was not the initial interviewer) and finalists by the board of directors. Of those suitable candidates, the director should make the final decision as to which he feels he could work with most comfortably. Ideally, there is general agreement among the board, the consultant, and the director.

That there is no clear source of house managers is currently a problem for the halfway house movement. But as the number of community residences increases, pressures will mount for the development of a new class of mental health worker explicitly trained for the job. Even so, some basic difficulties are likely to persist. For one thing, most married couples will not want to remain for more than a year or two in a position which is so intrusive upon their privacy. For another, workers who do want to stay for a long time may become "chronic" if they remain in the same milieu for a prolonged period, like the state hospital nurse who has been on a ward for twenty years with the same twenty patients.

One solution is to employ young married couples, where the husband or wife is a graduate student in a mental health field such as social work, psychology, vocational rehabilitation, or nursing. The managers in such a case would clearly be mobile, growing, and committed to the rehabilitation of the residents. In this model, the couple is usually allotted one and one-half positions, rather than two. One spouse is then free during the day and, like the residents, may be off at work or school. The other attends to administrative duties, as outlined in the job description.

Alternatively, a mature couple whose children are grown can do the job with equal vigor and competence—especially if in the initial year intensive supervision and consultation are available.

Another solution is to have the house manager position divided between two couples, with neither moving into the community residence totally. Each couple would spend three to four nights per week at the house. This can facilitate longer tenure of managers, but it tends to break up the "family" feel of the facility, and it repeats ever so slightly the changing-shift phenomenon of the hospital ward.

The problems of finding good live-in managers have led some programs to compromise on staff who were neither married nor live-in. Under this arrangement, full-time staff, whether married or not, work from 3:00 P.M. to 11:00 P.M., when the residents are at the house for dinner and socializing. During the day all residents attend their daily programs away from the residence. Sleeping is unsupervised, but a staff member is on call. This staffing pattern is halfway between the traditional community residence model and the cooperative apartment. Here again the "family" feel is sacrificed to some extent; but the reader should be aware of the various possibilities, as creativity is the only solution to the realities of a given situation. If the staff understands and is committed to the rehabilitative principles, then good results are feasible.

Other Clinical Staff

Relief managers should have all the attributes of the managers. They generally work only two days per week. Sometimes it has been useful to give the managers long weekends or an additional evening per week off, depending upon the intensity of their work. The house managers should also have about three weeks' vacation per year, so a complete change of scene is possible.

Additional clinical personnel are sometimes used if the program is larger than twenty adult residents or ten young adolescents, has elderly residents in need of special care, or has very desocialized residents who need much individual life-skill training.

Executive Director

The director is ultimately responsible for the implementation of the entire program, working as a close liaison between the managers and the corporate board. In starting a community residence the board will, as soon as financially feasible, hire the director to coordinate all of the initial steps outlined at the beginning of this chapter. It is especially important that the director be involved in developing the program description and the community entry strategy, recruiting managers, establishing liaison with referring agencies and ancillary rehabilitative resources, drawing up the budget, and implementing compliance with all codes and regulations.

Psychiatric Consultant

Another key person is the psychiatric consultant. As reviewed in chapter 6, in Massachusetts this position can draw on any one of a variety of mental health disciplines. The consultant should meet at least weekly with the director and house managers to review each resident's course as well as overall residence interaction. Sometimes the psychiatric consultant attends house meetings. In addition, the consultant should participate in applicant screening and in the development of the initial program plan for each new resident. The consultant should be knowledgeable in individual and group psychodynamics and be conversant with the pharmacotherapies. Ideally, he or she should be a "real person," enthusiastic about the program, and an able community spokesperson.

Other Staff

Rounding out the staff complement will be people providing secretarial assistance, bookkeeping and accounting, and, in a larger facility, heavy-duty cleaning services. Since all people who work in the residence are by definition members of the "family," innate clinical skills should be given high priority in recruitment of *all* staff. The entire staff should attend house meetings, special parties, and so on.

Finding and Furnishing a Suitable Building

Selection of the building is the final component in establishing a home for the community residence program. Above all else, the physical premises should have a homelike quality. The obvious means to this end is the selection of a dwelling that has been a large old home. The Victorian homes found in both urban and rural areas are often ideal. These turn-of-the-century houses offer a great deal of space, often at a good price. Such grand homes are not always available however. A church or other community group sometimes offers the sponsoring group a building that has not been used as a home. The feasibility of using any building as a community residence should be assessed according to a number of architectural components.

A primary consideration is adequate space. The building should not feel cramped. Adequate bedrooms and a separate suite (bedroom, bath, and sitting room) for the house managers are also a necessity. A residence housing ten to fourteen residents plus live-in house managers would require six to eight bedrooms.

The public rooms must comfortably accommodate the number of people living in the residence. All of the house members should be able to eat together at one sitting, family style. Similarly, the house meetings must be in a room large enough to accommodate all. Adequate living-room space will facilitate socializing. A cramped living room will tend to serve the social isolation of the vulnerable resident, who will allow himself to be "pushed out" of the common living area.

The spatial interrelationship of the public rooms is also of interest. Spaces that are visually accessible are preferable to discrete, cellular spaces. A resident who is tentative in his capacity to relate to others may be comfortable reading alone in a corner of a room. If that room is visually open to connecting rooms—as through a large doorway or archway—then the resident will not be totally removed from others. This represents a psychosocial principle expressed through architectural design: visually interconnected spaces create a capacity for privacy and separateness without isolation.

Lighting is another important component of the interior milieu. Natural daylight from plentiful windows and adequate artificial lighting contribute to a bright, open feeling. Inadequate windows and lighting create a dark, dismal, depressing mood that allows a resident to recede into the shadows.

Textures and colors of the walls, floor coverings, and furnishings are also important. Wall coverings that have texture and natural colors contribute warmth. Flat, painted grays and blues replicate a cold, institutional environment. Shades of brown, yellow, gold, and orange in burlap, cork, or textured wallpapers give a warm, cozy feeling. Paint is less costly and in these colors, with the addition of pictures and posters, helps to achieve approximately the same effect. Carpeting and rugs are preferable to bare floors, which are cold, noisy, and reminiscent of the hospital.

Furniture in the public rooms should be soft and comfortable. The penchant for artificial leathers on overfirm chairs, which supposedly provide maximum durability, sacrifices warmth and natural comfort. Fabrics are now available that provide equal durability without such a sacrifice.

Finally, there should be adequate recreational and entertainment facilities. Games such as checkers, cards, and chess, a ping-pong or pool table, a piano, and a television are all foci around which natural social activity occurs.

Developing a Budget and Locating Funds

Capital Start-Up Expenses

Start-up expenses vary so much with the individual program that it is difficult to generalize about them. There are two major expenses: personnel services, and building acquisition and renovation.

The donation of personnel services in the process of development of a program and its community entry is vital to a low-cost start-up. The planning and preparation in all the areas described can be carried out by volunteers from the organizing group or others recruited by them.

The building can be acquired by renting or purchasing. Renting requires a cooperative landlord who understands the building-code requirements, will support the program in the community entry phase, and will guarantee a long enough lease to assure the program a secure home. These conditions having been met, the advantage of little or no capital expense is gained.

Purchasing a building has the advantage of securing the property, as well as long-term benefits from any improvements to the building. The problem is getting the money for the down payment (mortgage payments can be drawn from residents' rent payments). A facility that is part of a community mental health center can apply for a grant from the National Institute of Mental Health under Public Law 94-63. Others can try to raise funds through public appeals, private grants, state grants, or special bank loans.

Once the property is acquired, it can be renovated at minimum expense through donations from local skilled workers, such as plumbers, electricians, painters, and carpenters. Sometimes a trade school will offer some of these skills through a class project—such as wiring a fire-detection system.

Once the building is acquired and renovated, it must be furnished. Obtaining needed beds and bureaus as well as all of the living-room, dining-room, and other public-room furniture is a substantial project. When the house is being rented or purchased, the sponsoring group should be alert to the possibility of acquiring furniture already in the dwelling. This can often be had at little or no additional expense. If this is not feasible, ads should be placed in a variety of media requesting donations. The response will usually produce much of what is needed, and the remainder can often be acquired through charitable donations or at-cost purchases from local furniture dealers. Some money, however, should be budgeted for such contingencies.

Additional funds will be required for essential appliances. These will be heavily used and be subject to much wear and tear, so "heavy-duty" models should be obtained if possible. In addition to a stove and a refrigerator, a dishwasher, a garbage disposal, and a clothes washer and dryer should be acquired.

Careful screening and preparation of applicants should occur shortly before opening, so that the house fills with paying residents promptly. This avoids an unnecessary start-up operating deficit.

Operating Budget

The major operating expenses are for staff, rent or mortgage payments, utilities, and food. Lesser items include repairs, insurance, transportation, and supplies. The budget varies as a function of the size of the program and the degree of pathology of the residents.

Economies of size take on survival significance when the resident population ranges from eight to twenty residents. Within this interval the size of the staff usually remains constant, and the additional expenses of a larger program are more than made up by increased revenue. Thus, it is far more economical to have a program with at least fifteen residents than a smaller one, since the per-resident cost becomes much lower. A higher per-resident cost means either shorter stays, fewer residents who can afford the program, or higher subsidies per resident. (Some programs do require increased staff-resident ratios, including those for the young adolescent, the elderly, the more debilitated chronic schizophrenic patient in need of life-skill training, and the resident with significant components of retardation.) An increased number of residents requires a larger building and consequent increases in rent or mortgage payments, utilities, and upkeep. It also increases the amount of paperwork and bookkeeping, as well as the food bills. However, the increased expenses of the larger program are offset by the increased revenue from the residents, until the number or type of residents becomes so great as to require a larger staff.

Income must come either entirely from the resident or from supplemental government or health-insurance subsidization. As of January 1977, Supplemental Security Income will pay the shared living rate for residents of halfway houses of $202.60 per month, or about $6.75 per day. The resident with only SSI income could pay $5 per day to the residence and keep about $1.75 per day as spending money.

Bearing in mind the potential programmatic variability, a sample budget for a community residence for fifteen modal residents, in 1977 dollars, is suggested in table 13. Assuming 100 percent occupancy, this amounts to $14 per day per resident. Thus, a $9 daily subsidy would be necessary for the resident with only SSI income. If all residents can pay only $5 per day, then with the total annual cost for a residence of fifteen at $76,650, the annual subsidy required would be $49,275. It should be borne in mind, however, that some residents will be able to pay more than $5 per day, because they will receive salaries from competitive employment or other funds from their families.

TABLE 13. Sample Budget of a Group Residence for Fifteen

Item	Percentage of Full-Time	Yearly Cost
Staff		
Director	50	$ 8,760
House managers	150	16,206
Relief managers	50	5,402
Professional consultant	5	2,920
Clerk or bookkeeper	67	5,840
Total staff		$39,128
Rent or mortgage		$ 7,738
Utilities		$ 4,044
Food ($3 per day per person)		$18,104
Other operating expenses		
Repairs, improvements		$ 1,314
Telephone		292
Supplies		1,460
Insurance		730
Transportation		1,650
Furniture, appliances		730
Services (trash collection, etc.)		730
Miscellaneous		730
Subtotal		$ 7,636
Grand total		$76,650

Income is potentially available from a number of other sources. Medical insurance will usually cover community residential care only if it can be shown that such care is part of a medically prescribed rehabilitation program. However, the state may have a program offering subsidies to the community residential program if it is operated by a nonprofit corporation and serves the state-owned hospital system.

Federal funds are available, but they are inadequate and unevenly distributed. Federal sources include:

1. Operations and planning grants under Public Law 94-63. These funds are insufficient, especially because the residential pro-

gram is in competition with every other service of the community mental health center.

2. Title XX under the Social Security Amendment. This provides social services as administered by the states in accordance with their comprehensive area service plan.

3. A variety of current programs administered by the Department of Housing and Urban Development through its central, regional, and area offices, including sections 8 and 202 and the traditional public (low-income) housing program. These can be used to purchase, construct, renovate, or subsidize rentals of buildings used as community residences. In all of these programs, the community residence is in competition with other uses, and the requirements are not easily met by housing for the mentally handicapped.

4. The Rehabilitation Services Administration. This agency has contributed funds for community residence programs in some states.

The Program Statement

A statement dealing with the issues covered in this chapter should be compiled to inform the public about the program. If the work has been done carefully, the community residence will be on solid ground and in a position to present itself with pride. This statement should include the organization and name of the sponsoring group; document the target population; establish the community's need for the program; identify the services that will be made available; introduce the staff; describe the budget; and assure compliance with all laws and codes.

The community residence is then ready to go into operation.

CHAPTER 11

Clinical Operation

The family-modeled clinical program lies at the heart of a community residence facility. I have already discussed this program from several different perspectives. In chapter 5, I discussed the house program as it interrelates with external systems, such as the state department of mental health. We have also seen how the program affects the individual resident (chapters 3 and 4). In chapter 10, I discussed in detail the residence program and the interrelationship of programmatic parts. In this chapter, my concern is to present an integrated view of clinical operations, first from the point of view of the residents (who experience the program in a chronological sequence), and second from the point of view of the staff (who experience the program as clinical goals, problems, and concrete tasks). A graphic representation of how these and other perspectives interrelate is shown in figure 4.

Entering the Community Residence Program

It is crucial that the prospective resident have a realistic perception of the community residence from the outset. Each prospective resident harbors his own preconceptions about what the residence is; it may be seen as a haven from a chaotic family, an easy way out of the hospital, or a place to grow and to reintegrate a troubled life. It is the residence's responsibility to identify its functions accurately. The house should present itself as a place to which the applicant comes by choice, where he can enhance his maturational development. Through a careful assessment of the applicant's strengths,

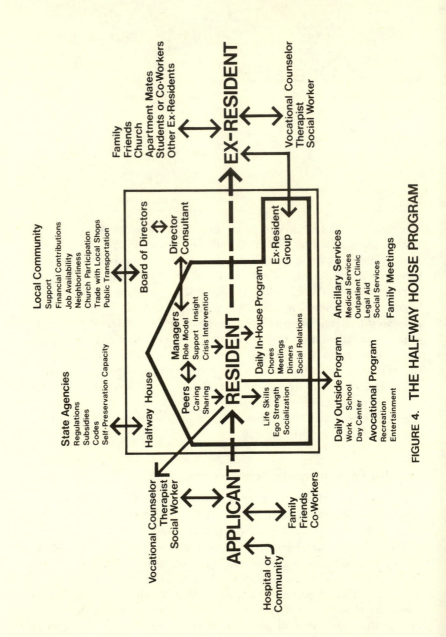

FIGURE 4. THE HALFWAY HOUSE PROGRAM

weaknesses, and current needs, the house can plan a program to foster his growth. The first tasks are to facilitate a sensitive application procedure and to help the new resident overcome the initial difficulties of moving into a new domicile.

Application Procedure

Generally, the applicant should seek a place in the community residence on his own initiative. He should not be the passive vessel of an active mental health professional who is dictating such a disposition to him. Accordingly, it is the resident who should make the ultimate decision to accept a placement if it is offered. No one should move into a community residence who does not want to live there, for coercion only defeats the rehabilitative goal. If the applicant experiences the house as a place to which he is being sent with no alternative, hostile dependence and negativism can result.

The initial contact between the applicant and the house is ideally based on what the applicant has heard or read about the program. The residence should have a brochure available to introduce its program to the prospective resident. (The text of the brochure used by Berkeley House is reproduced in Appendix 5.) Following consultation with a mental health professional, the applicant decides whether he wants to investigate the program further. If he does, the applicant telephones the house managers and requests an opportunity to visit. He can visit one evening, have dinner with the residents, tour the house with them, and speak with them about their experiences. He then meets with the house managers, who discuss such features of the program as house meetings and dinners, expectations regarding the daily program outside the house (work, school, or sheltered day care), and house policies covering behavior. A written house policy statement should be made available at this time (see Appendix 6). In turn, the managers try to elicit a comprehensive history from the applicant covering his past difficulties and recent advances. Current hopes, needs, expectations, and worries should be openly explored. Beyond this exchange of information, this meeting ought to communicate to the applicant that he is in the company of warm, understanding people who have reasonable expectations of him.

If the applicant decides he wants to live at the house, he requests application forms. He receives one for himself (Appendix 7) and different forms for the mental health professionals involved in his care (therapist, administrative psychiatrist, social worker, and so on). It is his responsibility to make out his own form and to distribute the others. This procedure familiarizes the applicant with the questions that are being asked of his mental health team and demystifies such communications.

The application form requires the resident to think through his own life. It asks about the events precipitating his initial difficulties, what he understands of his own vulnerabilities, what problems remain, and what he hopes to accomplish in the halfway house program. He is asked to outline his anticipated daily program while at the house, and to delineate his goals for the future. The intent of this exercise is to identify the halfway house as a way station in the applicant's pursuit of improved mental health and adaptive functioning. Completing a carefully thought-out application can itself be a therapeutic experience.

The application speaks directly to potential problems, asking the applicant whether he has taken illicit drugs (when and what sort), has an alcohol problem, or has attempted suicide. If suicide has been attempted, the applicant is asked to describe the circumstances surrounding the event, and his understanding of the precipitants. A medical history—including physical illness, physicians of record, and medications—and current sources of income round out the application form. The initial form is intended to communicate a balanced picture of the applicant as a person with strengths and problems, worthy of serious consideration.

Following receipt of the completed forms, the applicant is interviewed by the house consultant and the director. An admission meeting is then scheduled, bringing together the clinical team that has been working with the applicant and the community residence staff. It is explained to the applicant that the foremost purpose of the application procedure—interviews and meeting—is to get to know him better, to help the community residence staff work with him and his team, to formulate an effective and appropriate rehabilitative program. The applicant is told that, in addition, an assessment is made as to whether the program is suitable for his needs. If the applicant is initially thought to be unsuitable by the community residence staff, the meeting is frequently still held. This impression should be shared with the applicant's clinical team, for they may shed new light that alters the initial assessment. Even when such an impression is sustained, the meeting provides a careful consultation on the applicant's future program.

In addition to the applicant's clinical team and the community residence staff, representatives of the ancillary services that will be playing a critical role in the applicant's rehabilitation should also attend. These include (in addition to the community residence staff) the applicant's therapist, representatives of the inpatient back-up facility, the applicant's social worker, his vocational counselor, representatives of day care or sheltered workshop facilities, and representatives of hospitals where the applicant has previously been treated. The meeting can open discussion on disagreements (if any) among the staff involved in prior treatment, and on differences which may crop up during the meeting between prior care givers and residence staff. In general, the meeting should have the quality of a careful consultation, with the consultant to the community residence program, as well as the rest of the community residence staff, becoming increasingly expert in judging the readiness of an applicant for community residential living. Critical issues to be reviewed are: the psychosexual and psychosocial development of the applicant; the dynamics that contributed to his acute illness; the family's relationship to the applicant; the house's approach to the applicant's family; the role of continuing therapy; the status of medication; services required to ensure that medication is maintained and monitored; the applicant's physical health; his proposed outside daily program and transportation to the program; his history of peer relationships and interpersonal difficulties in this regard as they relate to planning a house milieu program; arrangement for potential inpatient back-up if necessary; the applicant's special talents, interests, and strengths; and planning the applicant's transition into the community residence.

Beyond these specific points, there are several important general issues. In the first place, the meeting establishes personal contact among all clinical participants in the applicant's rehabilitation program. This face-to-face discussion familiarizes the participants with one another's roles and points of view, and symbolically opens communication lines among all participants. Phone numbers should be exchanged to ensure mutual availability in the event that anyone believes the resident is doing poorly and beginning to slip. Rapid intervention in the face of potential or suspected relapse is the first line of defense against such an eventuality.

Second, the meeting provides a forum for discussion of, and agreement on, an essential axiom: *There shall be no more than one significant change in the applicant's life situation at a time.* This means that there should never be change in more than one of three key areas: the living situation; the job situation; and therapy. New situations created by gains or losses in these areas subject the vulnerable applicant to significant stress. Change in any one of them requires careful preparation and support, and change in more than one area simultaneously is likely to be intolerable. Unnecessary turmoil and relapse are the result of planning that overlooks this axiom. A two-week interval between change in one area and change in another is considered minimal.

A third general concern of the initial meeting relates to the applicant's daily program. It is generally preferable for the day program to be set up, and the applicant fully engaged in it, at least two weeks before he moves into the community residence. Experience has shown that this sequence can help motivate the more passive applicant to get going on his daily program. If he is allowed to move into the halfway house first and is already comfortably situated in new quarters, there is little leverage to get him to a daily program about which he is anxious. The same is true for the applicant's therapy, if appropriate; it should be initiated before the applicant moves in.

Finally, the admission meeting should address long-range future disposition, with the anticipated length of stay in the community residence in mind. Postresidence social housing, where appropriate, should be planned far in advance. One possibility projects the applicant moving out with fellow residents into independent apartment living. Alternatively, the applicant may need a more sheltered living arrangement, moving from the live-in community residence with houseparents to a cooperative apartment arrangement with regular visiting staff. Planning the ultimate disposition helps the clinical staff to prepare the resident for this step in the future.

Applicant Evaluation

In general, the community residence clinical staff, together with the applicant's clinical team, decides whether the applicant is suitable for the program without other consultation. The house may have specific admission criteria. Conditions that usually disqualify an applicant for admission include: destructive impulses toward the self, others, or property which are not in good control; ongoing narcotic addiction; unremitting abuse of alcohol; and uncontrolled sexual promiscuity. Characterological problems may or may not disqualify an applicant. The negativistic, stubborn applicant who refuses to get up and go to any meaningful activity may be taken on by a particular house as a challenge. As a resident, however, this applicant poses special problems which ought to be made explicit from the outset. If accepted, the applicant might break down the group expectation that all residents engage in meaningful daily activity off the premises; he might demand unreasonable attention and staff time; and he might breed resentment toward himself that would only recycle his negativism. Psychopathic characters also constitute a special problem (see chapter 10).

Some halfway houses ask current residents to vote on an applicant's acceptability. This is a poor procedure that smacks of fraternity elitism; the blackball has no place in a community residence. The clinical staff should take responsibility for decisions with regard to the overall needs of the house. Nevertheless, when an applicant has particular attributes that may be offensive or cause problems for the house, the staff may present the nature of the problem to the residents at a house meeting. The residents could then be asked about their feelings and ideas regarding the problem, and about their willingness to assist in the management of the problems of this particular resident. This is not so much a question of whether the residents will *accept* the difficult housemate as one of whether they will *actively help* him. Such help would include openly setting limits on a difficult resident with insufficient inner controls, or encouraging a retarded resident to do his best as opposed to belittling him.

Experience teaches that careful screening of the applicant and intensive work toward acquiring a thorough grasp of his dynamics, strengths, and weaknesses go a long way toward ensuring successful entry and tenure in the community residence program. The house managers ultimately review with the applicant all of the concepts and plans resulting from the application process.

Moving In

The applicant should usually move into the house gradually. A typical applicant entering the residence from a hospital setting might sleep in the house two or three nights the first week, three or four nights the second, and move in full time the third week. Where financial constraints mitigate against this, more rapid entry can be achieved. Similarly, an applicant who is moving out of a particularly noxious living situation in the community may want—and need—to move into the house promptly. In general, however, gradual entry aids the new resident both in adjusting to the new location and in saying good-bye to the old one.

In a house for young adults, and especially in houses for young adolescents, the applicant's family of origin meets with residence staff, at least initially. Regular family meetings, focusing on specific family issues, can enhance the family's capacity to reintegrate the young resident. The frequency and degree of involvement by the family (of origin or procreation) with house activities is a function of the resident's problems, his age, and the interest and commitment of the family. At a minimum, however, the family should be informed of the house program at the outset of the resident's stay. Further, whatever the age of its residents, the community residence staff should be aware of the typical dynamic patterns that create problems between the resident and his family.

For several reasons, it is advantageous for the applicant to live with roommates, rather than having a bedroom to himself. Wherever possible, the house management should match roommates who have a chance of becoming friends. This facilitates socialization and creates a "buddy" system, making the house a safer place. Roommates, over time, increasingly tend to look after each other's well-being. They help each other through crises. A resident will come to the house managers if he feels his roommate is in some secret difficulty that he cannot manage alone—suicidal feelings, drug problems, surreptitious avoidance of day activities, despondency over a lost lover—to obtain additional assistance. Double occupancy, then, provides checks and balances with regard to the house's clinical program and its behavioral codes, helping to prevent illicit drinking, sex, drugs, or antisocial behavior.

During the resident's transition into the house, the house managers can profitably meet with him after dinner, reviewing with him his feelings about moving into his new environment. During these interviews the managers get to know the resident more intimately, and the resident ideally comes to trust the managers and feel safe with them. The managers also review the critical issues that can facilitate the new resident's sense of security and well-being. (One mandatory procedure is the house managers' supervision of the "capability of self-preservation" test.)

Another area of concern is the resident's progress in developing life skills. The managers can ensure that the resident knows how to handle money. They can teach him how to open and maintain a checking account, and may even walk him down to a local bank. A careful review of the costs of the house and the resident's method of payment can provide a practical method of instruction. The managers can help the resident become familiar with all of the resources in the neighborhood by posting and referring to a large map or aerial photograph. A long walk with a manager or an experienced resident can show the new resident the location of shops, the nearest fire box, the library, various churches, recreational facilities, and the nearest general hospital emergency room. One by-product of routine chores such as trips to the market or post office is such orientation to the community. To become a fully functioning, responsible, and secure member of the residence, the resident needs to be taught how to use the house's stove, cleaning appliances, refrigerator, garbage disposal, and dishwasher, and how the interior fire-safety system operates. Fire-safety rules are reviewed, as are the location of posted emergency numbers and telephones.

The house managers can facilitate the new resident's social integration by participating with him in such social activities as cooking together, playing bridge or Monopoly, watching television, and going to the movies in a group. All these activities are avenues for the managers to facilitate the resident's social integration into the house.

To know where the resident will be during the day, the managers need an hour-by-hour schedule, describing the resident's whereabouts. The schedule includes a description of the daily activities, telephone numbers, addresses, and the days and hours of attendance at, for example, sheltered workshops, the day activity center, or competitive employment; the schedule of therapy appointments (family, individual, vocational rehabilitation counseling, and so on); other medical clinic appointments; and social club or other meetings. Providing the schedule meets the new resident's responsibility of letting others know where he can be reached, just as a family member has some obligations in this regard.

Like a family member, too, the new resident shares responsibility for household chores. These include the regular upkeep of his room, cooking, cleanup after meals, house cleanup, and outdoor grounds cleanup. Chores are rotated among the residents. The house managers review assignments with the new resident, and the rotation itself can be reviewed in the house meeting.

The House Milieu in Action

A delicate dynamic interplay between two essential forces characterizes the successful community residence milieu. One force for growth and development is warm, understanding, and insightful managerial care. The managers support, nurture, and, when necessary, intervene in crises. At other times they prod, challenge, and stimulate the resident to scale new heights. The second force in the dynamic balance is the residents' capacity to care for themselves and one another. This can be fostered by the managers and the milieu, through individual and group techniques. The ideal result of the interplay here is a gradual lessening of the resident's dependence upon the managers and other staff, and a greater reliance on himself and his fellow residents. Throughout, the managers remain trusted allies, available in times of unusual duress.

In this context, the manager's role is parental, in the very best sense of the term. At the outset, it requires an intuitive, insightful, and caring person, one who can provide a supportive base for the residents' growth and development. Later on, as the residents develop more mature capacities, the manager's more active parenting function recedes. This pattern recapitulates the essential dynamics of normal family-based development. It stands in distinct contrast to those programs which sustain the resident in an infantile and helpless position.

The House Managers' Role

In chapter 10, I presented a detailed job description for the house managers. In the present, clinically oriented discussion I will expand on some of these job requirements. The most important clinical task the house manager performs is maintaining a knowledge of the whereabouts and clinical condition of the residents at all times. This central responsibility may seem overwhelming at the outset, but after a few months the managers generally acquire a good sense of each resident's nuances of mood, and they can pick up early clues of social isolation, depressive feelings, delusional retreat, or a hyperexcited state. Sharing a household with the residents eases the accomplishment of this task, which does not require implementation of formal, specific procedures. Moreover, the responsibility becomes increasingly shared as the house managers are able to create a therapeutic milieu with the cardinal ethic of mutual help.

In the event that the house managers perceive a mood change in a resident, and if it appears to worsen despite the milieu's best efforts to intervene, it is of paramount importance that one of the house managers meet with the resident. Together they can review what is going on in the residents life that may be causing him to revert to earlier pathological modes. This is crisis intervention in action, at the earliest possible moment, probably earlier than in an outpatient clinic where the client is seen weekly. In a clinic setting, the clinician would likely be in a position to notice pathological change only *after* it had begun to develop into a full-blown regression.

The work that the managers have put into the relationship in the transition process and early weeks in the house pays dividends at this time. It has formed the foundation of the resident's trust, so that the resident knows the managers have his interest as their foremost concern. This facilitates the resident's confiding in the managers about the precipitants that have caused his move toward relapse. Frequently an altercation or a difficult interpersonal relationship with a resident or a co-worker, or the reopening of an old family wound lies at the root of the problem. The resident may feel enraged or rejected (or both); he may want to retaliate, yet fear the consequences. The manager who knows the precipitating causes can make a strategic intervention that assists, supports, and helps the resident "problem-solve."

Problem-solving includes the careful conceptual delineation of the precipitating event, and the recognition of the reasons for the resident's particular vulnerability to this event, followed by the exploration of the best method of dealing with the resident's strong reaction. Sometimes just the recognition that the precipitant reactivated an old rage or grief, which is understandable in relation to the past but unreasonably strong in relation to the present, will alleviate the upset. In other circumstances, the situation might call for action on the resident's part in the form of talking with one of the persons involved, or moving to extricate himself from the noxious situation.

The house managers have additional resources available if they are unable to alleviate the crisis entirely through their verbal intervention. These resources include contacting the residence consultant, considering (with medical assistance) administration of anti-anxiety or antipsychotic medications, or suggesting an increase in the dosage of ongoing medication to help weather the crisis. Sometimes a meeting between the resident, his family, and significant others to identify the nature of the crisis and to enlist everyone's support and understanding can reassure the resident that his sudden bleak outlook is not justifiable.

If the resident, in spite of these efforts, continues to be agitated, or if he is seriously depressed with suicidal potential such that he requires continual presence of staff support, and if the disturbance begins to interfere with his sleep, then the use of inpatient back-up for short-term night care can often be instrumental in shortening the duration of the disturbance. Ideally, such action should be taken with the cooperation of the resident, with the explicit understanding that his bed at the halfway house is being saved for him.

In reviewing the central role of the house managers, it cannot be overemphasized that their ultimate task is to foster an environment characterized by resident self-reliance and mutual care. A healthy milieu minimizes the need for staff intervention. Only in the event of a crisis which overtaxes this supportive milieu do the house managers need to intervene more actively.

Fostering Growth, Self-Reliance, and Mutuality

The value system of the program should be apparent in all aspects of the milieu. The fundamental principles are that each resident has both healthy and troubled parts of his personality, and that the healthy parts can increasingly understand and master the areas of difficulty. The acquisition of new skills strengthens healthy functioning and contributes to an inner sense of mastery. The resident increasingly feels himself to be competent and capable—a person of value. The old concept of the self as defective and valueless slowly withers in reponse to this growth force. No less than the residents, the staff support this growth ethic through their own commitment to it. All members of the milieu are expected to look honestly at themselves, to recognize their weaknesses, and to address themselves to improvement and growth. Although the staff are presumably at a more advanced level of growth, they participate in and benefit from this process. Smug, self-satisfied, patronizing staff have no place in a community residence.

These goals and values saturate the whole community residence, and they are obvious to the resident (and potential resident) from his first contacts with the program. From the program's brochure (Appendix 5), to the first admission meeting, and throughout the moving-in process, the resident is valued as a whole human being, not just a specimen of psychopathology. At this stage, the managers' careful nurturing of a trusting relationship prepares the resident for the future task of developing self-awareness, mastery, and new executive and social skills.

Every setting in the community residence program ought to provide opportunities for learning and growth. Both the house routines and informal exchange can foster the growth ethic. Dinners, shopping, working, chores, avocational activity—all of these are settings where growth can occur. The resident learns that growth is sustained and reality is tested in relation to significant others. Again, the house managers set the tone by establishing a relationship based on trust and self-disclosure. Peer relationships in the house should follow. Friends in the house share leisure activities, support the resident in times of stress, and confront his distortions. An authentic reality sense is thus sustained through continual interplay with peers. The importance of significant others, the capacity to share oneself with them, and group awareness of the growth ethic are learned first and foremost in the house meeting.

The House Meeting

A variety of issues pertain to the institution of house meetings in a community residence.

Two basic rules.   There are two fundamental rules in the residence: the first is that it is absolutely mandatory that all members of the milieu attend the house meetings; the second is "no illicit drugs." The first rule is needed to let the program thrive; the second, to keep it from being destroyed. Both rules ought to be communicated to potential residents so that they understand them. Anyone who cannot comply with these two requirements has no place in the program. The universal attendance rule is based on the experience that the house meeting is indispensable in promoting group solidarity and preventing fragmentation. It helps keep the residents from breaking into several isolated cliques; it helps keep the more isolated involved and relating to the more gregarious; it helps keep the staff from being treated as adversaries by the residents; and it helps keep the staff from making the "we-they" distinctions typical of a hospital ward.

Content. The house meeting does not confine itself to administrative issues alone, but rather runs the gamut of all possible issues. These range from run-of-the-mill, everyday announcements, to important administrative changes, planning parties and outings, and in-depth consideration of individual and group issues. Outside crises such as the death or illness of a family member are important fare for the meeting.

Leadership. The administrative leadership of the meeting—calling it to order and taking up the agenda—may be rotated through staff and residents. Given the scope of the meeting, however, the natural leader will be the person who has the most expertise in individual and group dynamics. This is usually the director, but the house manager or the consultant (if he is identified as a member of the milieu and attends faithfully) may also serve. The leader facilitates the discussion when it reaches important clinical issues. The leader is an educator, especially in the program's opening months. After some months of operation, the residents become increasingly knowledgeable about their own individual and group dynamics, and they should increasingly handle most of the clinical issues as a group. The leader's role then recedes until a unique or difficult topic is on the floor—or until, as in a transitional facility, a new, less sophisticated, group forms.

Time. The meeting is usually scheduled once a week, at a fixed time. Dynamically, the structured meeting time promotes a sense of group boundaries and enhances the members' sense of a safe space.

It also permits all members of the milieu to plan their other activities well in advance and avoid conflicts. Exceptions to this routine ought to be very rare and should be discussed with the whole group.

Setting. The meeting takes place in a large room with seating arranged so each is visible to all. The group sits in a large circle; if the room is too small to accommodate this arrangement, double circles may be used, with the inner circle sitting on the floor. Ideally, inexpensive "stack chairs" should be available for use during the meeting.

The Meeting in Action

Over the years, we have developed a particularly effective format for the house meeting. Initially the leader asks for general issues, and residents and staff respond with general announcements of varying importance. This is the time for the discussion of any administrative changes—including changes in staff, rates, public transportation schedules, or dinner procedures, or any issues regarding keys, cleanup, neighbors, rent collection, or use of new appliances.

As an essential function that contributes to house solidarity and helps prevent resident-staff splitting, it is recommended that the house policies be discussed, formulated, and adopted by consensus in the house meeting. These policies are a written statement on critical matters such as sex, nudity, alcohol and illicit drug use, handling prescribed medication, noise, neighbor relations, chores, visitors, hours of coming and going, fees, and collection of rent. In some sense these policies represent a concretization of the values of the house. In other respects they are a common-sense set of guidelines that makes group living for fifteen people more organized and tolerable. The policies of Berkeley House are available to the reader in Appendix 6. These have proved to be quite stable despite many reviews over a seven-year period. Groups moving out into their own apartments have often adopted similar policies regarding such issues as chores, noise, and messages, as they find that these are essential to harmonious living, with each member fulfilling his responsibilities to the group. These ground rules are similar to, but

perhaps more explicit than, those guiding the intersecting responsibilities of a family.

In some areas, outside constraints affect the content of house
policies. One of the critical functions of the staff is to educate the
residents as to the sources and likely impacts of these constraints.
For example, the group may explore the fact that permitting promiscuity or illicit drugs would shortly bring down the wrath of the
community, as well as the law, on the residence, threatening its
very existence. On another level, the group might explore the fact
that such practices would inevitably produce chaos and attract the
attention of the professional community. Referrals would stop, in
effect closing down the house. Such discussions exemplify the way
the "open society" of the house approaches necessary constraints, in
contrast to the "closed society" of the hospital, where rules are
simply passed down from those in authority. The group as a cohesive whole adopts the policies in response to their recognition of
their dependence upon society's respect and legitimation of the
program. Constraints such as those relating to alcohol and illicit
drugs are also made partly in relation to the growth ethic, for they
are accurately viewed as promoting escapism.

In other policy areas (such as those relating to house chores,
noise, visitors, and messages), the house is free from outside constraints. Accordingly, the residents have greater freedom in developing policies that suit their needs and wishes. All of these
policies are periodically reviewed in the house meeting as the population gradually turns over so that all residents continue to feel
represented in their content.

During the discussion of general issues, the group notes the absence of any member of the milieu due to such untoward events as a
medical illness requiring hospitalization, a death in the family, or an
emotional crisis requiring psychiatric inpatient treatment. In such
cases, the members of the milieu discuss the meaning and causes of
the absence and plan communication to the absentee—be it a get-
well card, a visit, or a sympathy note. This is the group's method of
keeping the person aware that he is missed and expected back as a

vital part of the group. This kind of input is especially helpful to the resident who is psychiatrically hospitalized. It is not appropriate when a person leaves the house *persona non grata*, owing to serious noncompliance with house policies.

The concern of any resident or group of residents about group or subgroup issues in the house is also a focus during the initial stages of the meeting. This is the time for both positive and negative appraisal and planning. Parties and outings are planned, or committees are appointed to plan such affairs. Group dissatisfaction with individual residents or staff and individual dissatisfaction with aspects of group functioning are also aired at this time. These issues include such matters as group dissatisfaction with smoking during house meetings; problems in receiving telephone messages accurately or at all; a lack of heat in midwinter, or a surfeit of it in the summer; disagreement with a particular staff member's actions or words; or dissatisfaction with a troublesome resident about whom the group is angry or worried. Some members of the group may feel that other members who have formed an exclusive subgroup are undermining the house in some way—and this is where all the wash should be hung out. The entire group may be castigated for its messy ways by a more fastidious member, and sometimes this stimulates group members to greater efforts.

After the general issues, including the group issues, the meeting turns to individual matters. If a particular member of the milieu is in a very pressing crisis, he will usually bring up his individual situation by himself, with a definite understanding that this is expected of him.

If there is no such crisis, the routine of the meeting proceeds as follows: Someone in the circle starts the proceedings by reviewing with the group his past week, and his future plans and activities. This is the time that he reviews problems he is having at work, or at school, with a roommate, with a therapist, or with teachers, or with difficult tasks at work or school. A distressing phone call from a parent or a disappointment with a friend can also be shared. The resident may be anticipating a vacation or a visit home and be anxious about the reception he will receive. All such issues are reviewed with the entire group, and they generally elicit sympathetic—and often knowledgeable—responses from other residents with similar experiences. The staff need say little when the residents themselves are effectively addressing the issue. Only if there is confusion or disagreement about how to approach a problem should the staff member intervene with his own solution. Upon completion of this discussion, a staff member may support the group's solution by adding a personal example, illustrating his own recent recourse to the same solution in a similar situation.

The resident reviews not only his problems but also his successes. For the resident who announces to the group that he has just landed a job after weeks of painful looking and rejection, this is a time for sharing joy and satisfaction. After weeks of listening to the resident's discouragement, lending him moral support, and sustaining his resolve through the difficult period, all the residents share in a well-earned sense of accomplishment. They feel that they also got something in helping their housemate. And so it goes, each person in the circle addressing the group, one after the other, until everyone in the group (including the staff) has related his troubles, successes, failures, and anticipated crises to the entire group.

These interactions produce a number of crucial clinical effects. First, each member, in spite of his shyness or isolation, learns to speak about meaningful issues with the entire group. If a particular member chooses to say nothing, and sustains his withdrawal, significant group pressure is exerted upon him. This is done, not malevolently, but sympathetically; nevertheless, it is unremitting. Because everyone communicates something to the entire group, no one is seen as so sick or so special as to be excluded. If a resident refuses to speak in the house meeting, it is experienced as a sign of significant crisis by all. This is especially the case where muteness afflicts a person who is usually more open. For others, the process of opening up is slow and gradual, but not *too* slow, as group pressure to speak is quickly perceived as more troublesome to deal with than the supposed safety of silence.

Second, the member who speaks discovers through the feedback he gets that he is not so strange, or his problem so unique, as he may have believed. He is not alone.

Third, through the help of housemates, the resident learns both to master the problems themselves and to improve his capacity to relate them effectively.

Finally, by listening and relating to others, the resident learns that those who may have seemed unapproachable or hostile were really troubled about matters in which he was not involved. His assumption that he was at fault, or that there was something unacceptable about himself, is undercut. This has two significant consequences: he feels more acceptable to others; and he feels better about approaching his fellow housemate because he understands what is really at issue.

In summary, each person's sharing diminishes his own isolation, enhances his self-understanding, and promotes his accessibility. Each of these gains for the individual carries a reciprocal gain for the whole group. Openness on both the individual and the group levels facilitates a mutuality, a closeness, a common helping and support, that carries over into the milieu, beyond the limits of the house meeting. This effect, too, is reciprocal: group solidarity and increasing pride in the milieu contribute to a feeling of strength and capacity in the group to do further meaningful work.

Growth Through Daily Routine

Daily house routine provides opportunities to learn, grow, and relate in a variety of areas and formats. The morning is clearly a time to arise, wash, dress, tidy one's room, and have breakfast in preparation for the day's activities. Remaining in bed and avoiding the daily routine should not be sanctioned. The arising phase requires motivation, organization, a positive sense of social responsibilities, and some basic knowledge and skill. Some or all of these capacities may be difficult for certain residents. The depressed resident may feel like remaining in bed, unable to face a world he considers overwhelming in its foreboding lack of gratification. The disorganized resident may arise at the wrong hour and totally miss his initial outside morning obligations. The asocial resident may wittingly or unwittingly neglect to bathe regularly so that his arrival for breakfast is preceded by an offensive scent. The developmentally disabled resident may, without assistance, arrive for breakfast unkempt, and unable to negotiate preparation of his meal or travel to his outside workshop. Residents and staff alike should have an idea of the quirks of each member's morning behavior, in order to facilitate a good start for everyone. The "buddy" system works well here, with roommates or floormates helping each other out. The early riser serves as the floor alarm clock, while his housemate works as the morning cook and other members provide transportation to the morning activity. Again, as in the house meetings, pooling the strengths of all the residents makes the day start right.

All residents receive funds in one manner or another, either through wages or Supplemental Security Income benefits. When money is received, it must be wisely handled. One of the key responsibilities of the community residence is to charge (and promptly collect) rents that leave the resident enough money for such other essentials as clothes, toiletries, entertainment, and hobbies (avocational activity *is* essential to health). The residence should also help the resident learn how to budget, save, and bank funds, and to see that he receives adequate payment from jobs or social agencies. The resident is thus helped to earn, budget, save, and spend wisely.

Shopping for house goods with funds generated partly through his rent is a multipurpose activity for the resident. In the company of knowledgeable housemates or the manager, the resident learns the route to and location of the supermarket, the hardware store, the pharmacy, and the department store. He becomes familiar both with the selection of goods available and with the personnel in these local businesses. The capacity to shop with confidence, ask appropriate questions, and manage purchasing in accordance with available funds is practiced in this setting. Once the goods are in hand, the resident can participate in "finishing" them at the house. The experience of buying the raw materials for a dinner at the market and preparing, cooking, and serving them at the house can be particularly rewarding. It is a special gift to one's housemates to plan and execute a good meal; it builds a capacity that enhances the quality of independent living after leaving the residence. The same can be said for acquiring the materials and skills involved in such minor house repairs as replacing light bulbs or fuses, putting up wallpaper, or painting a shabby room. They contribute to the hominess of the residence and to the resident's increasing sense of readiness for his own apartment. Even doing the daily chores contributes to a sense of group solidarity and unity, especially when schedules and responsibilities are part of the group process.

At the end of the day, dinner is an occasion for gathering together again, exchanging the small triumphs and defeats of the day over a hearty meal. Just as all members are expected to leave the house for their outside activities each day, so it is expected that the "family" will come together again over the evening meal. A resident who has had a traumatic day and needs special attention from the group can look forward to getting it here. After-dinner activity is usually unstructured, a time that each resident uses according to his needs, wishes, and current social capacity. The managers can act as catalysts if they feel the group needs organization or activity. The evening is a good and reasonable time for reading or listening to music. Generally, however, the manager encourages group social activities by starting a bridge or Monopoly game, watching television together, or going as a group to a movie or concert.

Special Events

Planning special events is an opportunity for residents to exercise new executive skills and enhance social capacities. On a grander scale than the daily routines, these events contribute to a sense of group tradition. Christmas, New Year, Halloween, and Thanksgiving festivities, if they become annual events (and if ex-residents are routinely invited to them) significantly contribute to longitudinal stability. Ex-residents know that there are certain times of the year when they are again a special part of the house activities. Continuing contact with ex-residents is also important to current residents, who see the ex-residents as role models and as proof of the viability of the family model, in which membership outlasts residence in the house.

Leaving the House

The resident who leaves the house should ideally depart for an established program, with a functioning psychosocial network. The postresidence program should have several important features. The ex-resident should be moving into a living arrangement with known others, not living alone. He should have a daily program of familiar activities which challenge but do not overtax his capacities. The ex-resident should be in an ongoing therapeutic relationship with someone—a psychotherapist, a clinical psychiatrist, or a community residence staff member—whom he trusts and to whom he can turn when in trouble. The ex-resident's medication should be stabilized, and provisions should have been made for medical monitoring where appropriate. There should also be some stabilization of the ex-resident's relationship with his family of origin, such that old pathological patterns will not reemerge without some provision for checking them and preventing relapse. Finally, an ongoing relationship with the residence through an ex-resident program and personal ties to the house, is highly desirable. In sum, the entire program of the resident who is moving out should be intact and stable. This is another example of the axiom that there should be no more than one significant life change at a time.

While the whole community residence program can be seen as preparation for moving out, the event itself should be preceded by a structured process. Lasting some weeks, the exiting process should prepare the resident psychologically and practically, and will involve current residents, ex-residents, and the community residence staff. Important factors are the selection of an apartment (if that is the destination) of adequate size, in a good building and a safe neighborhood, close to necessary services, with access to transportation to the daily activity and the ex-resident program. Moving out is taken a step at a time, as was entry into the residence. After moving out, the ex-resident continues to draw on—and to expand—the psychosocial system generated by the residence experience. (The concept and function of the psychosocial network and the ex-resident program are described in detail in chapter 4.)

Clinical Staff Meetings

It is recommended that the clinical staff meet regularly, preferably weekly, to review the house operation. At a minimum, the house managers, the consultant, the director, and the relief managers should attend. Secretarial and other personnel who work in the milieu can also contribute to the give-and-take of the meeting, as they carry out administrative action and may be called upon from time to time to assist in some clinical task. An agenda for the clinical meeting is suggested here.

The first order of business is a global assessment of how the house is working as a social system. What is the general perceived atmosphere? How is the group working together? What appears to be the group dynamics of the house meeting? How is the group handling chores and responsibilities in the house? Does the staff feel the group is working together in a positive way? Are there cliques that are destructive? Are the house policies being carried out? Or is there concern that there is a rebellious, negative mood? How is the group relating to the loss of a resident or other significant figure? How are the staff members relating to each other? Do they feel mutually supported? Is there a common understanding of and approach to house problems? Is there important disagreement about clinical, administrative, or community issues that should be resolved? How is the staff relating to its corporate board? Is there a smooth working relationship, or are there strains over disagreements in executive policy?

There should be a review of the residence's community relations. Have any untoward situations arisen with immediate neighbors that need review? Are there any problems with police protection or the fire department? Has there been harassment by an external licensing agency? Is the building inspector due, and is everything in order to satisfy his inspection? Is the nearby hospital emergency room working well with the house in time of medical crisis? Are the ancillary psychiatric services functioning to the satisfaction of the house staff? Has the house been notified that a resident missed his appointment for medication, or been absent from his sheltered workshop position? Are sources of referral satisfied with the progress of their clients, or have there been complaints? Is the house accurately portrayed by affiliated mental health associations and agencies?

The in-house, activity, evening, weekend, and avocational programs of each resident, as well as his health status, family relations, and life-skill development, ought to be carefully evaluated. Trends of gradual improvement or subtle deterioration should be watched for; and stressful situations that the resident will shortly enter should be anticipated, when possible, and planned for.

Departing and applying residents warrant a specific slot on the agenda. Careful planning is required to accommodate simultaneously the needs of both these vulnerable groups and their likely impact on the social and financial life of the program.

There should be a review of the physical plant and other administrative aspects of the house program. Is the house in need of repair? Have recent repairs been adequately made? Is the quality of the food up to standard? Can it be obtained more economically? Is equipment needed and is existing equipment working smoothly? Should there be a preventive maintenance program?

This careful and thorough weekly review of the entire program by the staff contributes significantly to the staff solidarity and rapport which is essential to the successful operation of the house. There is no question but that high staff morale accompanied by careful, thorough, clinical work lends a feeling of comfortable security to the house in which the residents feel safe and cared for.

House Manager Supervision

The house managers are supervised by the consultant or the director. Supervisors ought to be aware of the special demands made on live-in, married house managers, who must work in concert with their spouses. This can create stresses on both marital and work relationships. Regardless of their marital status, the managers are living day and night in a setting with emotionally disturbed housemates, to whom they are expected to relate with dignity, warmth, judgment, and objectivity.

In the supervision situation, special attention should be given to the identification of residents who are troublesome to the managers. This gives the managers an opportunity to express their hostilities and frustrations, and to examine possible countertransference issues dynamically. This eases the managers' work. It is important to review the managers' procedures for delegating and deflecting work which is not their responsibility. The exploration and recognition of family or health crises in the managers' lives is also essential. A common problem is that the conscientiousness of the managers leads to overwork. The supervisor has to ensure that managers take enough time off for recuperation from the pressures of the job.

The availability of the director as immediate clinical back-up for the managers, together with his recognition of the importance of their private lives, makes the entire program feasible. Some programs have encountered unnecessary difficulties, or collapsed altogether, because of lapses in this area. The director can act in the milieu, helping the residents recognize the managers' personal needs as an important reality they must face. This is in the interest of the managers, but it also serves the residents' capacity to delay their own demands and consider the needs of others.

CHAPTER 12

A Follow-up Study of Berkeley House, a Psychiatric Halfway House

with Mollie C. Grob and Judith E. Singer

Evaluation is a fundamental concept in public administration, one closely allied to the issue of accountability. Taxpayers, service consumers, and service providers agree that the basic question posed by program evaluation—How well is this program doing what it was set up to do?—deserves a serious answer. Taking this question as a point of departure, an evaluation can serve as a guide for program improvement. Further, if a study demonstrates that programmatic goals are being fulfilled, it can be instrumental in sustaining community, financial, and professional support.

In the case of a community residence facility, there are three major designs for answering the basic evaluative question. The first approach compares residents with a nonresident "control group," who share some important characteristics with the residents and differ primarily in their lack of exposure to the community residence program. The second, the so-called departure design, describes the resident's status immediately upon leaving the residence, using vocational, domiciliary, and clinical measures as evidence of the program's success. The third approach takes the form of a follow-up study, checking on the resident's condition at a specific interval, or intervals, after he or she has left the residence.

Each of these approaches has advantages and drawbacks for the

Mollie C. Grob is Director of the Evaluative Service Unit of McLean Hospital. Judith E. Singer is the former Co-Director of the Evaluative Service Unit and Assistant Clinical Professor of Psychology in the Department of Psychiatry at the Harvard Medical School.

evaluator trying to strike a balance between practicality and adequate methodology. Control group studies, for example, are extremely impractical in ongoing clinical programs, as reflected in their paucity in the literature on community residential facilities. Departure studies, by contrast, are practical; but because they fail to measure the long-term impact of the program, they leave much to be desired methodologically. Nevertheless, of the twenty-eight studies analyzing the success of community residential programs, twenty-three employ this evaluation format.[1] Only five studies have sought to determine the status of the ex-resident at a given interval after departure from the halfway house.[2]

Beyond the issue of design, there are difficulties in selecting the criteria to be measured. For example, hospitalization or rehospitalization is frequently taken as a measure of a program's failure to achieve lasting therapeutic change. All five follow-up studies of community residential programs used this criterion and reported rates of rehospitalization ranging from 15 to 48 percent, with a mean rate of 27 percent. The validity of this criterion is an open question, however, given the fact that it is variously used to describe: (1) the destination at the time of departure from the community residence; (2) an event that occurred some time after departure from the community residence, with the patient no longer in the hospital; or (3) the status of the ex-resident at the time of the follow-up study. Moreover, duration of hospitalization is rarely given in these studies, which further reduces the opportunity for critical appraisal of their significance. If hospitalization itself were a useful criterion, then a longitudinal assessment that includes duration of hospitalization prior to, and following, the halfway house experience would facilitate judgment of the impact of the house on the resident. Finally, these problems are compounded by concern that patients are dumped into the community irrespective of their capacity for adaptation to it. The fact that a patient is in the community no longer necessarily has any clinical significance. It is clear that an unprepared patient can be far worse off in the community than in the hospital.

This chapter reports on a study which, given these problems in assessment, attempts to obtain as global a picture as possible of the rehabilitative result of a halfway house experience. The investigation of Berkeley House, a psychiatric halfway house in Boston, was initiated by McLean Hospital in cooperation with the Simmons College School of Social Work.[3] A number of questions were raised: How was the former resident functioning with respect to his personal-social and occupational adjustment following the Berkeley House experience? Did Berkeley House achieve its goal of preventing or reducing hospitalization? What was the former resident's use of the house following his departure? What were the former resident's reactions to his halfway house experience? Our rationale in undertaking this follow-up as a method of evaluation of outcome is based on the assumption that the effectiveness of a residential program may be measured, though not conclusively, from *presumptive* evidence of the rehabilitative status of former residents.

Background of the Study

Setting

Berkeley House is a high-expectation, transitional, psychiatric halfway house which was the first facility of its kind in the United States to be affiliated with a private psychiatric teaching hospital—McLean Hospital. It is a five-story townhouse in downtown Boston, in a residential area within ten minutes' walk of schools and colleges, jobs, and ample recreational facilities. Twenty-three residents, male and female, live in the house, with an expectation that the stay will be no longer than one year. A married couple serves as house managers. The house itself has two whole floors of common rooms; bedrooms and some office space occupy the upper levels. In spite of its size, it was originally a private residence, and it still has a warm family-home feeling to it.

Berkeley House was designed as a relatively small, family-modeled living arrangement, functioning as an open social system, integrated within (rather than isolated from) the surrounding community.[4] The concept of Berkeley House is that the health and strength of a person can be asserted during daily activity at school or on the job. The resident can seek understanding and support from fellow residents and house staff during the evening. A required weekly house meeting at which each resident shares his struggles with the entire house community enhances group awareness and reinforces mutual development of problem-solving skills. As a result, each resident becomes increasingly alert and helpful to his fellow residents. The resident learns his vulnerabilities and also learns to anticipate and cope with situations which may be particularly stressful to him. Nightly family-style dinners and planned avocational activities are natural foci around which social capacities are strengthened and maintained.

The attainment of the capacity to tolerate affect, to solve problems, to work, to play, and to learn of and anticipate one's problems is portrayed as a sensible way of coping with life, rather than as treatment for sick people. Through a comprehensive ex-resident program, the house aims to function as a continuing social center supporting its alumni. Because residents often leave in clusters, the house helps build a social fabric in which ex-residents continue to grow, rather than drifting into social isolation, after departure.

If a resident in crisis begins to show signs of relapse, either while in residence or after departure, early, brief hospitalization is used as a crisis-intervention technique. In this event, however, the house maintains contact with the former resident. It is hoped that this early intervention and demonstration of "continuing care" will help prevent a major relapse and consequent long hospitalization, and that it will enhance the ex-resident's chance of early return to the house or the community.

Sample and Method

The sample population included all residents (male and female) who lived at Berkeley House from its opening in June 1970 and who left prior to September 1973 (four months before the follow-up interviewing period). There were seventy-eight such residents.

Data were collected in several ways. Relevant information regarding the former resident's background and previous hospitalization experience was obtained from medical records at McLean Hospital. Follow-up interviews with former residents were carried out in person or by telephone. The interviewers were thirteen psychiatric social work graduate students who used a lengthy, pretested questionnaire to elicit both objective and subjective data.[5] Objective data included specific information about aspects of the former resident's situation at the time of follow-up, including living arrangements, marital status, occupation, social activities, contact with the family, clinical status, and treatment experience. Subjective data included the ex-resident's own assessment of his adjustment in these areas and his perceptions about the Berkeley House experience.

The first set of analyses involved obtaining frequency distributions of the many variables describing the preadmission, hospitalization, and follow-up characteristics of the sample population in order to provide an overview of their status. The next step included an examination of the interrelationships between selected variables in an attempt to identify some of the factors influencing outcome. Chi-square values and significance levels were recorded for those variables found to be significantly related.

Results

Description of the Sample

Seventy-five of the 78 ex-residents in the sample were former McLean Hospital patients, all but 5 of whom came to Berkeley House directly after discharge. The 3 other residents came directly from other inpatient sources. Approximately two-thirds were male, one-third female. All but one were white. Although they ranged in age from sixteen to fifty-two when they came to Berkeley House, the large majority (90 percent) were between seventeen and twenty-four. The median age was twenty. Most of the sample were single (71 residents). Of the 7 who had married, 6 were women. Only 1 of these had an intact marriage; 3 were divorced, 2 others were involved in divorce proceedings, and 1 was separated.

With only a few exceptions, the sample was representative of the middle and upper classes socioeconomically. Ex-residents for the most part came from intact families (72 percent had grown up with both parents). The remainder came from families broken by death or divorce. The majority of ex-residents' mothers and fathers had advanced training beyond high school, with fathers predominantly professional or in business (85 percent). Diagnosed mental illness was apparent in the medical records of parents of 15 percent of the families—7 mothers and 5 fathers.

At the time of their admission to Berkeley House, almost two-thirds of the sample had already completed high school, with 40 percent having had some years in college. Two rather conspicuous and contrasting features stood out in the histories of the group: on the one hand, the predominance of academic problems (noted for 60 percent) and behavioral problems in the school situation (53 percent); and on the other, the high frequency of outstanding scholastic, athletic, and artistic achievement (33 percent). An assessment of cognitive functioning made at the time of hospitalization indicated an above-average level for 80 percent of the group.

Six of the most frequent problems noted at admission to McLean were: (1) inability to function even minimally; (2) severe problems with interpersonal relationships; (3) heavy drug abuse; (4) long-standing antisocial behavioral patterns; (5) severe depression or other mood disturbance; and (6) multiple or serious suicide attempts. [6] Thirty-three percent were assessed at admission to have had either no significant interpersonal relationships or only significantly self-destructive relationships. Fully 39 percent of the total sample were considered by their doctors to have serious suicidal potential. In general, these patients were sufficiently impaired in their functioning to require long-term hospitalization to prevent suicide, illicit drug intake, or antisocial behavior, or to promote socialization in the severely withdrawn. This population was ultimately diagnosed at discharge from McLean Hospital as follows: 60 percent schizophrenic disorders with varying degrees of affective component (of this group of schizophrenics, 38 percent were "chronic"); 33 percent personality disorders; and 5 percent affective disorders.

The median length of stay at McLean Hospital was twelve months. Two-thirds of the sample had had at least one previous hospitalization, with three months the median cumulative inpatient stay. Slightly more than one-half of the rehospitalized group had been admitted once before; the rest from two to six times. During the McLean hospitalization, the patients had received a variety of therapies, including individual psychotherapy (92 percent), psychotropic medication (91 percent), and milieu and other rehabilitative treatment. Slightly more than half of the sample continued their education while in the hospital at the Arlington School, a high school on the hospital grounds.

These patients were referred to Berkeley House because they were considered to be high-risk patients, likely to relapse if sent directly into the community. The median length of stay at Berkeley House was 217 days (approximately seven months), with a range of 35 to 755 days. Nine percent of the residents stayed less than three months, and 10 percent stayed over one year. Berkeley House's goal of functioning as a transitional facility with a length of stay ranging from three months to one year was thus met for 81 percent of the sample.

Former Residents at Follow-up

In all, follow-up information was obtained for 54 former residents, or approximately 70 percent of the sample population (66 percent from primary respondents, 4 percent from substitutes). Fifteen percent of the sample refused to participate, and another fifteen percent were inaccessible or could not be located. Respondents and nonrespondents were compared extensively across a number of variables in an effort to determine the representativeness of the group which participated. The slightly higher response rate of females was related to the higher proportion of males who could not be located, rather than to the refusal rate. Underrepresented in the follow-up sample were males who had been under the age of twenty at the time of admission to Berkeley House; individuals with histories of hard drug abuse; the personality disorder category; and those with a briefer length of stay at the house. All of these variables proved to be significantly interrelated. In addition, the follow-up sample was biased by a predominance of individuals with a history of more inpatient hospital days, suicidal symptomatology, and continued contact with the house following departure.

Follow-up interviews were completed for 54 former residents who had been out of the house at the time of the interview for a median of fifteen months, with the range extending from four to twenty-four months. The median age of the respondents was twenty-three; for the most part, they were viewed by the interviewers as responsive to the follow-up process and as reliable in their presentation of the data.

Living Situation: Residence

Table 14 shows the living situations of former house residents at the time of leaving Berkeley House and at the time of the follow-up study. At the time of follow-up, 91 percent, or 49 of the 54 former residents, were living in the community. Five were in the hospital. Of the 49 ex-residents living in the community, 28 were living in apartments with roommates, 8 were living alone, 5 were with families of origin, 4 with families of procreation, 3 were in college dorms, and 1 was in a halfway house.

TABLE 14. Living Situations of Ex-Residents

Living Situation	At Time of Departure		At Time of Follow-up	
	Number	Percentage	Number	Percentage
In apartment with roommate	30	56	28	52
In apartment alone	3	5	8	15
With family of origin	7	13	5	9
With family of procreation	3	5	4	7
In college dormitory	2	4	3	6
In halfway house	0	0	1	2
Traveling	2	4	0	0
At YMCA	1	2	0	0
Total in community	48	89	49	91
In psychiatric hospital	6	11	5	9

An examination of the residential pattern of the former residents at the time of departure from Berkeley House reveals that 48 of the 54, or 89 percent, established residence in the community, with 6 returning to a psychiatric hospital. It is interesting that, with few exceptions, those remaining in the community chose to live with others, rather than alone. Quite often former residents became roommates upon leaving.

Although the figures for the time of leaving and the time of follow-up do not seem dissimilar, 'there had been considerable shifts in living arrangements. Also, of the 6 former residents who had been rehospitalized at departure from Berkeley House, 3 were still hospitalized at the time of follow-up.

Occupational Status

The occupational status portion of the study revealed that 40, or 74 percent, of the respondents were engaged in occupations of some kind: 24 were at work, 14 were at school, and 2 were homemakers (table 15). Six others, or 11 percent, were actively seeking employment between jobs. Eight were unemployed, not at school, and not making attempts to enroll or find a job.

Twenty-one former residents were employed full time at follow-up, working 35 to 55 hours each week. Five of these fully employed were in school part time as well, while 4 did volunteer work in addition, usually working with exceptional or deprived children. The average length of employment of the full-time workers was eight months. Work histories indicated that 8 of the respondents had held the same job since leaving Berkeley House. Eighty-seven percent of the full-time workers rated their work good to excellent, and 67 percent rated their work improved over their performance prior to entering Berkeley House.

There were 13 full-time students who carried twelve to fourteen hours of classes each week. Two of the 13 were doing graduate work, and the rest were undergraduates. Four of the 13 students were enrolled at Harvard, 2 at Boston University, 2 at out-of-state universities, and 5 at various other colleges in the Boston area. The average length of time at school was 13 months. Most of these students

TABLE 15. Occupational Status

Activity	Number	Percentage
Employment		
Full-time	12	
Full-time, and part-time school	5	
Full-time, and volunteer work	4	
Part-time	3	
Subtotal	24	44.4
School		
Full-time	5	
Full-time, and part-time job	5	
Full-time, and volunteer work	3	
Part-time, and volunteer work	1	
Subtotal	14	25.9
Household management (homemaker)	2	3.6
Not employed, but actively seeking work	6	11.0
Not employed or at school	8	15.0

held part-time jobs or were involved in volunteer activities as well. Seventy-six percent of the full-time students rated their school work improved over their performance prior to entering Berkeley House.

Family Relationships

Table 16 shows that more than half of the respondents saw their families either monthly or weekly. It is of interest that 60 percent of the respondents reported the relationship with their mothers as either excellent or good; 26 percent, fair to poor; and 14 percent, variable. Overall, 61 percent said the relationship was better than before moving into Berkeley House. Seventy percent of the respondents reported the relationship with their fathers as excellent or good and 30 percent, fair-to-poor, with two-thirds saying it was better than before moving into Berkeley House. Of those who said that the relationship had changed for the better, the reason most often given was "a growing-up process" in either the respondent or the parent. The striving for independent maturity was manifested in the establishment of separate living arrangements for these young people and their parents.

TABLE 16. Frequency of Family Interaction

	Number	Percentage
Rarely	2	4
Yearly	10	22
Every few months	4	9
Monthly	12	27
Weekly	12	27
Daily	5	11

Social Adjustment

Improvement in social relationships since departure was reported by 70 percent of the respondents. Despite the report of improvement, only 56 percent rated their social life as excellent or good, compared to 34 percent fair and 10 percent poor (table 17). The majority expressed an interest in changing their social life in some way, a statistic that is perhaps not remarkable for a group of young, unmarried adults. At the same time, most respondents spoke of friendships, with 54 percent admitting to "difficulty" and 46 percent reporting ease in making friends (table 18).

Clinical Status

The majority of respondents, 72 percent, rated their "mental status" as excellent or good. Fully 92 percent reported that they had made progress in some areas, referring to intrapsychic growth as the dimension in which they experienced the most change. This subjective sense of well-being was supported by the relatively few reports of clinical symptoms. A typical answer in this category included "better stability, more confidence, being more easy-going, and having more realistic expectations."

Only one suicide attempt was reported, an encouraging finding considering the serious suicidal potential noted in the background of 54 percent of the ex-residents interviewed.

A review of the therapy and medication experiences of respondents following departure from Berkeley House reveals that although many former residents are not yet independent of these services, there has been a gradual decline in their use. During the

TABLE 17. Respondents' Social-Life Ratings

Rating	Number	Percentage
Current social life		
Excellent	6	12
Good	22	44
Fair	17	34
Poor	5	10
Compared to time of Berkeley House entry		
Better	35	70
Same	6	12
Worse	7	14
Varies	2	4

Berkeley House stay, all were in therapy; after leaving, 85 percent continued; and at the time of follow-up, 70 percent were in therapy. During the Berkeley House experience, 28 percent were reported to be receiving no medication; at follow-up this had increased to 47 percent.

The total incidence of hospitalization for the 54 former residents in the sample over the entire period following departure showed that 19, or 35 percent, of the entire group had been in the hospital at some point. The median of the total cumulative duration of all hospitalization time for the 19 former residents was four months. It should be remembered that 65 percent of the 54 former residents (with a median of sixteen months previous hospitalization time)

TABLE 18. Ease in Making Friends

	Number	Percentage
Very easy	6	12
Easy	17	34
Somewhat difficult	13	26
Difficult	9	18
Very difficult	5	10

never returned to the hospital, and 91 percent were in the community at follow-up.

Interrelationship of Several Selected Variables

Using the chi-square test, we found no significant statistical relationship among sex, age, diagnosis, length of stay at Berkeley House, and mental status ratings at outcome. However, when we examined the relationship between mental status and other measures of rehabilitation at follow-up (occupational status, social relationships, relationship to mother or father), we found that good mental status was significantly related to occupation and good social relationships ($p < .01$). Also, rehospitalization after leaving Berkeley House was significantly related ($p < .05$) to fair-to-poor outcome.

Use of the House After Departure

Thirty-nine of the 50 respondents providing data (78 percent) had contact with the house some time after leaving. Only 11 had no contact. Sixteen, or almost a third, were visiting the house at the time of follow-up. This indicates a pattern of decreasing involvement in house activities. However, almost 60 percent reported that they continued to remain in contact with other ex-residents, although most of them had left the house more than a year previously. This suggests that the social matrix of former Berkeley House residents was established and continued to survive following a dropping off of direct Berkeley House contact. This supports the hypothesis that the house was able to create or enhance the psychosocial kinship system.

Reactions to the Berkeley House Experience

The reactions of the former residents to the Berkeley House experience was of interest in terms of their perceptions of its impact on them. Over 75 percent of the respondents in follow-up interviews felt that Berkeley House helped at least somewhat in the areas of social and emotional adjustment. Approximately half felt that the house helped prevent rehospitalization. Thirty-eight percent said that they were helped in school or work (see table 19).

TABLE 19. Helpfulness of Berkeley House

	Helpful		Partly Helpful		Not Helpful	
	No.	Pctage.	No.	Pctage.	No.	Pctage.
Social adjustment	26	53	12	24	11	23
Emotional adjustment	27	54	11	22	12	24
Preventing rehospitalization	23	49	2	4	22	47
Vocational adjustment	13	26	6	12	31	62

The residents rated their subjective general reaction to the house (table 20). Sixty-four percent rated the house high or fairly high. Fifty-one respondents then rated what they liked most about the house (table 21), yielding 76 responses. The largest number of comments (32) related broadly to people at Berkeley House, both residents and staff; typical comments related to appreciating the sense of community and sharing, the family model. Related to this was the high rating given the group gatherings—house meetings and dinner. Personal freedom was also highly rated on the scale, and was often contrasted with the restrictive hospital environment. Table 22 shows that responses to the question "Who was most helpful" produced a fairly even distribution among houseparents, director, and residents. The high rating of "other residents" supports

TABLE 20. Personal Satisfaction with Berkeley
House Experience

Rating	Number	Percentage
High	17	33
Fairly high	16	31
Fairly low	9	18
Low	8	16
Refused to categorize	1	2

TABLE 21. What People Liked About Berkeley House

Staff	10
People and sense of community	32
Specific aspects of house routine	8
Transitional shelter	4
Aspects not directly related to halfway house function	9
Personal freedom	7
Stress on health	1
Everything	1
Nothing	4

the hypothesis that the house achieved its goal of helping residents learn to help each other.

When asked whether the house was different from the hospital, 97 percent of the former residents responded yes. Those replying positively were asked to describe the difference (table 23). The 48 respondents gave 57 replies. The greatest number of responses (28) emphasized freedom. Another 12 people focused on personal responsibility in jobs, relationships, and other areas of life.

Summary and Discussion of Findings

An examination of the sample population with a fifteen-month median departure time from Berkeley House suggests improved functioning along a number of dimensions: 91 percent of the ex-

TABLE 22. Most Helpful People at Berkeley House

Houseparents	30
Director	24
Other residents	27
No one	1
Everyone	1
Other	10

TABLE 23. The Difference Between Berkeley
House and the Hospital

More freedom at Berkeley House	28
More responsibility at Berkeley House	12
Less pressured than hospital	3
Berkeley House emphasis on normalcy	8
Staff	2
Did not describe difference	3

residents were living independently in the community; 74 percent were at work or in school (with another 11 percent actively looking for employment between jobs); family and social relationships had improved for the majority; treatment histories showed a reduction in the use of treatment resources and a considerable change in the hospitalization pattern from one of extensive length of stay to either no rehospitalization (for 65 percent) or a four-month median stay (for 35 percent). Furthermore, a majority expressed general satisfaction with the house experience and had made use of the house as a source of support in their later efforts to adjust in the community.

It would appear from the reporting of the former halfway house residents interviewed for this study that the rehabilitative outcome was favorable for the majority. Although the self-ratings may have been somewhat inflated, the objective evidence with respect to independence of living situation, occupational status, family and social contacts, lessening of dependence on therapeutic resources, and heightened sense of well-being attests to considerable growth in a population with a history of serious pathology and extended hospitalization.

One may argue that the bias created by the nonparticipation of 30 percent of the total sample may have affected the results. Certainly, we cannot speak for the underrepresented group—young males with a history of heavy drug-taking, briefer hospitalizations,and briefer stays at Berkeley House, with previous diagnoses of personality disorder. However, the reporting sample was highly representative of schizophrenic patients, those with histories of lengthier hospitalization and of serious suicidal potential, individuals who stayed longer at the house and maintained somewhat more contact after leaving.

Another question arises from the absence of collateral data from family or "significant others" to establish greater reliability, at least for some of the variables. A number of follow-up studies carried out at McLean Hospital over the years included both the former patient and his family as sources.[7] Family or "significant others" were excluded here by design because of the Berkeley House philosophy of working toward the establishment of the resident's emotional independence from parental intervention. The other McLean studies have demonstrated a fairly high level of reliability of findings; when differences existed, the former patients tended to assess themselves more positively than did their relatives.

The particular population studied—a middle- to upper-class group socioeconomically, with its concomitant highly advantaged characteristics—raises questions about the generalizability of the results. As one consequence of this limitation, it is not possible to make direct comparisons between the results of this study and those of other follow-up investigators cited earlier. Previously studied populations for the most part came from state hospital settings. Some differences in outcome between the populations at follow-up are highlighted in a recent publication by Grob and Singer and in a study which speculates as to whether middle-class schizophrenics actually have greater rehabilitation potential.[8]

A number of follow-up investigators have noted the difficulty in obtaining conclusive evidence of the actual effectiveness of ongoing clinical programs without the use of a controlled design.[9] The use of the former patient as his own control, however, provides promise of an adequate measure of change.[10] This method involves the development of clinical ratings of the premorbid level as a baseline against which to establish the level of adaptation after leaving the halfway house. Our data lend themselves to this type of comparison and await further analyses for a more definitive interpretation of their meaning. Short of this rigor, the present study can serve as a kind of close approximation.

An important by-product of this study has been the proven feasibility of using graduate students in such follow-up work. Their participation not only provides the means that make the follow-up work possible, but also develops the students' appreciation of the importance of evaluation in their future roles as practitioners.

A Final View

Too often it is thought that the halfway house residential experience is itself the final rehabilitative measure. We strongly believe that it is only one stage in the establishment of a social network for the former resident. Upon leaving the halfway house, the resident can begin to move out into the community, living with others, relating less and less directly to the house—but always using it if a crisis arises. Through this continued availability of the house and the social network it helps to generate, the community experience of the formerly hospitalized patient is supported and enhanced.

The Challenge Ahead

Recognizing the psychiatric halfway house as a social system, functioning within society, and operating with benefit to its residents, where do we find ourselves today? We are on a crest that has taken three decades to build. In the 1950s the psychotropic medications brought once unruly patients under control and increased their opportunities for living in the community. Through the 1960s we saw a cultural movement away from the impersonality of the large institution and toward small groups. The 1970s have brought a judicial and legislative revolution. The courts for the first time have defined the right of mental patients to live in the community in the least restrictive setting feasible. Public Law 94-63 made the halfway house an essential service of the community mental health center.

In response to all of these influences, mental health professionals are attempting to discharge those incarcerated and to avoid institutionalizing new patients entirely. Effective community treatment is clearly the goal for these patients, and adequate community residential programs must be available if they are to be rehabilitated. Yet these programs are clearly not available in adequate numbers. Certainly it takes time to develop appropriate residential programs and the necessary ancillary rehabilitative services. Nevertheless, there are still serious impediments to the program. What are these constraints? What is the challenge ahead?

Staffing these programs with trained and effective workers continues to be an important goal. It is essential that community residential programs continue to be operated by people with a commitment to growth and rehabilitation. The spark of enthusiasm accompanying creativity and innovation should not be lost, for it fosters a lasting renewal of spirit that keeps the program vital and relevant to both the residents and the community. More and better staff will be needed in the future. Educational institutions must address this new field of community residential care in planning curricula in the human services. Staff from phased-out institutions as well as new students must be educated in the principles of community and residential care outlined in this book.

A community's building code can too often be a veiled expression of community opposition aimed at exclusion. A code such as the one described in this book nullifies this kind of subterfuge and simultaneously ensures the safety of the residents. The rationale and details of such a code must be disseminated and adopted, however, if it is to serve this purpose.

There has also been concern that rigid programmatic standards set by governmental agencies would render the programs sterile and encumber them with expensive institutional trappings. This has not occurred, nor is it likely to occur in the numerous states yet to develop standards, if the precedents of other states and the guidelines in these pages are followed.

Two other roadblocks to the program, inadequate funding and community opposition, are more difficult to overcome. In this instance, we must pursue the slow process of educating the public and setting society's priorities to cope with these complex issues.

Community residential programs are caught in the funding intricacies of a mental health delivery system in evolution. Innovative programmatic concepts and court orders ensuring the constitutional rights of mental patients have not been matched by legislative appropriations. Allan Beigel, former chairman of the National Council of Community Mental Health Centers, recently reviewed some of these funding problems. He felt that there was a "basic problem" in there not being "enough dollars available to the mental health system." Because of this he warned that the "competitiveness between the institutions and the community programs is going to be a critical factor in determining the eventual outcome of the funding of our mental health service delivery system." Second, Beigel cited the "negativism toward coverage of mental health services by third-party payers" in spite of "documentation of the cost-effectiveness of underwriting mental health services." Finally, he described the confusion over whether the services are medical or social or both. "Should a community or an institutional mental health program be entitled to participate in both federal medical and social programs, such as Medicaid and Title 20 of the Social Security Act."[1]

Addressing the problem solely from the point of view of cost effectiveness, various investigators have shown the advantages of community programs.[2] In 1973 it was estimated that wards in general hospitals, private psychiatric hospitals, and community mental health centers had daily costs per inpatient of about $100, and state and county hospitals $30 per day, while the halfway house average daily cost was only $12.[3] Even though additional essential rehabilitative services raise the overall direct costs of community treatment, the increase of productivity through work more than makes up for it.[4] Further, studies similar to the follow-up reported in these pages have shown that community-treated groups have "less symptomatology, score higher on measures of satisfaction with life, spend less time unemployed, and have more positive social relationships."[5] If future studies continue to demonstrate the economic and humanitarian benefits of community care, then those responsible for allocating private and public monetary resources must respond by funding community programs more adequately.

Finally, the success of community residential programs will ultimately depend upon their true integration into the fabric of society. This book has suggested that there is a reasonable way for the mentally ill and the community to live together. The basic premise is that community residential living ought to be accepted and legitimized in exchange for compliance with society's values. The courts should base their judgments upon this tenet in future zoning cases. As long as the mentally ill person adheres to the community's basic value system, he has the same right to live within society as any other citizen.

Even if community entry of these programs is supported by the courts, it is equally important that the neighbors accept these patients without harassment. True rehabilitation will only be achieved in an accepting, helpful atmosphere. Public education in the principles and aims of community mental health programs is essential to this goal.

The realization of these ideals will require a joint effort of the mental health profession and the community. The mental health profession is obligated to make every effort to ensure that community placement is recommended only for those patients able to live within the community's behavioral code. The community, in turn, should be increasingly knowledgeable about these programs and accepting of the people in them. All will ultimately reap the benefits of a society which is both more humane and better able to meet its obligations to deal with its own difficulties.

Appendices
Notes
Bibliography
Index

Massachusetts Department of Mental Health Community Residence Regulations

Regulation 5.2. "Private Facilities Providing Care But Not Treatment"

Part 5—Private Facilities Providing Care But Not Treatment

Sec.

5.01   Authority
5.02   General provisions
5.03   Physical structure
5.04   Personnel
5.05   Residence directorship
5.06   In-residence management
5.07   Professional consultation
5.08   Medical coverage
5.09   Optional personnel
5.10   Program
5.11   Records
5.12   Departmental inspection

§ 5.01   *Authority*

The Department is required by G.L. c. 19, s. 29(a) to make regulations for the operation of facilities providing care but not treatment of persons who are mentally ill or mentally retarded. This part is promulgated pursuant to this authority. See 1 CHSR 26.45.

§ 5.02   *General provisions*

(a) A halfway house, group home, group residence, cooperative apartment, or any similar residence offering to the public and representing itself as providing care but not treatment shall be subject to this part, and for purposes of this part shall be referred to as a "community residence."

(b) Individuals receiving care in a community residence shall be certified as capable of self-preservation pursuant to Part 13 and for purposes of this part shall be referred to as "residents."

(c) A community residence may be legally organized as a corporation (business or non-profit charitable), a partnership, an individual proprietorship, an unincorporated association, or a public agency.

(d) A community residence which is affiliated with a facility which provides other services shall conform to this part.

(e) Each community residence shall notify the Department at its inception annually, and more frequently in case of change, of the names and addresses of those persons who assume the legal responsibility for the operation of the community residence and of that person or persons to whom all correspondence from the Department shall be directed.

§ 5.03 *Physical structure*

(a) The community residence may be a dwelling house or houses, an apartment, or a combination of apartments within a dwelling house appropriate in size, structure and layout to serve the community residence program.

(b) Community residences shall meet all applicable local and state building codes and requirements for fire, safety, and health protection, and the requirements set forth in this paragraph.

(1) Each community residence shall provide the Department with a copy of a license or certificate from the Department of Public Safety or from local safety authorities where required indicating their approval of the safety of the structure.

(2) There shall be no more than four sleeping accommodations in any one room in a community residence unless authorized by the Commissioner or his designee.

(3) Manually operated fire-fighting equipment such as hand extinguishers shall be available to the custodian and other designated personnel.

(4) There shall be a telephone in the apartment unit or a public telephone in the building accessible to all.

(5) The community residence staff shall familiarize the residents with a conspicuously posted fire procedure which includes location of the local fire box. Fire drills shall be held at three month intervals by each community residence.

(6) All fires occurring in a community residence shall be reported to the Department by the community residence staff within forty-eight (48) hours of the fire.

(7) First aid supplies shall be kept in a convenient and accessible place

ready for use. The name of the medical facility or physician available in case of a medical emergency shall be conspicuously posted by community residence personnel.

§ 5.04 *Personnel*

No uniform staffing pattern shall be required for any community residence. Each community residence shall maintain the following personnel functions: residence directorship; in-residence management; professional consultation; and medical coverage. In the discretion of the residence director, and with the approval of the Department, the function of in-residence management may not be required. Personnel functions may be performed by one or more persons.

§ 5.05 *Residence directorship*

The community residence program shall have a residence director whose administrative duties and responsibilities shall include:

(a) implementation of policies, practices, and procedures of the community residence;

(b) preparation of all reports and documents required by the Department;

(c) formulation of budget, and handling all financial matters in accordance with the approved budget;

(d) overall supervision of the medical health, nutritional standards, education and general welfare of the residents;

(e) maintenance of community residence records relating to residents and finances; and

(f) supervision of the residence manager, and delegation of appropriate duties and responsibilities to him when such manager is required.

§ 5.06 *In-residence management*

(a) The community residence program may have a residence manager living on the premises. The community residence manager shall have demonstrated qualities of ability to relate effectively to all residents of the community residence for the purpose of carrying out the community residence program.

(b) The duties and responsibilities of the residence manager shall include:

(1) promotion of a congenial atmosphere in the community residence;

(2) handling all matters relating to daily living in the community residence;

(3) assisting residents in problems relating to work or school adjustments; and

(4) carrying out all duties and responsibilities delegated by the residence director.

§ 5.07 *Professional consultation*

(a) A community residence shall have a written affiliation with one or more professional consultants in one or more of the following fields: psychiatry, psychology, social work, special education, vocational rehabilitation or any other field which is directly related and pertinent to the needs of the residents.

(b) The professional consultant shall have earned a graduate degree or degrees in an acknowledged specialty and a license or certification where required under Massachusetts statute. However, upon application of the community residence and in the discretion of the Department, experience and expertise may be considered in lieu of academic degrees or licensure.

(c) The professional consultant or consultants shall consult with the program at least once per month.

§ 5.08 *Medical coverage*

(a) A community residence shall have an arrangement with a medical facility or individual physician or physicians licensed under Massachusetts law.

(b) Such medical arrangement shall ensure twenty-four (24) hour availability for medical emergencies.

§ 5.09 *Optional personnel*

In addition to personnel responsible for the required personnel functions, there may be appropriate ancillary personnel, professional or non-professional, providing needed services to the community residence.

§ 5.10 *Program*

The community residence shall develop a written statement of its program, policies and practices. Such statement shall describe the program goals; the services, training and care offered by the community residence; the kinds of activities and facilities offered; the group or groups of persons to be served including any sex or age characteristics; admission and discharge policies, including parameters of length of stay; and limitations, if any, on sources of referral. The community residence shall develop rules regarding safety and health and these shall be communicated to the residents by the community residence staff.

§ 5.11 Records

(a) The community residence shall keep a record on each resident. Such record shall be confidential and not open to public inspection without the consent of the resident.

(b) Each community residence shall submit the following information to the Department on forms prescribed by the Department:

(1) an initial description of the community residence, including its program, facilities, organizational structure, staffing patterns; and

(2) an annual report relating to residents, budget, and personnel.

(c) Reports and records required by and submitted to the Department shall be confidential and not open to public inspection except in the discretion of the Commissioner for the purposes of research approved by the Department pursuant to Part 7. No studies disseminated to the public based on these records shall identify the community residence by name without its consent or any resident by name without his consent.

§ 5.12 Departmental inspection

Community residences are subject to inspection by a representative of the Department at any reasonable time for such inspection. There shall be at least one inspection annually.

Massachusetts Building Code

Section 424.0. Group Residence in the Commonwealth of Massachusetts

424.1. *Definition:* A premise, licensed or operated by an agency of the Commonwealth of Massachusetts for the residential care in any single building of not more than twelve (12) unrelated persons between the ages of seven (7) and fifteen (15) inclusive, or up to twenty-five (25) unrelated persons sixteen (16) years of age or over, as may be approved by the licensing or operating state agency, who are capable of self-preservation. The use of such accommodations provided for a group residence as defined herein shall be considered the same as a normal single-family residence for the purpose of these regulations and shall not be construed as being similar to a boarding house, lodging house or dormitory. These provisions will apply to group residence uses providing accommodations for the care of not more than twenty-five (25) individuals.

424.2. *New and Existing Occupancies:* These regulations apply to existing buildings, which are to be used as group residences as defined in section 424.1 of this Code, and to buildings and/or structures hereinafter erected or altered, which are to be used as group residences as defined in section 424.1 of this Code.

424.21. *Plans and Specifications:* Any existing building whose occupancy is altered for use as a group residency under the provisions of section 424.0 shall have filed with the local building department a complete set of plans showing in detail all rooms, doors, corridors, windows, stairs and stairways, hazard vertical openings (section 424.51), and the location of all fire detection equipment, alarms, and fire suppression equipment.

424.3. *Hazard of Contents:* Any household contents, which represent a fire hazard greater than that which could be expected of ordinary household furnishings, shall not be allowed.

424.4 *Means of Egress:* A means of egress shall be a continuous path of travel from any point in a building to the open air outside at ground level.

424.41. *Principal Means of Egress:* There shall be a principal means of egress normally used by the occupants to leave the building. Under fire conditions this exit would be the first choice for exiting.

424.42. *Escape Route:* There shall be a back-up, or escape route, available to each occupant from any occupied portion of the building to preclude any possibility of entrapment in the event that the principal means of egress is blocked by fire, smoke or structural collapse. This escape route shall be so determined as to minimize the likelihood that it can be deliberately compromised.

424.43. *Time for Egress:* The time taken to accomplish total evacuation of the building shall not exceed one (1) minute per floor, with a maximum time of two and one-half (2½) minutes as determined by and to the satisfaction of the licensing agency in accordance with Section 9.1 of 9 CHSR S. 51 Title 9 Code of Human Services Regulations, promulgated by the Executive Office of Human Services of the Commonwealth of Massachusetts.

424.44 *Requirements for Egress and Escape Routes:* All main egress doors must swing in the anticipated direction of egress or escape where practicable.

424.5 *Fire Protection Features.*

424.51. *Hazardous Vertical Openings:* Hazardous Vertical Openings such as laundry chutes, dumb waiters, heating plenums or combustible concealed spaces shall be enclosed or protected with a minimum of three-eights (⅜) inch gypsum sheet rock on the side of the expected exposure to delay the spread of fire and smoke. Automatic detection systems as specified in Section 6 shall be provided in each space.

424.52 *Smoke Screens:* For the purpose of this Code a solid bonded core smokestop wood door with an automatic closer will be acceptable as a divider in providing two noncrossing, independent, egress routes.

424.53. *Interior Finish:* Only Class A and B Interior Finishes shall be permitted in the principal means of egress (to flame spread of seventy-five (75)). In the refinishing of any area, materials with a flame spread rating in excess of two hundred (200) are not allowed.

424.6 *Alarm Detection System:* An approved automatic fire/smoke detector system and alarm system shall be provided.

424.61 *Types and Locations of Detectors:*

Type	Location
Products of Combustion	Principal means of egress on each floor.
Smoke Detectors	Living-Dining-Recreation Areas.
Rate of Rise Detectors	Boiler Room-Kitchen-Bedroom.
Fixed Temperature Detectors	Closets and vent shafts, and concealed spaces.

424.62. *Types and Locations of Alarms:*

Type	Location
Manual Sending	Each exit of principal means of egress.*
Manual Sending	One outdoor alarm of a type acceptable to local Fire Departments; maximum two hundred (200) feet from building.*
Automatic Connection to Manual	From each detector.

424.63. *Alarm Sounding and Visible Devices:* Alarm sounding devices shall be provided of such character and so distributed as to be effectively heard in every room above all other sounds. Visible alarm devices may be used only in conjunction with an approved back-up system, and where specifically approved.

Every alarm sounding device shall be distinctive in pitch and quality from all other sounding devices.

424.64. *Maintenance and Supervision:* Each detector (or system) and alarm shall be provided with a signal (either visible or audible) to indicate when it is not capable of functioning according to its designed purpose; and shall be periodically inspected and certified by the licensing agency. The entire electrical alarm and detector system circuit shall be designed so that the disruption of any part of the continuous circuit will set off an alarm.

424.7. *Fire-Fighting Equipment.* Manually operated fire-fighting equipment such as hand extinguishers, shall be available to the custodian and other designated personnel.

424.8. *Inspection:* Inspections shall be made frequently by authorized inspectors to insure conformance with this Code. The results of such inspec-

---

*To municipal fire department as well, wherein practicable.

tions shall be reported to the licensing agency on a prepared checklist and signed by the authorized inspector.

424.9 *Final Certification of Occupant:* After preliminary certification by those qualified certifying personnel as specified in 9 CHSR S.51 Title 9 Code of Human Services Regulations, Section 51, each occupant must be certified at regular intervals but not less than once every quarter at the place of proposed residency by the licensing agency.

Capability of Self-Preservation

Part I—Orienting Information

Capability of Self-Preservation: A Requirement for Citizens Living in Group Residences Licensed by Human Services Agencies of the Commonwealth

The Executive Office of Human Services, in collaboration with the Massachusetts State Building Code Commission, has developed a unique dual set of requirements which will insure that citizens living in group residences licensed by agencies of the Commonwealth will be safe in case of fire.

The State Building Code Commission has adopted a building code which enables group residences to retain a family, home-like quality and to be safe at the same time. This building code emphasizes maximum opportunity for safety from fire based on a philosophy of a safe, speedy exit from the building rather than finding refuge within it. To make this possible, the code calls for adequate fire prevention, detection, alarm and adequate escape routes.

In developing this code, the Commission stipulated that residents must be certified to be *capable of self-preservation,* i.e. able to take care of themselves and evacuate the residence in case of fire. This instruction sheet is a narrative summary of regulations promulgated by the Executive Office of Human Services to insure capability of self-preservation (9 CHSR S.51). *As of January 1, 1975, these regulations will be promulgated by individual licensing agencies of the Commonwealth.* These regulations provide that residents must have:

a) sufficient capacity to recognize the physical danger of fire;

b) sufficient judgement to recognize when such danger requires immediate egress from a group residence;

c) sufficient capacity to follow a prescribed route of egress; and
d) sufficient physical mobility to accomplish such egress.

The following points highlight the tenor of the regulations:

1. All persons living in group residences will have to be formally certified by a uniform test as capable of self-preservation. No resident or applicant (potential resident) may be admitted or sleep overnight in a group residence unless they have been given and have passed one of these tests (51.15). Persons who are residents on the effective date of these regulations must be certified within ninety (90) days.

2. The Capability of Self-Preservation test has two sections. The first section (Questions 1–3) may be administered at a referral site as a means of pre-screening the applicant. If all three questions are answered satisfactorily, the second part of the test must then be administered at the proposed group residence site. Where there has been no referral, the entire test may be administered at the proposed group residence.

3. Personnel who administer the tests for capability of self-preservation must be qualified by training or experience. The appropriate requirements are to be determined by the agency or program which employs such personnel (51.16).

4. If a person cannot pass the *standard* test for capability of self-preservation, a *modified* test may be given. This modified test will be used in the event that the individual being tested has difficulty in understanding abstract ideas (e.g. mental retardation) or in articulating answers verbally. If necessary, pictures are available to assist in illustrating the questions.

5. Persons tested according to the standard or modified test may be given general or limited certification. *General Certification* means that a person is capable of self-preservation from all locations within a group residence. *Limited Certification* means that a person is capable of self-preservation only from a certain location(s) within the group residence. In this latter case, the resident would receive limited certification, with the limitation placed on his living situation specified on the testing instrument (51.20).

6. If the person in charge of a group residence has reason to believe that a resident has become incapable of self-preservation, he must readminister the capability of self-preservation instrument. If the resident fails the test, the person in charge of the group residence shall arrange for alternative residential arrangements, as quickly as possible (51.22).

7. If a resident terminates his living arrangement at a group residence but

seeks to return at any time, he must then be retested for capability of self-preservation (51.23).

Appeals, confidentiality of records, reexamination of residents and further details are outlined in the regulations themselves. More explicit instructions for administering the test(s) are included with the testing instrument.

Questions concerning these regulations or the testing instrument should be referred to the relevant group residence office of the licensing or operating agency.

Code of Human Services Regulations

Title 9—Human Services

Chapter I—General Provisions

Part 51—Certification of Capability of Self-Preservation

Subpart A—Purpose, Authority and Effective Date

§ 51.01 *Purpose*

In order to qualify as a group residence, a residential care facility licensed or operated by a state agency must show that its residents are capable of self-preservation. This part establishes the procedures for complying with this requirement.

§ 51.02 *Authority*

This part is promulgated by the Secretary pursuant to G.L. c. 143, § 1. This citation of authority conforms to the requirements of 1 CHSR 26.45.

§ 51.03 *Effective date*

This part shall take effect on September 30, 1974.

Subpart B—Definitions

§ 51.05 *Meaning of terms in this part*

As used in this part, unless the context otherwise requires, terms shall have the meanings ascribed in this subpart.

§ 51.06 *Applicant*

"Applicant" means a person who has applied to become a resident or who is being referred to a group residence.

§ 51.07 *Capable of self-preservation*

"Capable of self-preservation" means having, as determined pursuant to this part, the following capabilities in an emergency situation:

(a) sufficient capacity to recognize the physical danger of fire;

(b) sufficient judgment to recognize when such danger requires immediate egress from a group residence;

(c) sufficient capacity to follow a prescribed route of egress; and

(d) sufficient physical mobility to accomplish such egress.

§ 51.08   *Group residence*

"Group residence" means a premises, licensed or operated by a state agency, for the residential care in any single building of not more than twelve unrelated persons between the ages of seven and fifteen inclusive, or of not more than the number of persons sixteen years of age or over as may be approved by the licensing or operating state agency, who are capable of self-preservation.

§ 51.09   *Resident*

"Resident" means a person living in a group residence for the purpose of receiving residential care.

§ 51.10   *State agency*

"State agency" means any department or agency of the Commonwealth.

Subpart C—Certification Procedure

§ 51.15   *General rule*

Applicants shall be individually certified as capable of self-preservation before beginning to live in a group residence; provided, however, that persons who are residents on the effective date of these regulations pursuant to § 51.03 shall be so certified within ninety days thereafter.

§ 51.16   *Qualification of certifying personnel*

Personnel who administer tests for capability of self-preservation shall be qualified to do so by training or experience or both. Each agency, facility or program which employs such personnel and each group residence shall establish appropriate requirements of training or experience for such personnel.

§ 51.17   *Administration of tests*

Capability of self-preservation shall be determined by administration of a test or tests prescribed by the Secretary. The person administering any such test shall be qualified pursuant to § 51.16 and shall record both the questions asked and the responses. Each such test shall measure the following capabilities:

(a) physical sensory perceptions, i.e., whether the applicant can see or hear sufficiently to recognize the physical danger of fire;

(b) physical mobility, i.e., whether the applicant possesses the necessary physical mobility to leave a dangerous place quickly;

(c) mental ability to identify and judge the kinds of danger requiring immediate exit; and

(d) mental ability to understand communication and to follow a route of egress.

§ 51.18 *Tests at group residences; evacuation time*

Each such test shall include a part which shall be administered at the group residence in which the resident resides or the applicant intends to reside. The test at the group residence shall include a test of the time taken by the resident or applicant to evacuate the building. The time taken to accomplish total evacuation of the building shall not exceed one minute per floor, with a maximum time of two and one-half minutes.

§ 51.19 *Training and retesting; interval of twenty-four hours*

Any person who fails a test administered pursuant to this part may be trained and retested; provided, that there shall be an interval of at least twenty-four hours between completion of training and the administration of the test.

§ 51.20 *Limited certification*

A person who cannot be certified as capable of self-preservation with respect to every location in a group residence may be certified on a limited basis as capable of self-preservation in particular locations within that group residence. Such person shall be given an opportunity for site visits and training in self-preservation at the group residence conducted by the appropriate licensing or operating agency, referring agency, facility, program, or group residence. Appropriate certifying personnel qualified pursuant to § 51.16 shall then administer, in the group residence, a test prescribed pursuant to § 51.17. If the person passes, he shall be certified as capable of self-preservation in particular locations only within that residence. The precise nature of his disability, the nature of his training, and the limitations placed on his living situation (e.g., room on the first floor), shall be part of his certification record.

§ 51.21 *Reexamination*

Each group residence shall conduct a quarterly reexamination of each resident to determine capability of self-preservation. Such reexamination shall be conducted by personnel qualified to make certifications pursuant to § 51.16. The group residence may execute a new certification instrument at the time of such reexamination but it shall not send a copy of such instrument pursuant to § 51.26. The group residence shall annually send a checklist showing that it has complied with this section to the agency which licenses or operates it; provided, that any group residence which is licensed by the Office for Children but which has a contract with any other state agency shall send such copies to the state agency or agencies with which it contracts.

§ 51.22 *Persons who may not be capable of self-preservation*

If the person in charge of a group residence has reason to believe that a resident has become incapable of self-preservation, he shall promptly cause his capability of self-preservation to be determined pursuant to § 51.15. If the resident fails the test so administered, the person in charge of the group residence shall immediately make alternative residential arrangements or contact the resident's guardian or closest relative or the state agency, facility or program which referred the resident to the group residence. Such guardian, relative, agency, facility or program shall make alternate residential arrangements as quickly as practicable.

§ 51.23 *Termination of living arrangements*

If, in the judgment of the staff of a group residence, a resident terminates his living arrangements at such group residence, but seeks to return at any time, his capability of self-preservation shall again be determined pursuant to § 51.15.

Subpart D—Certification Records

§ 51.25 *Instruments executed* partially at referring agencies

Each referring agency, facility or program shall execute a certification instrument for each applicant but shall not execute that part of the instrument which is to be executed at a group residence pursuant to § 51.18. The group residence shall complete the instrument pursuant to § 51.18 and shall return a copy of the completed instrument to the referring agency, facility or program.

§ 51.26 *Instruments executed entirely at group residences*

Except as provided in § 51.21, each group residence shall send a copy of any certification instrument executed entirely at the group residence (i.e., where there has been no referral) to the agency which licenses or operates it within seven days after the certified person becomes a resident; provided, that any group residence which is licensed by the Office for Children but which has a contract regarding such resident with any other state agency shall send such copy to such state agency. Any such copy shall include the first name, last initial and date of birth of the person so certified but shall not include any other identifying information. In the case of persons who are residents on the effective date of this part pursuant to § 51.03, such copies shall be so sent within seven days after they are executed.

§ 51.27 *Retention of certification records*

Each group residence and each agency, facility, or program which receives a copy pursuant to §§ 51.25 and 51.26 shall retain a copy of the certification instrument for each resident for at least the period of his residence.

§ 51.28 *Confidentiality*

All certification records shall be confidential. No person or agency other than the applicant or resident, the group residence, its licensing or operating agency, the referring agency, facility or program, if any, and the EOHS shall have access to an applicant's or resident's certification records, except as provided in this part.

Subpart E—Appeals

§ 51.30 *Rights of appeal*

An applicant or resident shall have the right to appeal a determination that he is not capable of self-preservation. He shall also have the right to appeal a determination pursuant to § 51.21 that he is capable of self-preservation only in a particular location within a group residence.

§ 51.31 *State agency to which appeal is made*

Any appeal under § 51.30 shall be made to the state agency, if any, which made the determination, otherwise to the state agency operating or licensing the group residence in which the appellant lives or seeks to live.

§ 51.32 *Appeal procedure*

A person who appeals shall avail himself of the state agency's existing appeal procedure, if any. If none, the state agency shall devise an appeal procedure which fairly protects the rights of the appellant.

§ 51.33 *Appeal not to delay alternate arrangements*

An appeal of a resident shall not operate to delay the procedures pursuant to § 51.22 for making alternate residential arrangements for the resident.

§ 51.34   *Prompt admission of successful appellants*
A successful appellant shall promptly be declared eligible for admission
or readmission to the group residence.

Part II—Test Material

This packet includes the tests for capability of self-preservation. A person
must pass either the *Standard or Modified Certification Test* in order to live
in a group residence for the purpose of receiving residential care. The
person's answers to the questions on the test should be recorded on the
testing form with *A PIECE OF CARBON PAPER INSERTED BETWEEN
THE ORIGINAL AND SECOND COPIES.* The forms must be filled out by
an individual qualified to certify capability of self-preservation as specified
in the accompanying regulations (PART I—ORIENTING INFORMA-
TION).

Both the Standard and the Modified Tests may be administered in one of
two ways:

1. Questions 1–3 may be administered at the referral site as a means of
prescreening the applicant. If all three questions are answered satisfactorily, the second part of the test (Question #4) must then be administered *at
the proposed group residence site.* The group residence shall complete the
instrument and shall return the carbon copy of the completed instrument to
the referring agency, facility or program.

2. Where there has been no referral, the entire test may be administered
at the proposed group residence. If the applicant is certified as capable of
self-preservation, the group residence shall send the carbon copy of the
certification instrument to the agency which licenses it within seven days
after the certified person becomes a resident; provided that any group
residence which is licensed by the Office for Children but which has a
contract with any other state agency shall send the carbon copy to the state
agency with which it contracts for that individual. Any such copy shall
include the first name, last initial and date of birth of the person so certified
but shall not include any other identifying information.

If a person fails the Standard Test he/she may be given the Modified Test
immediately *or* may be trained and re-tested with the Standard Test, provided that there be a twenty-four hour interval between the last training
and the testing day. If the individual fails the Modified Test, he/she may be
trained and re-tested, provided that there is a twenty-four hour interval
between the last training and the testing day.

General and Limited Certification

Persons tested according to the Standard or Modified Test may be given General or Limited Certification.

General Certification means that a person is capable of self-preservation from *all* locations within the group residence.

Limited Certification means that a person is capable of self-preservation only from a certain location(s) within the group residence. For example, a person with a physical handicap might be capable of leaving the residence within two and half minutes from the ground floor only—in this case, she/he would receive limited certification with the limitations placed on his living situation *specified on the instrument.*

I: STANDARD CAPABILITY OF SELF-PRESERVATION TEST

NAME OF PERSON BEING TESTED: _____

                            First Name   Last Initial   Date of Birth

PROPOSED GROUP RESIDENCE: _____

ADDRESS: _____ PHONE: _____

TESTING DATE (Day/Month/Year): _____

REFERRAL SITE (If any): _____

ADDRESS: _____ PHONE: _____

TESTER AT REFERRAL SITE (If any): _____

TESTER AT GROUP RESIDENCE: _____

               ****

1. Name some ways you can tell when there's a fire: _____

_____

    NOTE: To answer this question satisfactorily, three of the following six
           indicators must be mentioned. If not enough accurate answers are given,
           tester should ask "WHAT ELSE?"

		SAT.	UNSAT.
1.	Seeing smoke	_____	_____
2.	Smelling smoke	_____	_____
3.	Seeing flames	_____	_____
4.	Feeling heat	_____	_____
5.	Hearing an alarm bell	_____	_____
6.	Hearing someone yell "FIRE"	_____	_____

2. What would you do if the house you were in were on fire? _____

_____

    NOTE: To answer this question satisfactorily, the answer must include mentioning
           leaving, getting out of the house, etc.

                                        SAT. _____   UNSAT. _____

3. This question is to be asked only if the first part of the test is administered at a referral site. If the entire test is administered at a community residence, skip this question and go on to #4.

> "Please open the door and come back."

NOTE: Applicant must open the closed door. As soon as this is accomplished, tester should ask him/her to return.

TIME TAKEN: _____
> (This should be accomplished within 30 seconds)

> SAT. _____   UNSAT. _____

4. This question must be tested at the proposed group residence.

A. "Please leave this house."

NOTE: Person must be able to leave the residence from the sleeping quarters by the main route of egress. Maximum time acceptable: 2 1/2 minutes.

TIME TAKEN: _____

> SAT. _____   UNSAT. _____

B. "Please leave this house."

NOTE: Person must be able to leave the residence from the sleeping quarters by an alternative route of egress while the main route is temporarily blocked. Maximum time acceptable: 2 1/2 minutes.

TIME TAKEN: _____

> SAT. _____   UNSAT. _____

CONCLUSIONS OF TEST ADMINISTRATOR:

	SAT.	UNSAT.
Question #1	_____	_____
Question #2	_____	_____
Question #3	_____	_____
Question #4A	_____	_____
Question #4B	_____	_____

To be capable of self-preservation there must be no unsatisfactory scores.

_____ Capable of self-preservation at this time.

> _____ General

> _____ Limited (Specify restrictions) _____

_____ Not capable of self-preservation at this time.

II: MODIFIED CERTIFICATION TEST

This test may be used instead of the Standard Certification Test. It may
be administered verbally, and if thought necessary the pictures in the accompanying
booklet (Part III) may be used to accompany each item in Questions #1 and #2.

NAME OF PERSON BEING TESTED: _____

                       First Name   Last Initial   Date of Birth

----

PROPOSED GROUP RESIDENCE: _____

ADDRESS: _____

TESTING DATE (DAY/MONTH/YEAR): _____

REFERRAL SITE (If any): _____

ADDRESS: _____

TESTER AT REFERRAL SITE (If any): _____

TESTER AT GROUP RESIDENCE: _____

----

1. Is there a fire?   YES   NO

    a. If you see a lot of smoke?   _____   _____

    b. If you see flames?   _____   _____

    c. If you smell a flower?   _____   _____

    d. If you hear a fire alarm?   _____   _____

    e. If you hear a watch ticking?   _____   _____

        (CORRECT ANSWERS: YES=A,B,D;   NO=C,E)

                                  SAT. _____   UNSAT. _____

2. If there is a fire, should you   YES   NO

    a. Stay in bed?   _____   _____

    b. Leave the house?   _____   _____

    c. Hide in the closet?   _____   _____

        (CORRECT ANSWERS: YES=B;   NO=A,C)

                                  SAT. _____   UNSAT. _____

3. This question is to be asked only if the first part of the test is administered at a referral site. If the entire test is given at a community residence, skip this question and go on to #4.

"Please open the door fast and come back."

NOTE: Applicant must open the closed door. As soon as this is accomplished, tester should ask him/her to return. Maximum time acceptable: 30 seconds

TIME TAKEN: _____

SAT. _____   UNSAT. _____

4. This question must be tested at the proposed group residence.

A. "Please leave this house."

NOTE: Person must be able to leave the residence from the sleeping quarters by the main route of egress. Maximum time acceptable: 2 1/2 minutes.

TIME TAKEN: _____   SAT. _____   UNSAT. _____

B. "Please leave this house."

NOTE: Person must be able to leave the residence from the sleeping quarters by the alternative route of egress while the main route is temporarily blocked. Maximum time acceptable: 2 1/2 minutes.

TIME TAKEN: _____   SAT._____   UNSAT. _____

CONCLUSIONS OF TEST ADMINISTRATOR:

	SAT.	UNSAT.
Question #1	_____	_____
Question #2	_____	_____
Question #3	_____	_____
Question #4 A	_____	_____
Question #4 B	_____	_____

To be capable of self-preservation there must be no unsatisfactory scores.

_____ Capable of self-preservation at this time.

_____ General

_____ Limited (Specify restrictions) _____

_____ Not capable of self-preservation at this time.

Proposed Zoning Law

An Act to Regulate the Numbers of Group Residences in Cities, Towns, and Wards

Section 1. Chapter 23B of the General Laws is hereby amended by inserting after section 5A the following section:—

Section 5B. There shall be within the department a group residence appeals committee consisting of seven members, including the five members of the housing appeals committee established under section five A of this chapter, one member to be appointed by the secretary of the executive office of human services who shall be an officer or employee of said office or of a department within said office responsible for operating or licensing group residences and one member to be appointed by the director of the office for children who shall be an officer or employee of said office. Members shall serve for terms of one year and may be reappointed. The commissioner shall designate one of the members to serve as chairman.

A member of the committee shall receive no compensation for his services, but shall be reimbursed by the commonwealth for all reasonable expenses actually and necessarily incurred in the performance of his official duties. Said committee shall hear all petitions for review filed under section twenty-three C of chapter forty B, and shall conduct said hearings in accordance with rules and regulations established by the commissioner.

The department shall provide such space and clerical and other assistance as the committee may require.

Section 2. Chapter 40B of the General Laws is hereby amended by inserting after Section 23 the following sections:—

Section 23A. The following words, whenever used in this section and in sections 23B to 23D, inclusive, shall, unless a different meaning clearly appears from the context, have the following meanings:—

"Group residence," a premises, licensed or operated by or under contract
to a department or agency of the commonwealth, for the residential care in
any single building of not more than twelve unrelated persons between the
ages of seven and fifteen, inclusive, or of not more than the number of
persons sixteen years of age or over as may be approved by the licensing,
contracting, or operating department or agency, who are capable of self-
preservation as certified in accordance with procedures established by the
Secretary of Human Services.

"Infeasible," any condition caused by any single factor or combination of
factors which unreasonably restricts the establishment or operation of a
group residence.

"Consistent with community needs," requirements and regulations shall
be considered consistent with community needs if they are reasonable in
view of the need to protect the health or safety of the occupants of the
proposed group residence of the city, town, or ward and if such requirements and regulations are applied as equally as possible to all housing.
Requirements or regulations shall be consistent with community needs
when imposed by a board of zoning appeals after comprehensive hearings in
a city, town, or ward are in excess of five percent of the housing units
reported in the latest decennial census of the city, town, or ward.

"Policy objectives of the Commonwealth relative to group residences,"
the policy objectives of the Commonwealth are that mentally, physically,
and socially handicapped persons should to the maximum extent possible,
have the opportunity to receive care in group residences where they can
live in normal residential surroundings rather than in large impersonal
institutions. County and municipal zoning ordinances and building codes,
and other ordinances and administrative interpretations thereof, should not
unreasonably obstruct the creation and operation of group residences. Each
city and town in the commonwealth should be prepared to assume some
responsibility in the placement of group residences; however, no city or
town should bear a disproportionate share.

"Local board," any town or city board of survey, board of health, board of
subdivision control appeals, planning board, building inspector or the officer or board having supervision of the construction of building or the power
of enforcing municipal building codes, or any city council, board of aldermen, or selectmen, or town meeting.

"Person," any individual, partnership, corporation, association or organization or any department, agency or institution of the federal government
or of the Commonwealth or any political subdivision thereof.

Section 23B. Any person proposing to build or to operate a group residence may submit to the board of appeals, established under section fourteen of chapter forty A, a single application to build or operate such group residence in lieu of separate applications to the applicable local boards. The board of appeals shall forthwith notify each such local board, as applicable, of the filing of such application by sending a copy thereof to such local boards for their recommendations and shall, within thirty days of the receipt of such application, hold a public hearing on the same. The board of appeals shall request the appearance at said hearing of such representatives of said local boards as are deemed necessary or helpful in making its decision upon such application and shall have the same power to issue permits or approvals as any local board or official who would otherwise act with respect to such application, including but not limited to the power to attach to said permit or approval conditions and requirements with respect to height, site plan, size or shape, or building materials as are consistent with the terms of this section. The board of appeals, in making its decision on said application, shall take into consideration the recommendations of the local boards and shall have the authority to use the testimony of consultants. The provisions of section seventeen of chapter forty A shall apply to all hearings. The board of appeals shall render a decision, based upon a majority vote of said board, within forty days after the termination of the public hearing and if favorable to the applicant, shall forthwith issue a comprehensive permit or approval; provided, however, that the board of appeals shall not issue any permit or approval that would permit the building or operation of a group residence unless the applicant is able to substantially comply with the building code applicable to group residences and is licensed or operated by or under contract to a department or agency of the commonwealth, or can show that such license will issue or such contract be signed upon granting of such comprehensive permit or approval. If said hearing is not convened or a decision is not rendered within the time allowed, unless the time has been extended by mutual agreement between the board and the applicant, the application shall be deemed to have been allowed and the comprehensive permit or approval shall forthwith issue. Any person aggrieved by the issuance of a comprehensive permit or approval may appeal to the court as provided in section twenty-one of chapter forty A.

Section 23C. Whenever an application filed under the provisions of section twenty-three B is denied or is granted with such conditions and requirements as to make the building or operation of such group residence infeasible, the applicant shall have the right to appeal to the group residence appeals committee in the department of community affairs for a review of the same. Such appeal shall be taken within twenty days after the date of the notice of the decision by the board of appeals by filing with said committee a statement of the prior proceedings and the reasons upon which the appeal is based. The committee shall forthwith notify the board of appeals by filing of such petition for review and the latter shall, within ten days of the receipt of such notice, transmit a copy of its decision and the reasons thereof to the committee. Such appeal shall be heard by the committee within twenty days after receipt of the applicant's statement. A stenographic record of the proceedings shall be kept and the committee shall render a written decision, based upon a majority vote, stating its findings of fact, its conclusions and the reasons therefor within thirty days after the termination of the hearing, unless such time shall have been extended by mutual agreement between the committee and the applicant. Such decision may be reviewed in the superior court in accordance with the provisions of chapter thirty A.

Section 23D. The hearing by the group residence appeals committee established by section five B of chapter twenty-three B shall be limited to the issue of whether, in the case of the denial of an application, the decision of the board of appeals was consistent with community needs and with the policy objectives of the commonwealth relative to group residences. In the case of an approval of an application with conditions and requirements imposed, the group residence appeals committee shall determine whether such conditions and requirements make the establishment or operation of such group residence infeasible and whether they are consistent with the community needs and the policy objectives of the commonwealth relative to group residences. If the group residence appeals committee finds, in the case of a denial, that the decision of the board of appeals was unreasonable and not consistent with community needs and the policy objectives of the commonwealth relative to group residences, it shall vacate such decision and shall direct the board to issue a comprehensive permit or approval to the applicant. If said committee finds, in the case of an approval with conditions and requirements imposed, that the decision of the board makes the establishment or operation of such group residence infeasible and is not consistent with community needs and the policy objectives of the commonwealth relative to group residences, it shall order such board to modify or remove such conditions or requirements and to issue any necessary permit or approval; provided, however, that the committee shall not issue any order which would permit the establishment or operation of a group residence unless the applicant is able to substantially comply with the building code applicable to group residences and is licensed or operated by or under contract to a department or agency of the commonwealth, or can show that such license will issue or such contract be signed upon granting of such comprehensive permit or approval.

Decisions or conditions and requirements imposed by a board of appeals that are consistent with community needs shall not be vacated, modified or removed by the committee.

The group residence appeals committee or the petitioner shall have the power to enforce the orders of the committee at law or in equity in the superior court. The board of appeals shall carry out the order of the group residence appeals committee within thirty days of its entry and upon failure to do so, the order of said committee shall, for all purposes, be deemed to be the action of said board, unless the petitioner consents to a different decision or order by such board.

Berkeley House Brochure

Berkeley House: A Good Place to Live is an illustrated, attractively printed brochure that is distributed to mental health agencies, prospective applicants, and others. It includes the telephone numbers of the director and house managers, a statement of ownership, and a request for donations. Only the text is reproduced in this appendix.

What Berkeley House Is

Berkeley House is a private lodging house which is owned and operated by the McLean Hospital Division of the Massachusetts General Hospital. It has been established for the purpose of providing a good place to live for people who have been troubled emotionally. It provides a transitional living arrangement, intermediate between psychiatric hospital and home. Lack of such facilities has meant that some hospitalized people have been either delayed in leaving the hospital or have had an unnecessarily stormy and difficult time in achieving independent living. The existence of such a facility means that others for whom hospitalization is not yet indicated can now gain from the beneficial milieu and temporary detachment from their homes which can be provided by such a lodging house—perhaps preventing the necessity for hospitalization in the future.

The aim of Berkeley House is to provide a warm, familylike atmosphere that can help people who are eager to grow in their capacity to live rich, meaningful lives. The goal is to help the resident not only increase his ability to be appropriately close to others, but also to more fully develop his strengths in being independent. It is hoped that this will be achieved through the cooperative efforts of all of the members of the House—both residents and house managers. Mutual exchange of ideas and experiences, sharing of problems encountered at work and at school, supporting a fellow resident at a time of stress, going together to a ball game, movie or concert,

243

helping in house cleaning—all of these are potential avenues that can help lead the resident toward trusting, respecting, affectionate relationships with his fellows. Simultaneously, he will be increasing his skills in independent living.

The House itself is a five-story townhouse located in Boston in the vicinity of the Public Garden. There are accommodations for up to twenty-four residents, male and female. All rooms are doubles except for one triple and three single rooms. There are also ample common rooms for social activity, including a living room and TV room on the first floor and a large area on the ground level which has a soda machine, a washer and dryer and room for TV and a ping pong table.

The location of Berkeley House is optimal for multiple functions. Jobs are readily available due to the nearness of downtown Boston stores and businesses. Several schools and colleges are in the immediate neighborhood. Entertainment and recreation facilities that are within walking distance include many movie theaters, the Prudential Center and War Memorial Auditorium and the Charles River Esplanade. Churches of all denominations, the Boston Public Library and Fenway Park are also nearby. For accessibility to activities not within walking distance, MBTA rapid transit is only three short blocks away.

Responsible for the house in its day to day operations is a married couple who act as the House Managers. They live in the House, collect the rent and oversee the general maintenance of the House. They are devoted and committed to the goal of fostering a warm, supportive and, at other times, appropriately demanding environment for people to live in. They meet with the residents in regular House meetings to discuss issues concerning the entire group. At other times they are available as friends, bridge partners, confidantes, travel guides, bull sessioners and sailing instructors.

After leaving Berkeley House, alumni who live nearby continue to relate to the House through its ex-resident program. This includes informal use of the House for maintaining continuing friendships, occasional dinners and social gathering, as well as intermittent meeting with staff members when appropriate. The alumni may join the ex-resident group which meets weekly and focuses on common problems of independent living.

Berkeley House is in full compliance with Massachusetts Department of Mental Health regulations which apply to private facilities of its type.

Overall responsibility for the operation of the House is retained by a Director who is a psychiatrist holding a staff appointment at the McLean Hospital Division of the Massachusetts General Hospital.

What Berkeley House Is Not

Berkeley House is explicitly *not* a hospital nor a clinic—it is not a medical treatment center. There are no nurses. The House is left unattended by the Managers at times. Residents and their families should understand this explicitly. Anyone living at Berkeley House should be responsible and healthy enough to maintain himself without the intensive care characteristic of a hospital.

Who Lives in Berkeley House

Berkeley House is available for anyone who is in psychiatric treatment outside of the House, who is at least 17 years of age, and who has a bona fide program that occupies him during the day outside of the House such as school, a job, or in some cases an outside psychiatric day care program. Agreement of the outside therapeutic team and the family of the resident is required. Acceptable applicants include not only people who are leaving inpatient psychiatric services but also any person in treatment who may never have been hospitalized but who could benefit from a place to live that offers the special advantages of Berkeley House. Acceptable applicants who are discharged from McLean Hospital will be accommodated with priority; however, remaining space will be available to other applicants.

Berkeley House in the Neighborhood

Being a good neighbor in the community is another vital part of the life at Berkeley House. As any other residence in the area, we are committed to the maintenance of the quality of the neighborhood and readily take on our responsibility in good neighborliness. This is expressed in the external upkeep and cleanliness of the property and in participation and support of neighborhood cleanups. Just as any family would, we naturally maintain proper and appropriate restraint on our social behavior to avoid unpleasant intrusion into the peace and privacy of our neighbors, such as excessive noise and outside horseplay.

Financial Arrangements at Berkeley House

The resident will be expected to pay his own rent at the end of each month. All residents should have their own checking accounts to facilitate payment. Residents who are receiving financial aid from their families should make arrangements with them to insure a reasonable monthly bank balance. The details of the rate are found on the card inserted in this brochure.

Length of Stay at Berkeley House

The House is conceived of as being a place to live for not longer than a year. Residents moving out may, when desirable, easily live in one of the innumerable nearby apartments or rooming houses and continue to retain social contacts at the House through the ex-resident program. Thus, a smooth transition from the House to even more independent living is available. The House reserves the right to terminate the stay of any resident at the end of a year's residence or before if this is felt to be advisable by the House management.

Applying to Berkeley House

The applicant should telephone the House Managers to arrange an appointment with them at Berkeley House. At this meeting he will receive application forms to be completed by himself and members of his treatment team including therapists, administrative psychiatrist and social worker. It is the applicant's responsibility to distribute the various forms. The visit to the House will also give the applicant an opportunity to acquaint himself with the area, see the House and chat with residents and the House Managers.

When the House has received the completed forms the applicant will be notified, at which time he should arrange a meeting with the Director of the House. Finally, the entire treatment team meets with the House Managers and the Director. This meeting is to help them assess the suitability of the applicant for living at the House. Further, it provides an opportunity for the House management to meet the members of the treatment team to join in an effort at a common understanding of the applicant and his problems and to open communication lines between them. If the applicant is judged to be suitable for the House, he will be notified and arrangements made for moving in.

Applicants may be judged to be unsuitable for Berkeley House for a variety of reasons. The current population of the House may be felt to be unsuitable for the applicant—rather than the reverse. It may mean that an alternative living arrangement would be felt to be in the applicant's best interests—such as a foster home or an independent apartment. It may mean that the House management feels the applicant is not ready for the independence that is part of the House living. Finally, the applicant may be suitable but the House full. The applicant may then wish to be put on a "waiting list."

The final thinking of the House management will be reviewed in detail with each applicant. Even if an applicant is not judged to be suitable for the House, the House management hopes and intends that he or she will have had a growing, educational and worthwhile experience for having applied.

Berkeley House Policies

Robert and Cheryl Jolley

Instead of greeting each new resident at Berkeley House with a list of rules, our custom has been to talk over with them the house policies which have evolved since we opened and to hope that older residents would be helpful as well in orienting new people to the house. Over a period of time we, residents and management working together, have developed, especially through discussion at house meetings, a number of policies with reference to life in the house. To help avoid confusion and to help all our memories, this pamphlet outlines these basic policies according to which the house operates.

In Boston as in other large cities there are different kinds of rules by which people live. They are city codes, state regulations, and in most cases house standards, too. In the case of city and state regulations we have no jurisdiction, but most of the house policies have been worked out by those of us who are living in the house.

In the category of state laws, those which are relevant to operation of this house include laws against illicit narcotic drugs, a 5.7% state excise tax to be paid during the first 90 days of residence in a lodging house, and those relating to our status as a lodging house. Boston city laws affecting life in the house are numerous; included are those relating to fire safety and precautions, entrances and exits in the building, and the number of lodgers we may accommodate.

In the category of house policies we have generally operated on the basis of mutual understanding and consideration for the rights and privileges of all of the people living in the house. Even with this in mind, it has been necessary for us to be somewhat more definitive in certain areas.

Robert and Cheryl Jolley drafted these house policies when they were Berkeley House managers, 1970–1972.

Food and Meals

At Berkeley House we intend to provide plenty of wholesome, tasteful food. Residents make their own breakfasts and lunches with food supplied at the house. Some people drink a cup of coffee and others prefer a full hot breakfast to start their day. For those working or in school, sandwich meats, tuna fish, etc. are available to pack lunches, and those who happen to be eating in the house can usually find leftovers or soup in addition to sandwich materials.

The evening meal is a hot meal served family style each day Monday thru Thursday at 7:00, Fridays at 6:15, and Saturdays and Sundays at 6:00. Because of our feeling that the evening meal is an important aspect of life in the house, people are generally expected Monday through Friday for dinner. Exceptions have been for therapy, college classes, and other important activities. In order to plan for each meal we need to know in advance when people are not expecting to be here for dinner. Since more people do plan weekend activities out of the house, there is a sign-up sheet for Saturday and Sunday dinner which people are asked to check to indicate whether they will be in or out. On Sunday evenings the cook has a night off and we order out, usually chicken, pizza, or Chinese food. If you know you are going to be late, dinner can be saved if you let us know in advance.

There is generally snack food available, and both refrigerators, the freezer, and cupboards are open to residents for their use. With the exception of dinner, all dishes and cooking utensils used should be rinsed and placed in the dishwasher or washed and put away, and each person should be responsible for cleaning up after himself in the kitchen–dining room area. Dinner dishes and clean-up are done each evening except Sunday by two house residents. When the house is full this means that each person will be expected to take his turn two out of every three weeks.

House Meetings

House meetings are a vital part of the structure and program of the house. It is an important opportunity for discussing general issues regarding the house and personal issues. Currently our house meetings begin at 8:00 each Monday evening, and people are expected to attend.

Visitors and Guests

Guests at Berkeley House fall into a number of different categories: outside visitors, dinner guests, and overnight guests. Separate policies have been evolved dealing with each of these categories.

Outside visitors are encouraged to visit the house. House policy permits outside visitors in residents' rooms from 9 A.M. to 11 P.M. weekdays and from 11 A.M. to 1 A.M. on weekends. Community rooms on the first floor and lower level are always available for visiting.

Guests are likewise welcome to join us for meals. We need at least one day's advance notice unless checking with the cook indicates an abundance of food for that particular meal. In any event, there will be a $1.00 charge for any meal guest, payable to the house manager.

A provision has been made in order that overnight guests may be accommodated in the house. However, the responsibility for arranging an overnight visit must be taken by the resident. Only if there is an available bed in the house will overnight guests be permitted. There are times when residents have made arrangements to be out of the house on a given night, at which time their beds would become available for guests. It is to be understood that male guests will stay only in beds being used by males and that female guests will stay only in beds being used by females. It will be necessary for the resident expecting the guest to clear his plan in advance both with the resident whose bed will be used and with the house managers. When the guest arrives, both guest and resident will be expected to meet with the house managers to fill out a registration card, and to review with the managers relevant house policies. There is a $3.00 charge levied for each night a visitor stays, which includes dinner and breakfast. Lunch would be an additional $1.00.

Since some visitors in the house may not know about out status or people's connection with the hospital, we ask that you use your own best judgment and discretion in a situation where someone's date or friend is in the house as a stranger to you.

Sex

At Berkeley House we have tried to provide numerous areas on the lower floors where groups or couples can get together to talk, study, watch T.V., etc. These are public rooms which do have semiprivate niches. In any of the rooms above the second floor, however, any sexual behavior at all has been forbidden.

Drugs

There are people at Berkeley House who are taking prescribed medication. For each new resident, a small metal combination lock box is provided for medication and other valuables. Any use of, or possession of, any illicit or narcotic drugs in the house is strictly prohibited, and violation of this policy may be grounds for asking someone to leave the house.

Alcohol

Although some people at Berkeley House are old enough and mature enough to consume alcoholic beverages, others are not. Because it is illegal for those under 21 to be served and because of the detrimental effects drinking can have on some people, alcoholic beverages of all kinds are prohibited in the house. There are bars and lounges nearby for people who are of age and do desire an occasional drink.

Noise

We live in a neighborhood of close proximity to our neighbors and generally try to be as considerate of them as we expect them to be of us. Many realtors in Boston comply with a code limiting noise after 11:00 P.M. Although, we do not belong to that particular organization, we do try to cooperate. Our expectation is that stereos, radios, and other sound equipment will be turned down to a low volume after 11:00 P.M.

Nudity and Privacy

We are coeducational and because of the physical structure of the building, passages between bedrooms and bathrooms are not absolutely private. Although we have not specified proper or improper attire for late-night trips to the bathroom, it is expected that people will dress with a modicum of decency. The fire doors on each bedroom serve a dual function of fire protection and privacy, and it is expected that people will not appear nude in any of the upstairs halls or foyers.

Hours

Unlike some boarding schools and other such institutions, we have not found it necessary to create or impose curfews or bed checks. We do, however, want to know where people are, whether they are in or out and if out when they expect to return, particularly in the evening. We want to be notified before you leave where you are going, and when you expect to be in. A note on the hall table is sufficient notice. If you are not planning to be in by 12:00 midnight or for some reason cannot make it in by that time, we expect to be called. If we do not know we become concerned and would notify the director, your family, therapist, and the police in that order, if it became necessary. If we did not show up by the time we are expected we would want you to begin to make the same kinds of inquiries about us. If you are planning to be gone overnight, we need to be informed personally that you are leaving and need a name, phone number, and address where you could be reached should that become necessary. If you are planning to be gone from the house for more than two days, either the house managers or the director must be consulted in advance.

Keys

Each resident at Berkeley House is issued a front door key and a room key. A $3.00 fee will be charged for each lost key. It is the keys and not the $3.00 which we are interested in. If you do not have one, a key ring might be a wise investment.

Linen

We do have a linen service at Berkeley House and will provide each resident with a pillowcase and two clean sheets each week. Each resident is responsible for making his own bed and seeing that dirty linen gets put in the laundry bags on each floor by Monday morning early. Towels are not provided, and each resident is expected to provide his own. We do have a coin-operated washer and dryer on the lower level for the use of house residents. There are an ironing board and iron in the sewing room and numerous dry-cleaning establishments located within walking distance of the house.

Parking

Parking in downtown Boston is a problem for anyone with a car. Unfortunately we cannot help. The three spaces which we have in back of the house are reserved for the director, the managers, and hospital or other service and repair men. Street parking is an alternative—read the signs carefully as Marlborough Street meter maids seem to do an active business. The Boston Common Underground Garage is about a 15 minute walk, but the reservation waiting list gets lengthy each fall with the influx of students and the approach of winter. The St. James Street Garage on Berkeley and St. James Street is only a 10 minute walk but has no reserved spaces. Some people do manage to rent back-alley spaces from realtors. Most of our residents have managed very well using nearby public transportation.

Anonymity and Neighbors

One of our hopes about Berkeley House is that we can provide a setting much like the other apartment and lodging houses in our area. We feel it is beneficial to the house generally and to the individuals living here that we remain as anonymous as possible with regard to our McLean Hospital affiliation and the background of our residents. In order to maintain this anonymity it is necessary for each of you to be aware and careful in your dealings with neighbors, salesmen at the door, or guests of other house residents. All inquiries at the door or by phone should be referred to the house managers for them to handle.

Fire Precautions and Emergencies

In keeping with fire safety and prevention codes, there are a number of preventive measures with which each person in the house needs to be familiar. There are trash cans located on each floor in the back stairway where individual wastebaskets should be emptied. Keeping ashtrays and wastebaskets emptied will help keep the fire danger in the building low. There is a local in-house alarm with pull boxes on each floor in the central hallway. Each floor has its own fire extinguisher located on the back stair landing. There are heat detectors in each of the bedrooms in the house. Both stairways and central hallways are equipped with emergency lighting and smoke detector systems. Each of the doors leading to the bedrooms from the central hallway is a fire-rated door. There are fire escapes in front and back leading to the next building. For your own safety and the safety of others in the house please familiarize yourself with the location and use of each of the above. Each of the rooms has been provided with an Emergency Bulletin in case of a fire emergency.

Checking Accounts and Bill-Paying

Part of living in any lodging house is the necessity of paying weekly or monthly bills and being financially responsible in that way. This is also true at Berkeley House. We ask that each of you set up a checking account in your name from which your checks will be drawn to pay your own bills while you are living here. Bimonthly payments will be due the 1st and 16th of each month, and we will expect bills to be paid on time.

Resident Application Form

CONFIDENTIAL

RESIDENT APPLICATION FORM FOR BERKELEY HOUSE

Date: _____

Name: _____   Sex: ____ Age: ____ Birthdate: _____

Present address: (where you can   Draft Status: _____
be currently reached)
                                    Educational Level Achieved: _____

_____   Marital Status: ____ ____ ____ ____
                                                      Mar. Sin. Div. Wid.
Present phone: Spouse (if any) _____

                                    Children (if any): No.: _____

_____   Ages: _____

(Where items below are not applicable, please so state)
HOW DO YOU CURRENTLY SPEND YOUR TIME DURING THE DAY?

Present
Occupation: Job: _____   Title: _____

             Address: _____   Phone: _____

             How long have you been there? _____

             Employer: _____

Present
School: Name of School: _____ Grade Level: ____

             Address: _____ How Long: _____

Other Daily
Activity:

Other Activity: Are you active in other part time activity such as group work, committee work, AA, etc.?

What daily program do you plan to follow while living at Berkeley House? Be as specific as you can.

When were you initially hospitalized? Month: _____ Year: _____

What was the problem that led to treatment or hospitalization?

What problems remain?

What goals do you intend to achieve in the next year?

How do you hope the halfway house will help you achieve these goals?

Psychotherapist: Name: _____

Address: _____

Phone: _____

Frequency of meetings: _____

Date of Inception: Month_____ Year _____

Group Therapist: Name: _____

Address: _____

Phone: _____

Frequency of meetings: _____

Date of Inception: Month_____ Year _____

Administrative
Psychiatrist: Name: _____

Address: _____

Phone: _____

Frequency of meetings: _____

Date of Inception: Month_____ Year _____

Social Worker: Name: _____

                      Address: _____

                      Phone: _____

                      Frequency of meetings: _____

                      Date of Inception: Month_____ Year _____
Rehabilitation
or Job Counselor: Name: _____

                      Address: _____

                      Phone: _____

                      Frequency of meetings: _____

                      Date of Inception: Month_____ Year _____

Other: Name: _____
(Family therapy,
psychomotor   Address: _____
therapy, etc.)
                      Phone: _____

                      Frequency of meetings: _____

                      Date of Inception: Month_____ Year _____

Please list all psychiatric medications and doses that you are
currently taking:
Medication   Dosage
_____   _____
_____   _____
_____   _____

Do you have significant (nonpsychiatric) medical problems? _____

Do you have any allergies? _____ If yes, explain:

Do you take medications for these?____ If so, please name:

Do you have a special doctor for these problems? _____

   Name: _____ Phone: _____

   Address: _____

From what source of funds do you plan to pay your bills at Berkeley House? (If more than one source please allot portions.)

   1. Income from your job? _____

   2. Money from your family? _____

   Name: _____

   Relationship: _____

   Address: _____

   3. Other sources?____ If so, what?

Parents (or Guardian)

   Name: _____

   Address: _____

   Phone: _____

Have you taken at any time:

	NO	YES	If yes, date of last use
Marijuana	___	___	_____
Amphetamines	___	___	_____
LSD	___	___	_____
Barbiturates	___	___	_____
Heroin	___	___	_____

Have you ever had an alcohol problem? _____

Have you attempted suicide in the past?   If yes, please explain the circumstances.

What do you expect your goals to be upon leaving Berkeley House?

What are your long-range goals?

Notes

Preface

1. D. Landy and M. Greenblatt, *Halfway House* (Washington, D.C.: U.S. Department of Health, Education, and Welfare, Vocational Rehabilitation Administration, 1965); N. D. Rothwell and J. M. Doniger, *The Psychiatric Halfway House: A Case Study* (Springfield, Ill.: Charles C. Thomas, 1966); R. M. Glasscote, J. E. Gudeman, and J. R. Elpers, *Halfway Houses for the Mentally Ill* (Washington, D.C.: Joint Information Service of the American Psychiatric Association and the National Association for Mental Health, 1971); and H. L. Raush and C. L. Raush, *The Halfway House Movement: A Search for Sanity* (New York: Appleton-Century-Crofts, 1968).

Chapter 1. Crisis, Concept, and Challenge

1. M. Jones, *The Therapeutic Community* (New York: Basic Books, 1953); A. H. Stanton and M. S. Schwartz, *The Mental Hospital* (New York: Basic Books, 1954); and J. Cumming and E. Cumming, *Ego and Milieu* (New York: Atherton, 1963).

Chapter 2. In Search of a Conceptual Model: Historical Perspectives

1. H. L. Raush and C. L. Raush, *The Halfway House Movement: A Search for Sanity* (New York: Appleton-Century-Crofts, 1968), p. 207, quoting M. J. Schwartz and C. G. Schwartz, *Social Approaches to Mental Patient Care* (New York: Columbia University Press, 1964), pp. 301–02.

2. D. Landy and M. Greenblatt, *Halfway House* (Washington, D.C.: U.S. Department of Health, Education, and Welfare, Vocational Rehabilitation Administration, 1965), p. 26.

3. N. D. Rothwell and J. M. Doniger, *The Psychiatric Halfway House: A Case Study* (Springfield, Ill.: Charles C. Thomas, 1966), p. 9.

4. Raush and Raush, *Halfway House Movement*, pp. 11, 25.

5. Ibid., p. 12, quoting M. Jones, *The Therapeutic Community* (New York: Basic Books, 1953).

6. Ibid., p. 13, quoting R. N. Rapaport, *Community as Doctor: New Perspectives on a Therapeutic Community* (Springfield, Ill.: Charles C. Thomas, 1960), pp. 22–23.

7. Ibid., p. 14.

8. Ibid., pp. 15–16.

9. Ibid., pp. 19, 17.

10. Ibid., pp. 26, 28.

11. Ibid., p. 204.

12. Ibid., p. 192.

13. Ibid., pp. 191, 192.

14. Ibid., p. 192.

15. Elizabeth Zetzel, "A Developmental Approach to the Borderline Patient," *American Journal of Psychiatry*, 127, no. 7 (January 1971).

16. M. Greenblatt and R. D. Budson, "A Symposium: Follow-up Studies of Community Care," *American Journal of Psychiatry*, 133, no. 8 (August 1976):196–21; W. Kohen and G. Paul, "Current Trends and Recommended Changes in Extended-Care Placement of Mental Patients: The Illinois System as a Case in Point," *Schizophrenia Bulletin*, 2, no. 4 (1976); F. D. Chu and S. Trotter, *The Madness Establishment* (New York: Grossman, 1974); and M. Koltuv and W. S. Neff, "The Comprehensive Rehabilitation Center: Its Role and Realm in Psychiatric Rehabilitation," *Community Mental Health Journal*, 4 (1968):251–59.

17. R. Reich and L. Siegel, "The Chronically Mentally Ill Shuffle to Oblivion," *Psychiatric Annals*, 3 (November 1973):35–55.

18. H. R. Lamb and V. Goertzel, "Discharged Mental Patients—Are They Really in the Community?" *Archives of General Psychiatry*, 24 (1971):29–34.

19. M. Jones, "Community Care for Chronic Mental Patients: The Need for a Reassessment," *Hospital and Community Psychiatry*, 26 (1974):94–98.

20. N. W. Bell and E. F. Vogel, introduction to their *Modern Introduction to the Family* (New York: The Free Press, 1968).

21. E. M. Pattison et al., "A Psychosocial Kinship Model for Family Therapy," *American Journal of Psychiatry*, 132, no. 12 (December 1975):1247.

Chapter 3. The Halfway House as a Family-Modeled Social System

1. The concept of the family in this chapter draws heavily on Norman W. Bell and Ezra F. Vogel, "Towards a Framework for Functional Analysis of Family Behavior," in their *Modern Introduction to the Family* (New York: The Free Press, 1968). Direct quotations are noted by parenthetical page references in the text.

2. O'Connor v. Donaldson, 43 *U.S. Law Week* 4930 (June 24, 1975).

3. Erving Goffman, *Asylums: Essays on the Social Situation of Mental Patients and Other Inmates* (Garden City, N.Y.: Doubleday, 1961).

4. No. 74285 (C.C.D.C. 1974).

Chapter 4. Beyond the Halfway House: The Extended Psychosocial Kinship System

1. E. M. Pattison et al., "A Psychosocial Kinship Model for Family Therapy," *American Journal of Psychiatry*, 132, no. 12 (December 1975):1247, 1246.

2. K. C. W. Kammeyer and C. D. Bolton, "Community and Family Factors Related to the Use of a Family Service Agency," *Journal of Marriage and the Family*, 30 (1968):488–98; A. S. Alissi, "Social Work with Families in Group-Service Agencies: An Overview," *Family Coordinator*, 18 (1969):391–401; A. H. Collins, "Natural Delivery Systems: Accessible Sources of Power for Mental Health," *American Journal of Orthopsychiatry*, 43 (1973):46–52; W. R. Curtis, "Community Human Service Networks," *Psychiatric Annals*, 3 (1973):32–40; F. Feldman and F. Scherz, *Family Social Welfare* (New York: Atherton, 1967); and N. Hansell, "Patient Predicament and Clinical Service: A System," *Archives of General Psychiatry*, 14 (1967): 204–10.

3. F. D. Chu and S. Trotter, *The Madness Establishment* (New York: Grossman, 1974); M. Koltuv and W. S. Neff, "The Comprehensive Rehabilitation Center: Its Role and Realm in Psychiatric Rehabilitation," *Community Mental Health Journal*, 4 (1968):251–59; and R. Reich and L. Siegel, "The Chronically Mentally Ill Shuffle to Oblivion," *Psychiatric Annals*, 3 (November 1973):33–55.

4. H. R. Lamb and V. Goertzel, "Discharged Mental Patients—Are They Really in the Community?" *Archives of General Psychiatry*, 24 (1971):29–34; and H. Richards Lamb and Associates, *Community Survival for Long-Term Patients* (San Francisco: Jossey-Bass, 1976).

5. D. J. Rog and H. L. Raush, "The Psychiatric Halfway House: How Is It Measuring Up?" *Community Mental Health Journal*, 11 (1975):2.

6. M. A. Test and L. I. Stein, "Practical Guidelines for the Community Treatment of Markedly Impaired Patients," *Community Mental Health Journal*, 12, no. 1 (1976):72–82; H. B. M. Murphy, B. Pennee, and D. Luchins, "Foster Homes: The New Back Ward?" *Canada's Mental Health* (September 1972):1–17; and B. Weinman, R. Kleiner, J. H. Yu, and V. A. Tillson, "Social Treatment of the Chronic Psychotic Patient in the Community," *Journal of Community Psychology*, 2 (1974):358–65.

7. R. D. Budson, "The Psychiatric Halfway House," *Psychiatric Annals*, 3, no. 6 (1973):64–83.

8. In 1973, the office separated into two divisions, one for the mentally ill and one

9. Kammeyer and Bolton, "Community and Family Factors," p. 492.

10. Pattison et al., "Psychosocial Kinship Model," p. 1248.

11. Ibid., italics added.

12. P. R. Polak and M. W. Kirby, "Follow-Up Evaluation of an Inpatient Alternative Program," as summarized in M. Greenblatt and R. D. Budson, "A Symposium: Follow-Up Studies of Community Care," *American Journal of Psychiatry*, 133, no. 8 (August 1976):916; and L. I. Stein and M. A. Test, "Training in Community Living:

One-Year Evaluation, as summarized in Greenblatt and Budson, "A Symposium," p. 917.

13. Lamb and Associates, *Community Survival.*

Chapter 5. Government-Community Interaction in a Statewide Program

1. Barney Frank, "Even the Politicians Are Independent," in *Boston: The Liveable City, Boston Sunday Globe,* June 24, 1973.

2. For a brief summary of these cases, see Louis E. Kopolow et al., *Litigation and Mental Health Services,* pub. no. (ADM)75-261 (Washington, D.C.: Department of Health, Education and Welfare, 1975).

3. 325 F. Supp. 781 (M.D. Ala. 1971).

4. 43 *U.S. Law Week* 4930 (June 24, 1975).

5. No. 74285 (C.D.D.C. 1974).

6. Village of Belle Terre et al., Appellants v. Bruce Boraas et al., 38 *U.S. Law Week* 4475-81 (April 1, 1974).

7. City of White Plains v. Ferriaioli, 34 N.Y. 2d 300, 313 N.E. 2d 756, 357 N.Y.S. 2d 449 (1974).

8. In 1973, the office separated into two divisions, one for the mentally ill and one for the mentally retarded.

9. Murray Schumach, "Where Can Mental Patients Go?" *New York Times,* February 24, 1974.

Chapter 6. Legal Issues, Standards, and Regulations

1. R. D. Budson et al., *Developing a Community Residence for the Mentally Ill* (Boston: Commonwealth of Massachusetts, 1974), pp. i–ii.

2. Task Force on Community Mental Health Program Components, *Developing Community Mental Health Programs: A Resource Manual* (Boston: United Community Planning Corporation and Massachusetts Department of Mental Health, May 1975), pp. 50–51.

3. Each state was sent a short questionnaire in the fall of 1976 asking whether it had halfway house regulations or was drafting such regulations. Those states which did not respond to the survey were telephoned. Information on the various states is derived from the following sources:

Alabama. Alabama Department of Mental Health Standards for Community Mental Health Centers, adopted February 18, 1971, revised June 1975, 1976.

Arizona. Arizona State Hospital Regulations and Procedures—Boarding Home Standards, 1969.

Arkansas. W. R. Oglesby, Director, Community Mental Health Services, correspondence and survey reply, 1976.

California. Laws and Regulations Relating to Licensing of Residential and Adult Day Facilities. Excerpts from the California Health and Safety Code and the California Administrative Code (Title 22, Division 6—effective August 31, 1975).

Connecticut. Melanie Jones, personal communication, October 1976.

District of Columbia. Community Residence Facility Regulations, Title VII, amending the Health Care Facilities Regulation No. 74-15, pending 1974.

Florida. Guidelines Covering the Administration and Operation of Halfway Houses of Florida, proposed by the Florida Association of Halfway Houses, Inc., revised May 1973.

Hawaii. Walter H. Inouye, Department of Health, Program Support Services, correspondence, September 24, 1976, survey reply, 1976.

Indiana. Indiana Department of Mental Health Requirements for Halfway Houses, 1976; correspondence, November 4, 1971.

Iowa. Lowell Schenke, Psychology Consultant, Department of Social Services, correspondence, October 8, 1971; N. J. Grunzweig, Acting Director, Bureau of Mental Health Services, Department of Social Services, correspondence, June 18, 1973; survey reply, 1976.

Kansas. Standards for Certification of Payment to Residential and Transitional Homes for Social Services Provided . . . , January 15, 1975; authorized by K.S.A. 1973 Suppl. 75-3307b, effective January 15, 1975, Suggested Standards for Community Centers Serving the Mentally Ill, Mentally Retarded and the Alcoholic, draft, June 1970.

Maine. W. F. Kearns, Jr., Commissioner, Department of Mental Health and Corrections, correspondence, September 27, 1971.

Maryland. Guidelines for the Operation of Community Residences for the Psychiatrically Ill in the State of Maryland, Mental Hygiene Administration, September 19, 1975.

Massachusetts. Regulation 5.2, Private Facilities Providing Care But Not Treatment (Ref. M.G.L. ch. 19, sec. 29), November 1, 1971. (See Appendix 1.)

Minnesota. Rule 36, Department of Public Welfare Rule for the Licensing and Operation of All Residential Programs for Adult Mentally Ill Persons (pending).

Missouri. House Bill no. 43, 75th General Assembly, 1969, 202.645.

Nebraska. Section 71-2017-71-3020—Basic Standards, Nebraska Department of Health; further legislation pending.

New Hampshire. Stuart P. Howell, Coordinator of Community Mental Health Services, October 5, 1971; survey reply, 1976.

New York. Part 86, Operation of Community Residences, Department of Mental Hygiene.

North Carolina. Eugene A. Hargrove, correspondence, October 6, 1971.

North Dakota. Personal communication, October 1976.

Ohio. Roger M. Gove, Commissioner, Division of Mental Retardation, correspondence, October 15, 1971.

Pennsylvania. Bulletin no. 1409, Domiciliary Care Demonstration Program, Commonwealth of Pennsylvania, Department of Public Welfare, June 25, 1976; Domiciliary Care Service of Adults, sec. 29 A.

Rhode Island. Department of Mental Health, Retardation and Hospitals, Rules, Regulations and Standards for Licensing of Mental Health Group Residences, in accordance with provisions of chaps. 23-43.3 and 42-35 of the General Law of Rhode Island, February 14, 1975.

South Carolina. Rules, Regulations and Standards for Mental Health Facilities, Authority of Section 32-1034 through Section 32-1034.14, South Carolina Code of Laws, 1962; amended 1971; revised 1975.

Texas. Texas Rehabilitation Commission Standards for Halfway House Operations, November 1, 1972.

Utah. Guidelines for Group Homes, Utah State Training School, 1972.

Virginia. Chapter 8, Section 37.1.179-37.1.189, Licensing Private Institutions, Mental Hygiene and Hospitals; revised 1971; standards in process, 1973.

West Virginia. Jane D. Neal, Acting Director, Mental Health Licensing Program, Department of Mental Health, correspondence, April 11, 1972; survey reply, 1976.

Wisconsin. Chapter H 31, Residential Care Institutions, Type II Halfway Houses, Wisconsin Administrative Code, Department of Health and Social Services, July 1, 1971; revision in process.

Wyoming. Timothy O'Connor, Mental Health Consultant, Department of Health and Social Services, correspondence, September 28, 1971.

4. Accreditation Council for Psychiatric Facilities, Joint Commission on Accreditation of Hospitals, *Principles for Accreditation of Community Mental Health Service Programs,* 1976 (draft), p. 3.

Chapter 7. A Group Residence Fire Safety Code

1. *Basic Building Code,* Building Officials Conference of America, 1313 East 60th Street, Chicago, Illinois, 1970.

Chapter 8. Community Entry and Zoning Requirements

1. S. Rubenstein and J. Meehan, "Definition of Family in Zoning Ordinances," in *Developing a Community Residence for the Mentally Ill,* ed. R. D. Budson, J. Meehan, and E. Barclay (Boston: Commonwealth of Massachusetts, 1974), Appendix H.

2. Missionaries of Our Lady of La Salette v. Whitefish Bay, 267 Wisc. 609, 66 NW 2d 627; Carrol v. Miami Beach, 198, So. 2d 643 (Fla); Robertson v. Western Baptist Hospital, 267 SW 2d 395 (Ky); Alphone A. LaPorte, et al. v. City of New Rochelle, et al., 152 NYC 2d 916, affirmed 2 NY 2d 921, 141 NE 2d 917).

3. Marino v. Norwood, 77 NJ Super 587, 187 A2d 217.

4. Gloster v. Downey Side Inc., Equity #714.

5. Village of Belle Terre et al., Appelants v. Bruce Boraas et al., 38 *Law Week*, 4475–81.

6. City of White Plains v. Ferriaioli, 34 N.Y. 2d 300, N.E. 2d756 [1974]; rev'g 339 N.Y.S. 2d 27 [1972], reported at 25 *ZD* 241.

7. Mental Health Law Project, 1220 19th Street, N.W., Washington, D.C. 20036.

8. Edward Scott, Director, Mental Health Legislative Guide Project, Mental Health Law Project, personal communication.

9. California Welfare and Institutions Code (West Supp. 1974).

10. Defoe v. San Francisco Planning Commission, Civil No. 30789; Cal. Ct. App., filed May 30, 1973, cited in Laurence Kress, "The Community Residence Movement: Land Use Conflicts and Planning Imperatives," *New York University Review of Law and Social Change*, 5, no. 2 (Spring 1975):157.

11. A. A. Cupaiuolo, "Zoning Ordinances and Other Legal Issues in the Development of Community Residences," in *Gaining Community Acceptance: A Handbook for Community Residence Planners*, ed. Patricia Stickney (White Plains, N.Y.: Westchester Community Council, Community Residences Information Services Program, 1976), pp. 20–26.

12. Minn. Stat. Ann secs 252.28 subd. 3 (1) (Supp. 1976).

13. Cupaiuolo, "Zoning Ordinances," p. 25.

14. Governor's Commission on Citizen Participation, *Report* (Boston: Commonwealth of Massachusetts, December 1973).

15. I have modified my position on this somewhat, questioning the constitutionality of "quotas" of community residences in a community. See R. D. Budson, "Basic Human Rights of Mental Patients in the Community" (Paper presented at the Sixth World Congress of Psychiatry, Honolulu, Hawaii, August 3, 1977).

Chapter 9. Profile of a Statewide Community Residence Program

1. D. J. Rog and H. L. Raush, "The Psychiatric Halfway House: How Is It Measuring Up?" *Community Mental Health Journal*, 11 (1975):2.

2. R. D. Budson, "Community Residences," in *Developing Community Mental Health Programs* (Boston: Task Force on Community Mental Health Program Components, United Community Planning Corporation, and Massachusetts Department of Mental Health, 1975).

Chapter 12. A Follow-up Study of Berkeley House, a Psychiatric Halfway House

1. D. J. Rog and H. L. Raush, "The Psychiatric Halfway House: How Is It Measuring Up?" *Community Mental Health Journal*, 11, no. 2 (1975):155–62.

2. W. S. Gill, "San Antonio's Halfway House," *Hospital and Community Psychiatry*, 18 (1967):281; P. Gumrukcu, "The Efficacy of a Psychiatric Halfway House: A Three-Year Study of a Therapeutic Residence," *Sociological Quarterly*, 9,

no. 3 (1968):374–86; J. F. Wilder, M. Kessel, and S. C. Caulfield, "Follow-up of a 'High Expectations' Halfway House," *American Journal of Psychiatry*, 124 (1968):1085–91; F. H. Wright, J. E. Brown, J. R. McDaniel et al., "A Descriptive Report on Sixty-Five Halfway House Patients Over a Two and One-Half Year Period," *International Journal of Social Psychiatry*, 12 (1966):289–92; and D. Landy and M. Greenblatt, *Halfway House* (Washington, D.C.: U.S. Department of Health, Education, and Welfare, Vocational Rehabilitation Administration, 1965).

3. I acknowledge here the enthusiastic contributions of the second-year graduate students from this institution and their director of research, Dr. Helen Reinherz.

4. R. D. Budson, "The Psychiatric Halfway House," *Psychiatric Annals*, 3, no. 6 (1973):64–83.

5. I am grateful to the ex-residents of Rutland Corner House, Boston, Massachusetts, who participated in the pretest phase of the study, and to the administration of Rutland Corner House, who made this pretesting possible.

6. The admission referred to is that directly preceding the Berkeley House experience.

7. C. Altman et al., "The Psychiatric Patient One Year After Hospital Discharge: Part I" (M.S. thesis, Simmons College School of Social Work, May 1970); J. Boudeau, "The Psychiatric Patient One Year After Hospital Discharge: Part II (M.S. thesis, Simmons College School of Social Work, May 1971); M. Grob and J. Singer, *Adolescent Patients in Transition: Impact and Outcome of Psychiatric Hospitalization* (New York: Behavioral Publications, April 1974); and J. Singer and M. Grob, "Short-Term Versus Long-Term Hospitalization in a Private Psychiatric Facility: A Follow-up Study," *Hospital and Community Psychiatry*, 26, no. 11 (November 1975):745–48.

8. Grob and Singer, *Adolescent Patients;* and D. Landy and M. Greenblatt, *A Sociocultural and Clinical Study of Rutland Corner House—A Transitional Aftercare Residence for Female Psychiatric Patients* (Washington, D.C.: Department of Health, Education, and Welfare, Vocational Rehabilitation Administration, 1965).

9. E. Herrera, B. Lifson, E. Hartmann et al., "A Ten Year Follow-up of 55 Hospitalized Adolescents," *American Journal of Psychiatry*, 131, no. 7 (July 1974):769–74; Landy and Greenblatt, *Sociocultural and Clinical Study of Rutland Corner House;* and S. Washburn and M. Grob, "Psychiatric Day Care Patients: Their Four to Seven Year Outcome," *Massachusetts Journal of Mental Health*, 4, no. 1 (Fall 1973):16–36.

10. Landy and Greenblatt, *Sociocultural and Clinical Study of Rutland Corner House.*

Epilogue: The Challenge Ahead

1. A. Beigel, "The Politics of Mental Health Funding: Two Views, A Look at the Issues," *Hospital and Community Psychiatry*, 28, no. 3 (1977):194.

2. J. Gunderson and L. Mosher, "The Cost of Schizophrenia," *American Journal of Psychiatry*, 132, no. 9 (September 1975); J. G. Murphy and W. E. Datel, "A

Cost-Benefit Analysis of Community Versus Institutional Living," *Hospital and Community Psychiatry*, 27, no. 3 (March 1976); S. Sharfstein and J. C. Nafziger, "Community Care: Costs and Benefits for a Chronic Patient," *Hospital and Community Psychiatry*, 27, no. 3 (March 1976); and B. A. Weisbrod, M. A. Test, and L. I. Stein, "An Alternative to Mental Hospital Treatment: III. Economic Benefit—Cost Analysis," *Archives of General Psychiatry*, in press.

3. Gunderson and Mosher, "Cost of Schizophrenia," pp. 901–02.

4. Ibid., pp. 901–05; Weisbrod, Test, and Stein, "An Alternative to Mental Hospital Treatment."

5. Weisbrod, Test, and Stein, "An Alternative to Mental Hospital Treatment."

BIBLIOGRAPHY

Alissi, A. S. "Social Work with Families in Group-Service Agencies: An Overview." *Family Coordinator*, 18 (1969):391–401.

Anstice, E. "Halfway Home." *Nursing Times*, 69, no. 4 (1973):129–31.

Baganz, P. C.; Smith, A. E.; Goldstein, R.; and Pou, N. K. "The YMCA as a Halfway Facility." *Hospital and Community Psychiatry*, 22, no. 5 (1971):156–59.

Barnes, R. "Group Homes and Social Networks." *Health and Social Service Journal*, 83, no. 4343 (1973):1587–88.

Becker, R. E. "Group Preparation for Discharge and Group Placement of Chronically Hospitalized Schizophrenic Patients." *Diseases of the Nervous System*, 32, no. 3 (1971):176–80.

Beigel, A. "The Politics of Mental Health Funding: Two Views, A Look at the Issues." *Hospital and Community Psychiatry*, 28, no. 3 (1977):194.

Bell, N. W., and Vogel, E. F. *A Modern Introduction to the Family.* New York: The Free Press, 1968.

Berman, N., and Hoppe, E. W. "Halfway House Residents: Where do they Go?" *Journal of Community Psychology*, 4, no. 3 (1976):259–60.

Booth, P. W., and Bogguess, C. "Remotivation for Return to Community Life." *Journal of Psychiatric Nursing and Mental Health Services*, 5, no. 6 (1967):555–66.

Bowen, W. T., and Fry, T. J. "Group Living in the Community for Chronic Patients." *Hospital and Community Psychiatry*, 22, no. 7 (1971):205–06.

Breitmeyer, R. G.; Bottum, G.; and Wagner, B. R. "Issues in Evaluative Follow-up for a Residential Program." *Hospital and Community Psychiatry*, 25, no. 12 (1974):804–06.

Britten, C. S. "The Function of a Halfway House Within a Long-stay Ward." *International Journal of Social Psychiatry*, 20, nos. 1, 2 (1974):78–79.

Budson, R. D. "Basic Human Rights of Mental Patients in the Community." Paper presented at the Sixth World Congress of Psychiatry, August 31, 1977, Honolulu, Hawaii.

———. "Community Residential Care for the Mentally Ill in Massachusetts: Halfway Houses and Cooperative Apartments." In *Working Group on Cooperative Apart-*

ments: Proceedings of a Conference, edited by J. G. Goldmeier, F. V. Mannino, and M. F. Shore (Rockville, Md.: National Institute of Mental Health, 1978).
————. "Legal Dimensions of the Psychiatric Halfway House." *Community Mental Health Journal,* 11, no. 3 (1975): 316–24.
————. "The Psychiatric Halfway House." *Psychiatric Annals,* 3, no. 6 (1973):64–83.
————. "The Role of the Psychiatric Halfway House in Social Work Education." *Hospital and Community Psychiatry,* in press.
Budson, R. D.; Grob, M. C.; and Singer, J. E. "A Follow-up Study of Berkeley House—a Psychiatric Halfway House." *International Journal of Social Psychiatry,* 23, no. 1 (1977).
Budson, R. D.; Meehan, J.; and Barclay, E., eds. *Developing a Community Residence for the Mentally Ill.* Boston: Commonwealth of Massachusetts, 1974.
Cannon, M. D. *Selected Characteristics of Residents in Psychiatric Halfway Houses.* HSMHA, NIMH Statistical Note 93. Rockville, Md.: National Institute of Mental Health, August 1973.
Cannon, M. S. *Halfway Houses Serving the Mentally Ill and Alcoholics, United States, 1973.* Mental Health Statistics, ser. A, no. 16 (DHEW No, ADM 76-264). Rockville, Md.: National Institute of Mental Health, 1975.
Cassell, W.; Smith, C.; Grunberg, F.; Boan, J. A.; and Thomas, R. F. "Comparing Costs of Hospital and Community Care." *Hospital and Community Psychiatry,* 23, no. 7 (1972):197–200.
Chien, C., and Cole, J. O. "Landlord-Supervised Cooperative Apartments: A New Modality for Community-Based Treatment." *American Journal of Psychiatry,* 130, no. 2 (1973):156–59.
Chu, F. D., and Trotter, S. *The Madness Establishment.* New York: Grossman, 1974.
Collins, A. H. "Natural Delivery Systems: Accessible Sources of Power for Mental Health." *American Journal of Orthopsychiatry,* 43 (1973):46–52.
Cumming, J., and Cumming, E. *Ego and Milieu.* New York: Atherton, 1963.
Cunningham, M. K.; Botwinik, W.; Dolson, J.; and Weickert, A. A. "Community Placement of Released Mental Patients: A 5-Year Study." *Social Work,* 1969, pp. 1454–61.
Curtis, W. R. "Community Human Service Networks." *Psychiatric Annals,* 3 (1973):32–40.
Dailey, W., and Wellisch, D. "Managing Family Conflicts of Halfway House Residents." *Hospital and Community Psychiatry,* 25, no. 9 (1974):583–84.
Easton, K. "Residential Facilities for Hospital-Discharged Former Mental Patients: Aspects in Development." *New York State Journal of Medicine,* 74, no. 10 (1974):1762–65.
Engelsmann, F.; Murphy, H. B. M.; and Tcheng-Laroche, F. C. "Criteria for Post-Hospital Adjustment of Mental Patients in Sheltered Settings." *Canadian Psychiatric Association Journal,* 19, no. 4 (1974):375–80.

Fairweather, G. W.; Sanders, D. H.; and Maynard, J. *Community Life for the Mentally Ill: An Alternative to Institutional Care.* Chicago: Aldine, 1969.

Fakhruddin, A. K. M.; Manjooran, A.; Nair, N. P. V.; and Neufeldt, A. "A 5-Year Outcome of Discharged Chronic Psychiatric Patients." *Canadian Psychiatric Association Journal,* 17, no. 6 (1972): 433–35.

Feldman, F., and Scherz, F. *Family Social Welfare.* New York: Atherton, 1967.

Gill, W. S. "San Antonio's Halfway House." *Hospital and Community Psychiatry,* 18 (1967):281.

Glasscote, R. M.; Cumming, E.; Rutman, I.; Sussex, J. N.; and Glassman, S. M. *Rehabilitating the Mentally Ill in the Community.* Washington, D.C.: Joint Information Service of the American Psychiatric Association and the National Association for Mental Health, 1971.

Glasscote, R. M.; Gudeman, J. E.; and Elpers, J. R. *Halfway Houses for the Mentally Ill.* Washington, D.C.: Joint Information Service of the American Psychiatric Association and the National Association for Mental Health, 1971.

Goering, P. "A Bridge Between—The Transition from Hospital to Community." *Menninger Perspective,* 2, no. 4 (1971):26–29.

Goffman, Erving. *Asylums: Essays on the Social Situation of Mental Patients and Other Inmates.* Garden City, N.Y.: Doubleday, 1961.

Goldmeier, J.; Shore, M. F.; and Mannino, F. V. "Cooperative Apartments: New Programs in Community Mental Health." *Health and Social Work,* 2, no. 1 (1977).

Greenblatt, M., and Budson, R. D. "A Symposium: Follow-up Studies of Community Care." *American Journal of Psychiatry,* 133, no. 8 (1976):916–21.

Gumrukcu, P. "The Efficacy of a Psychiatric Halfway House: A Three-Year Study of a Therapeutic Residence." *Sociological Quarterly,* 9, 3 (1968):374–86.

Gunderson, J., and Mosher, L. "The Cost of Schizophrenia." *American Journal of Psychiatry,* 132, no. 9 (1975).

Hansell, N. "Patient Predicament and Clinical Service: A System." *Archives of General Psychiatry,* 14 (1967):204–10.

Hodgman, E., and Stein, E. "Cooperative Apartment." *Community Mental Health Journal,* 2, no. 4 (1966):347–52.

Hogarty, G. E. "Hospital Differences in the Release of Discharge-Ready Chronic Schizophrenics." *Archives of General Psychiatry,* 18 (1968):367–72.

Hopperton, Robert. *Zoning for Community Homes: Handbook for Local Legislative Change.* Ohio: College of Law, Ohio State University, Law Reform Project, November 1975.

————. *Zoning for Community Homes: Technical Assistance Handbook for Municipal Officials.* Ohio: College of Law, Ohio State University, Law Reform Project, December 1975.

Huessy, H. R. "Beyond the Halfway House." *International Journal of Social Psychiatry,* 15 (1969):235–39.

————. "Satellite Halfway Houses in Vermont." *Hospital and Community*

_ *Psychiatry*, 20, no. 5 (1969):147–49.

Jansen, E. "The Role of the Halfway House in Community Mental Health Programs in the United Kingdom and America." *American Journal of Psychiatry*, 126, no. 10 (1970):1498–1504.

Jones, M. "Community Care for Chronic Mental Patients: The Need for a Reassessment." *Hospital and Community Psychiatry*, 26 (1974):94–98.

———. *The Therapeutic Community*. New York: Basic Books, 1953.

Kammeyer, K. C. W., and Bolton, C. D. "Community and Family Factors Related to the Use of a Family Service Agency." *Journal of Marriage and the Family*, 30 (1968):488–98.

Kohen, W., and Paul, G. "Current Trends and Recommended Changes in Extended Care Placement of Mental Patients: The Illinois System as a Case in Point." *Schizophrenia Bulletin* 2, no. 4 (1976).

Koltuv, M., and Neff, W. S. "The Comprehensive Rehabilitation Center: Its Role and Realm in Psychiatric Rehabilitation." *Community Mental Health Journal*, 4 (1968):251–59.

Kopolow, Louis E., et al. *Litigation and Mental Health Services*, pub. no. (ADM)75-261. Washington D.C.: Department of Health, Education, and Welfare, 1975.

Kresky, M.; Maeda, E. M.; and Rothwell, N. D. "The Apartment Program: A Community Living Option for Halfway House Residents." *Hospital and Community Psychiatry*, 27, no. 3 (1976):153–54.

Kressel, Laurence. "The Community Residence Movement: Land Use Conflicts and Planning Imperatives." *New York University Review of Law and Social Change*, 5, no. 2 (1975).

Lamb, H. R. *Community Survival for Long-term Patients*. San Francisco: Jossey-Bass, 1976.

Lamb, H. R., and Goertzel, V. "Discharged Mental Patients—Are They Really in the Community?" *Archives of General Psychiatry*, 24 (1971):29–34.

———. "High Expectations of Long-Term Ex-State Hospital Patients." *American Journal of Psychiatry*, 129, no. 4 (1972):471–75.

Landy, D., and Greenblatt, M. *Halfway Houses*. Washington, D.C.: U.S. Department of Health, Education, and Welfare, Vocational Rehabilitation Administration, 1965.

Lynch, V., and Budson, R. D. "The Ex-Resident Program: Meeting the Needs of Former Halfway House Residents." *Hospital and Community Psychiatry*, 28, no. 8 (August 1977).

Mannino, F.; Ott, S.; and Shore, M. "Community Residential Facilities for Former Mental Patients: An Annotated Bibliography." *Psycho-Social Rehabilitation Journal*, 1, no. 2 (1977).

Mason, A. S.; Cunningham, M. K.; and Tarpy, E. K. "The Quarter-Way House: A Transitional Program for Chronically Ill Geriatric Mental Patients." *Journal of the American Geriatric Society*, 11 (1963):574–79.

May, P. R. A. "Adopting New Models for Continuity of Care: What Are the Needs?" *Hospital and Community Psychiatry*, 26, no. 9 (1975):559–601.

Murphy, H. B. M.; Engelsmann, F.; and Tcheng-Laroche, F. "The Influence of Foster Home Care on Psychiatric Patients." *Archives of General Psychiatry*, 33 (February 1976):197.

Murphy, H. B. M.; Pennee, B.; and Luchins, D. "Foster Homes: The New Back Ward?" *Canadian Mental Health*, September 1972, pp. 1–17.

Murphy, J. G., and Datel, W. E. "A Cost-Benefit Analysis of Community Versus Institutional Living." *Hospital and Community Psychiatry*, 27, no. 3 (1976).

National Institute of Mental Health. *Halfway Houses Serving the Mentally Ill and Alcoholics: United States, 1969–1970.* Rockville, Md.: National Institute of Mental Health, ser. A, no. 9.

Orndoff, C. R. "Transitional Housing." In *The Future Role of the State Hospital*, edited by J. Zusman and E. F. Bertsch, pp. 221–30. Lexington, Mass.: Heath, 1975.

Ozarin, L. D., and Witkin, M. J. "Halfway Houses for the Mentally Ill and Alcoholics: A 1973 Survey." *Hospital and Community Psychiatry*, 26, no. 2 (1975):101–03.

Pattison, E. M., et al. "A Psychosocial Kinship Model for Family Therapy." *American Journal of Psychiatry*, 132, no. 12 (December 1975):1246–47.

Rapaport, R. N. *Community as Doctor: New Perspectives on a Therapeutic Community.* Springfield, Ill.: Charles C. Thomas, 1960.

Raush, H. L., and Raush, C. L. *The Halfway House Movement: A Search for Sanity.* New York: Appleton-Century-Crofts, 1968.

Reich, R., and Siegel, L. "The Chronically Mentally Ill Shuffle to Oblivion." *Psychiatric Annals*, 3 (November 1973):33–55.

Richmond, C. "Expanding the Concepts of the Halfway House: A Satellite Housing Program." *International Journal of Social Psychiatry*, 16 (1970):96–102.

———. "Halfway House and Day Hospital Complement Each Other." *Hospital and Community Psychiatry*, 19 (March 1968):78–79.

———. "Therapeutic Housing." In *Rehabilitation in Community Mental Health*, edited by H. Lamb, pp. 114–35. San Francisco: Jossey-Bass, 1971.

Roberts, P. R. "Human Warehouses: A Boarding Home Study." *American Journal of Public Health*, 64, no. 3 (March 1974): 276–82.

Rog, D. J., and Raush, H. L. "The Psychiatric Halfway House: How It Is Measuring Up?" *Community Mental Health Journal*, 11, no. 2 (1975).

Rothwell, N. D., and Doniger, J. M. *The Psychiatric Halfway House: A Case Study.* Springfield, Ill.: Charles C. Thomas, 1966.

Schwartz, M. J., and Schwartz, C. G. *Social Approaches to Mental Patient Care.* New York: Columbia University Press, 1964.

Sevren, M., and Mendelson, L. "Characteristics of Family Caretakers." *Hospital and Community Psychiatry*, 20, no. 8 (1969):245–47.

Sharfstein, S., and Nafziger, J. C. "Community Care: Costs and benefits for a Chronic

Patient." Hospital and Community Psychiatry, 27, no. 3 (1976).
Sinnett, E. R., and Sachson, A. D. Transitional Facilities in the Rehabilitation of the
    Emotionally disturbed. Lawrence: University Press of Kansas, 1970.
Spivak, M. "A Conceptual Framework for Structuring the Housing of Psychiatric
    Patients in the Community." Community Mental Health Journal, 10, no. 3
    (1974):345–50.
Stanton, A. H., and Schwartz, M. S. The Mental Hospital. New York: Basic Books,
    1954.
Stickney, Patricia, ed. Gaining Community Acceptance: A Handbook for Community
    Residence Planners. White Plains, N.Y.: Westchester Community Council, Com-
    munity Residences Information Services Program, 1976.
Task Force on Community Mental Health Program Components. Developing Com-
    munity Mental Health Programs: A Resource Manual. Boston: United Community
    Planning Corporation and Massachusetts Department of Mental Health, May
    1975.
Test, M. A., and Stein, L. I. "Practical Guidelines for the Community Treatment of
    Markedly Impaired Patients." Community Mental Health Journal, 12, no. 1
    (1976):72–82.
Tunakan, B., and Schaefer, I. "The Community Boardinghouse as a Transitional
    Residence During Aftercare." Current Psychiatric Therapy, 5 (1965):235–39.
Weinman, B.; Kleiner, R.; Yu, J. H.; and Tillson, V. A. "Social Treatment of the
    Chronic Psychotic Patient in the Community." Journal of Community Psychology,
    2 (1974):358–65.
Weisbrod, B. A.; Test, M. A.; and Stein, L. I. "An Alternative to Mental Hospital
    Treatment: III. Economic Benefit—Cost Analysis." Archives of General Psy-
    chiatry, in press.
Wilder, J. F.; Kessel, M.; and Caulfield, S. C. "Follow-up of a 'High- Expectations'
    Halfway House." American Journal of Psychiatry, 124 (1968):1085–91.
Wright, F. H.; Brown, J. E.; McDaniel, J. R.; et al. "A Descriptive Report on
    Sixty-Five Halfway House Patients Over a Two and One-Half Year Period." Inter-
    national Journal of Social Psychiatry, 12 (1966):289–92.
Zetzel, Elizabeth. "A Developmental Approach to the Borderline Patient." American
    Journal of Psychiatry, 127, no. 1 (January 1971).

Index

Contemporary Community Health Series

MARRIAGE AND MENTAL HANDICAP
A Study of Subnormality in Marriage
Janet Mattinson

A METHOD OF HOSPITAL UTILIZATION REVIEW
Sidney Shindell and Morris London

THE PSYCHIATRIC HALFWAY HOUSE
A Handbook of Theory and Practice
Richard D. Budson

A PSYCHIATRIC RECORD MANUAL FOR THE HOSPITAL
Dorothy Smith Keller

RACISM AND MENTAL HEALTH
Charles V. Willie, Bernard M. Kramer, and Bertram S. Brown, Editors

THE SOCIOLOGY OF PHYSICAL DISABILITY AND REHABILITATION
Gary L. Albrecht, Editor

THE STYLE AND MANAGEMENT OF A PEDIATRIC PRACTICE
Lee W. Bass and Jerome H. Wolfson